D1555108

Paul
Leroy-Beaulieu and
Established
Liberalism
in France

Paul
*L*eroy-Beaulieu and
Established
Liberalism
in *F*rance

Dan Warshaw

 Northern Illinois University Press · *DeKalb* · *1991*

© 1991 by Northern Illinois University Press
Published by the Northern Illinois University Press, DeKalb, Illinois 60115
Manufactured in the United States using acid-free paper ∞
Design by Julia Fauci

Library of Congress Cataloging-in-Publication Data
Warshaw, Dan.
    Paul Leroy-Beaulieu and established liberalism in France / Dan
Warshaw.
        p. cm.
    Includes bibliographical references (p.   ) and index.
    ISBN 0–87580–159–5
    1. Leroy-Beaulieu, Paul, 1843–1916. 2. Economists—France—
Biography. 3. Economics—France—History. 4. Liberalism—France—
History. I. Title.
HB105.L38W37 1991
330'.092—dc20   90–28524

To Paul,

whose loving support made it possible

to finish this book.

Contents

Preface   ix

Acknowledgments   xi

Introduction   xiii

1   The Study of an Ideologist   3

2   Background and Youth: Leroy-Beaulieu in the Era of the Second Empire   10

3   The Journeyman Publicist   27

4   Leroy-Beaulieu during the War and the Conservative Republic   41

5   The Turning Point: Experiences and Reactions of the Late 1870s and Early 1880s   61

6   The Path to Imperialism: Leroy-Beaulieu on Colonial Empire, 1869-1881   78

7   The Mature Writings of Leroy-Beaulieu   106

8   The Last Twenty Years   132

9   Leroy-Beaulieu in the History of Liberalism   149

Notes   179

Selected Bibliography   233

Index   243

Preface

■ Leo A. Loubère in his *Radicalism in Mediterranean France* refers to his subjects as Radicals with a capital R so as "to distinguish this tendency and its adherents from other movements called radical."[1] For similar reasons, in this book I use a capital L for the word Liberalism. For me the word Liberal designates specific historical groups, with definite if shifting membership, and Liberalism signifies not a vague social-political outlook but instead a specific current of ideological thought, separate from other currents such as Conservatism and Socialism. I also tend to capitalize the names of social classes. I believe it is vital that we recognize the reality of social classes, their continuity from generation to generation, and the mutations of social structures over the course of centuries. It seems to me absurd to refer to the aristocracy of the Middle Ages and the Directing Class of "Late" Modern times with the same vacuous term, "the upper class." I do not ask others to follow my usage, but I believe it communicates my ideas more clearly.

Acknowledgments

■ After eight years of labor, I can finally get to one of the last and surely the most pleasant parts of being an author: paying tribute to those who helped me. Just before he died, Edward Tannenbaum encouraged me to undertake the book. I will always be grateful to him for the challenges he posed to me. Phyllis Stock-Morton read the earlier chapters and gave a number of useful comments. Four people read the entire manuscript once I had it completed: Thomas R. Osborne, Mary Lynn Stewart, David Gordon, and Steven Englund. Their critiques were astonishingly thorough and made my job of revision much easier than I had dared to hope. The comments of the readers for Northern Illinois University Press also helped considerably, and I am grateful for the care they took. The director of the press, Mary Lincoln, and the editors, Susan Bean and Wendy Warnken, put up with my eccentricities and guided me well through the process of preparing the final version of the book. The staff of the Fairleigh Dickinson University Library, particularly Judy Katz, Roz Marcus, Charlotte Hoffman, and Ken Cooper, were constantly going out of their way to assist me. Mme. Antoine of the Archives Nationales, Mme. Larnaudie of the Institute, and several other members of the staff patiently guided me through the complexities of their archives. I owe a very great debt to Andrew Rubenfeld, who took time off from his other commitments to publishers, to edit the last three chapters of the book. As everyone who knows us realizes, however, I owe more than anything can repay to Paul Banks, to whom this book is dedicated.

Introduction

■ A particular perspective is always found under the academic gown of "objective" history. This study is no exception. It is based on a desire to break through the stereotype of a single "nineteenth-century Liberalism" and break with the equation of that Liberalism with the belief in laissez-faire. Instead I propose that at least three currents existed within the stream of nineteenth-century French Liberal thought: Classical, Established, and Reformist Liberalism. The first was the expression of the Enlightenment; it merged into other currents soon after the end of the French Revolution. The second, Established Liberalism, sprang out of the reaction against the excesses of the Revolution, and it persisted throughout the nineteenth century. Leroy-Beaulieu was part of this current. The third, the Reformist current, which began to flow strongly in his lifetime, changed in the twentieth century into Welfare Liberalism, the ideology that championed the Welfare State as well as representative government. Whether or not the names Established Liberal, Reformist Liberal, and Welfare Liberal are well chosen, this book, along with the work of other scholars, makes clear the differences within the Liberal outlook that historians must take into account.

Established Liberal ideology reached its final form in the writings of Leroy-Beaulieu and like-minded thinkers in late nineteenth-century France. An examination of the beliefs of this archetypal figure of Established Liberalism indicates the impossibility of equating any significant school of French Liberals at the end of the nineteenth century with laissez-faire. A more nuanced interpretation is necessary.

This study of Leroy-Beaulieu, however, has been guided by a

concern, indeed a passionate concern, about the present as well as a historian's fascination with the past. The defeat the Established Liberals suffered through the creation of the Welfare State is now being contested by a new set of thinkers and political groups who share much of the spirit, and even some of the ideas, discernible in the Liberalism of Leroy-Beaulieu. Thus, as a contribution to judging current regimes in the West, it has become vital once again to reevaluate Liberalism in all its different forms; we need to reexamine our preferences for or against the Liberal Welfare State, the reforms that created it, and the rationales for those reforms. This author's bias is in favor of the Reformist position and of the Welfare State, in contrast to the form of the Liberal Regime that preceded it.

Leroy-Beaulieu's historical significance lies in the spirit he represents rather than the ideas or analyses he contributed to the Liberal tradition. He exemplifies an important current that has regained considerable force in the West. One component of that current is an elitism that celebrates the superiority of businesspersons and the academically educated over manual workers. This spirit also denigrates professional government personnel, manifesting a defiant and mistrustful attitude toward political agents and agencies and a preference for private (especially individual) activity. It also seeks to rely on moral reform and to invoke individual responsibility in connection with the improvement of living and working conditions.

Too often historians and other commentators regard this individualistic doctrine as the only ideology that should be labeled Liberalism. But today we can see what was often obscure during the creation of the Welfare State: its champions in the West remained in the Liberal spectrum of belief. They too supported private enterprise and wanted a relatively free market rather than central planning to allocate resources and guide production. They too accepted the distinction between intellectual and manual labor and defended inequalities of income and status based on the superiority of the former kind of activity. However, they were preoccupied with a problem that Leroy-Beaulieu and his reformist opponents had largely ignored: preventing business cycles. Consequently, they contended that central government must have a greater role in directing the nation's economic life. Moreover, many argued that the power of private concentrations of wealth must be curbed as a means of realizing the democratic potential of Liberal society. They believed that the power of the vote could counteract the dangers to individual freedom inherent in bureaucracy, and thus they enthusiastically endorsed universal manhood suffrage both before and after it was won, in France and elsewhere. Those of us who approve the Welfare State find the Reformist and Welfare Liberal view mostly correct—so far; we believe modern free institutions have kept the big state from becoming the ogre predicted by Established Liberals.

All forms of Liberalism emphasize the importance of the individual, but those who share Leroy-Beaulieu's convictions find it particularly difficult to grasp the reality and value of any group other than the nation. And their sense of the nation is full of unexamined feeling and empty of careful consideration of the nature of community. That is, individualism is stronger in this part of the Liberal stream of thought than it is in Welfare State Liberalism. Moreover, present-day champions of free enterprise also appear at times to echo Leroy-Beaulieu's class-based elitism. This combination of class feeling and fear of government action might lead to impasses similar to those in which Leroy-Beaulieu found himself during the last years of his career. His spiritual kindred in the United States in the late twentieth century, for example, are also extreme in their nationalist feelings, and these feelings impel them, despite their general suspicion of government controls, to propose limitations on individual freedom in the name of maintaining the world position of the United States—just as Leroy-Beaulieu turned his back on freedom of speech and the press on the eve of World War I.

Ultimately what condemns Paul Leroy-Beaulieu is that he promoted unrestrained economic development, fought social change, and promoted suffering in the name of a narrow class egoism, and that he helped unleash violence in the name of national egoism. It is troubling to see Liberals, often falsely calling themselves "conservatives," following the same path today. Who, if born in the United States during or after the New Deal and growing to maturity during or soon after World War II, would ever have dreamed that there would again be beggars all over the streets of a great city like New York? Those of us who spent time in the slums ourselves, on our way from student or dropout to comfortable (or, rather, insecure) middle-class status, would never have imagined that this human wreckage would include not just aged alcoholics who conceivably had washed themselves into the gutter, but young men and women as well. The right-wing Liberals who carried so much weight in the 1980s, and who still win majorities in many elections, proclaim that capitalist societies are superior to Soviet ones because in the former the individual is truly valued and in the latter he or she is subordinated to the state. Yet this same group has done very little to keep individual lives from going down the drain. What has this to do with Paul Leroy-Beaulieu and Established Liberalism? I believe we are witnessing again the same class egoism and national egoism that ruled his thought, distorting the heritage that cherishes freedom, equality, and human brotherhood and preserving or recreating human ills against which the original Liberalism and reformist Liberalisms have protested and struggled.

It should be apparent that I have strong feelings about the issues raised in this study. However, the historian must combine active engagement with the ability to stand back from his or her feelings. We must be both empathetic and analytical, but also faithful to the data. In addition, we have the obligation to be fair, which means the necessity to search for those instances where we have been unfair. I have tried to be just to Leroy-Beaulieu. It is for the reader to judge whether or not I have succeeded.

Paul *L*eroy-Beaulieu and Established Liberalism in *F*rance

1
The Study of an Ideologist

■ Few economists, especially ones who have actually existed, ever appear in fiction. Neither great ones such as Adam Smith nor the "vulgar economists" castigated by Marx have attracted the novelist's attention. One exception is a French writer and journalist of the late nineteenth century, Paul Leroy-Beaulieu. We encounter him, if briefly, in the pages of Marcel Proust's *A la Recherche du Temps Perdu*. In *Le Côté des Guermantes* the protagonist asks the Comte de Norpois for advice about achieving election to the Académie des Sciences Morales et Politiques, and the count replies that without the support of Leroy-Beaulieu a candidate will not be successful.[1] The presence of the economist in this monument of French literature testifies to his formidable personality and to the prominent place he held in French intellectual life during the 1800s. A number of studies have described Leroy-Beaulieu as the foremost advocate among French academics of the policy of colonial imperialism, but he was more than just an imperialist. Political figures and social thinkers during his own lifetime pointed to him as the representative spokesman for the views of the dominant social classes and mainstream academic opinions in France.[2] Today's historians also cite him regularly in works on the social and economic history of the period.

Although Leroy-Beaulieu was active in the realms of business, politics, and journalism, the main interest he holds for us is as a typical member of the Liberal Grande Bourgeoisie. He represented this class as a commentator on French life, a defender of the social and economic institutions that emerged in France after the French

Revolution, and an intellectual heir of generations of Liberal thinkers. By studying the whole of his social, political, and economic
thought, we can gain a fuller picture of a time, a social class, and
Liberalism itself.

Leroy-Beaulieu was both wide-ranging and eminently successful
in his intellectual endeavors. Born in Normandy in 1843, he wrote
indefatigably from the outset of his career, in the mid-1860s, until
just before his death in 1916. Between 1867 and 1870 he submitted
five manuscripts in competitions sponsored by the Académie des
Sciences Morales et Politiques, and in each case he won the prize.[3]
During the same period he launched a career as a journalist, becoming a commentator on social problems for a number of periodicals.
By the early 1870s he was contributing regularly to the *Revue des
Deux Mondes* and the *Journal des Débats*. In 1873 he founded his
own weekly, *L'Economiste Français*, which soon was considered the
outstanding publication in France devoted to business and economic
affairs.[4] As a teacher he also occupied a significant place. In 1872
he began lecturing on public finance at the Ecole Libre des Sciences
Politiques, and in 1880 he followed J.-B. Say, Pellegrino Rossi,
and Michel Chevalier as occupant of the Chair of Political Economy
at the Collège de France. The year before he had already achieved
election to the Académie des Sciences Morales et Politiques, and,
as Proust informs us, he soon played a highly visible role in that
branch of the Institut de France.

Leroy-Beaulieu won his position of eminence largely by eloquently restating the mainstream Liberal thought of his time. This
version of Liberalism, born in the early 1800s, had become a kind
of intellectual establishment in France, practically monopolizing the
teaching of economics in France until the late 1870s. The great depression of the 1930s and the triumph of Keynesianism and the Welfare State in the late 1940s and early 1950s seemed to put an end
to Leroy-Beaulieu's type of Liberalism, and he slipped into obscurity along with his school of thought. Although historians of
nineteenth-century France encountered him in the references of his
contemporaries, he was generally forgotten even in his own country.
However, his brand of social-political thought is once again influential in the public discourse of the West, and the French are regaining
an interest in forms of Liberalism kindred to the one he espoused.
Therefore, Leroy-Beaulieu's reputation and ideas may be getting
more attention.[5] This shift in ideological currents makes it particularly important to place Leroy-Beaulieu in the history of ideas and

ideologies. To do so we must review the role he played in his own era and reflect on the foundations of his thought.

Leroy-Beaulieu's career coincided with the first half of the Third Republic. Throughout this period his main role was as a spokesman. Before he turned fifty, he was an outstanding champion of imperialism, a leading advocate of free trade, and a preeminent defender of the interests of large industrial and commercial enterprises. However, as a thinker Leroy-Beaulieu was never original: he generally repeated formulas and arguments that his predecessors in the Liberal establishment had developed. Other well-known politicians, intellectuals, and journalists of his time propagated the same system of beliefs. Either Frédéric Passy, who preceded Leroy-Beaulieu into the Académie, or Maurice Block, who edited dictionaries of political economy and contributed numerous articles to the *Journal des Economistes*, could be chosen as a representative figure. Two other Liberals, Jules Simon and Léon Say, were more in the public eye than Leroy-Beaulieu during the first decades of the Third Republic and, until their deaths in the 1890s, played a far more important role in the political realm. However, since Leroy-Beaulieu wrote so much and since his works are so accessible, his words give us an especially complete entry into the values, beliefs, and dilemmas of mainstream Liberals during the early Third Republic.

Leroy-Beaulieu's intellectual efforts centered on confronting three challenges to the institutions he valued: the discontent of the Working Class, the development of arguments in favor of government intervention in economic life, and the emergence of a new political system in his country. Like previous generations of French Liberals, Leroy-Beaulieu and his colleagues in the establishment were preoccupied with the rise of Socialism and other radical movements among workers. But by the early 1880s, Marx, Lassalle, and trade unionism had replaced St. Simonian and Communitarian radicals as the foremost challengers of Liberal values. As for proposals for government intervention in the economy, the late nineteenth-century Liberal establishment shared its forebears' opposition; but beginning in the 1870s the demand for state action no longer came only from industrialists and merchants who wanted protective tariffs, subsidies, and other favors. Now reformers—some with respectable academic credentials—were calling on government to shape economic conditions and set up social-security systems. There was also a new political situation. Unlike the Liberals of the July Monarchy, the establishment figures of the late nineteenth century did not have to face agitation by the masses for the vote. The battle against the expansion of the right to vote had been lost, and universal suffrage had already become a powerful force in French political life. Leroy-Beaulieu and like-minded thinkers had to wrestle with the consequences of this change.

Despite the breadth of his concerns, only Leroy-Beaulieu's ideology of imperialism has been studied extensively. Notwithstanding his great output of books and articles on colonies, much more of his work defends the social and economic superiority of the Grande Bourgeoisie. In response to proposals for government intervention, Leroy-Beaulieu propagated free-enterprise solutions for the miseries of the Working Class. For decades he struggled to find a basis for circumscribing government involvement in economic life. However, from the late 1870s on, transformations in the political life of his country began to distress him, and he wrote extensively about the failings of the system of government that had been established after the fall of the Second Empire.

Fundamentally Leroy-Beaulieu acted as an ideologist, not an economist or social theorist. He never devoted himself to the investigation of society or the development of new economic theories. In early and late writings alike, Leroy-Beaulieu presented himself as champion of the group he called alternately the bourgeoisie and the middle classes, a group he described as composed of high, middle, and lower segments. Yet his basic allegiance was to preserving the status of the highest of the three segments, the Grande Bourgeoisie. He allied himself closely with the economic interests of one section of that elite: French manufacturers and merchants engaged in international trade. Thus he became a leading defender of free trade and of the concentration of firms into larger and larger enterprises.

To call Leroy-Beaulieu an ideologist is not to condemn him. His skillful defenses of Capitalism and the class system must have reinforced the confidence of many beneficiaries of those institutions. At the same time he developed an eloquent critique of the ideas and policies of his opponents, casting doubt upon the value of alternatives to the existing social and economic arrangements. In the area of politics he offered trenchant critiques of the republican regime, although he never succeeded in formulating an alternative that would have appealed across class lines. Leroy-Beaulieu's supporters believed that he identified major weaknesses in the outlook of reformers, socialists, and advanced republicans. Those who disagreed with his ideas confronted a powerfully argued ideology, an ideology that was a form of Liberalism.

*B*efore proceeding further we must clarify the meaning of the crucial term *ideology*. Lionel Trilling captured a central contrast between theorists and ideologists when he commented that a great Liberal of the eighteenth century "did not give new answers to old questions or propose questions never asked before. He possessed himself of the ideas of the philosophical originators of his own time and of the past; he chose among these ideas and made use of them."[6] Following Trilling, we can reserve the terms *philosophy* and *political theory* for a questioning, speculative mode of inquiry as opposed to the mainly practical, politically committed intellectual activity we will call *ideology*. Politically partisan thinkers, or ideologists, use the ideas already available in order to change the world in which they live or to prevent change.

To label someone an ideologist courts the danger of seeming to denigrate that person's ideas, for the word can connote rationalizations of selfish class interests, unworkable abstractions, and unscientific, distorted views of reality. Fortunately, some social scientists and historians employ a neutral definition that we can use in place of the pejorative ones. In this sense, "an ideology is a set of statements that purports to explain society while evaluating social institutions according to norms of justice or morality in such a way that these statements can be used to mobilize groups of people into a movement to defend, modify, or overthrow the existing institutions."[7] Often the best sign that we are dealing with such a doctrine is a combative tone. Whereas nineteenth-century theorists also were often quite polemical, individuals who are mainly oriented to social and political mobilization will normally have polemic as a basic trait, since they are fighting on a battlefield of ideas. We will usually find other traits, such as an emphasis on applying rather than on verifying theories, that tell us we are in the midst of an ideological struggle rather than a theoretical debate.

Few people look on themselves as ideologists, and thus they do not separate the ideological element from the totality of their thought. Leroy-Beaulieu was no exception, even though he operated more on the ideological level than on any other. Even his early books, which had a largely scholarly character, contain important ideological sections, designed to counter the prescriptions of social reformers. Yet we rarely find formal boundaries in his writing between the social scientist and the protector of the interests of business owners and the Grande Bourgeoisie. When we approach Leroy-Beaulieu's works as ideological statements, therefore, we must sometimes extract the ideological outlook because it is not on the surface. Since Leroy-Beaulieu stated his own views frequently and consistently, identifying the ideological side of his writings is seldom difficult.

Liberalism, Martin Seliger claims, is one of the most complete ideological systems,[8] but what essentially is Liberalism? This term presents problems even greater than those involved in defining ideology. There is such a variety of beliefs among those who have been identified as Liberals that no one has yet offered a widely acceptable statement of the essence of Liberalism. In addition, the fairly clear distinction that existed in the early 1800s between Liberalism and Conservatism has become blurred by an indiscriminate application of the term "conservative" to anyone who supports maintenance of the status quo. Another source of the difficulty is that the 1800s, in France at least, saw a growing rapprochement between people who thought of themselves as Liberals and people who considered themselves Conservatives, and thinkers created doctrines that contained elements from both ideological streams.[9]

Time must be a factor in our formulation of a conception of Liberalism, since this doctrine has a history. One can imagine Liberalism as a stream flowing through time, dividing into a number of branches and receiving a number of tributaries. Or the stream can be conceived of as composed of a number of currents. Although this stream is complex and still too much in development to permit a neat definition, we can place an individual such as Leroy-Beaulieu in a specific current of Liberal belief. One good indication of a Liberal in nineteenth-century France was that he or she rejected the Old Regime and approved the social, economic, and political life that emerged in the aftermath of the French and Industrial Revolutions. Liberals characteristically believed that the development and happiness of the individual are supremely important, that private property and the market are essential institutions, that transformations of technology and dynamic industrial growth are salutary, that parliamentary institutions and protection against arbitrary government action are vital for human existence, and that social mobility is essential for a good society. Before identifying someone as a Liberal we must verify that that person accepts the "Modern Regime."[10] Leroy-Beaulieu was a champion of that regime, and he moved contentedly in a particular current within the stream of Liberal belief systems, the current of Established Liberalism.

2

Background and Youth

Leroy-Beaulieu in the Era of the Second Empire

■ Paul Leroy-Beaulieu began his career by winning the favorable attention of a key bastion of the Liberal establishment. In 1867, when he was only twenty-four, the Académie des Sciences Morales et Politiques awarded him the first of the five prizes he would win over the next three years. This auspicious debut marked his first step up from the social status he had inherited from his father. During the next decade a series of successes won him social promotion into the ranks of the Grande Bourgeoisie. His writings reveal that Leroy-Beaulieu conceived of himself as a spokesman for this elite class. Yet he was not merely a paid mouthpiece since he became a representative member of the Grande Bourgeoisie not only in ideology but also in career, marriage, and in personal economic situation. Embarking on a career as a commentator on current social, economic, and political controversies, he made a secure place for himself within the Liberal establishment, and the leaders of this establishment assisted his rise in status. To understand Leroy-Beaulieu's thought, therefore, we must first outline his family background, the key developments of the time that he wrote about, the nature of Liberalism in mid-nineteenth-century France, and the character of the Grande Bourgeoisie.

According to some theorists, the class historians now tend to call the Grande Bourgeoisie was forged during the eighteenth century. By the 1820s it clearly existed as a self-conscious status group, expressing its interests through political organizations. The families in the Grande Bourgeoisie were rich, some extremely rich. Generally they could boast of more than one generation of family members who had been wealthy and conspicuous in public life. Following the fall of Robespierre in 1794 these families held great and sometimes dominant power in French political life. Along with the remnants of the aristocracy they controlled most decision making at least into the early years of the Third Republic. The class consisted of important financiers, the biggest industrialists, and landowners with large estates. The upper levels of the bureaucracy were members of these groups; an official promoted to an upper-level post gained entry for himself and his family into the nonnoble elite.[1]

At the time of Paul's birth his family belonged to the milieu of bourgeois landowners praised by Guizot in 1849 as the natural rulers of France. The family was rooted in the Calvados region of Normandy, and apparently during the French Revolution it rose to importance there.[2] As local notables, they held a status certainly superior to what we would call Middle Class today, but my impression is that they were still in the vague border area of families whose position was not solidly grand bourgeois. That is, the family was not sufficiently important in either its fortune, ancestors, relatives, or role to belong to the highest stratum of the bourgeoisie of the mid-1800s. Nevertheless, when Paul Leroy-Beaulieu was born, the family was moving up the social hierarchy. Pierre Leroy-Beaulieu, the future economist's father, was wealthy enough to be an elector at a time when that right depended upon possession of a considerable income. Furthermore, he combined landownership with an administrative career. Like his father before him, he became mayor of Lisieux, but his career did not stop there. In the late 1820s François Guizot became his political patron after purchasing Val Richer, an estate in the neighborhood of the Leroy-Beaulieu lands. Through this support, Pierre became subprefect at Saumur in 1843, and later Guizot obtained for him a promotion to the rank of prefect—still in his native department of Calvados where Lisieux was the seat of government. An article on Pierre in the *Dictionnaire des Parlementaires* cites a "biography" that declared that he "was completely devoted to the policies of Guizot" and "repaid him . . . in electoral and prefectoral zeal everything which he received in tokens of benevolence."[3] The association between the powerful minister of the July Monarchy and the bourgeois notable of Lisieux may have been more than just political. According to one lifelong associate of Paul

Leroy-Beaulieu, Pierre often took his son with him on visits to Val Richer, and that implies a degree of friendship.[4] The Revolution of 1848 temporarily checked the ambitions of this protégé of Guizot, but in 1849 he profited from the antirevolutionary tide and as a candidate of the "monarchic conservatives" was elected to the Legislative Assembly. After the coup d'état of December 1851, when President Louis-Napoleon Bonaparte made himself the dictator of France, Pierre succeeded in having himself adopted as an official candidate, and he presented himself to his electors in the following terms:

> At all times and from different official posts I have zealously served the Party of Order, and after the February Revolution, in the midst of the universal unrest, as soon as the name of Louis Napoleon came to the fore, I rallied enthusiastically to him as the sole figure who could save our imperiled society. . . . No one is more convinced than me of the immense services Louis Napoleon has bestowed on our France and of those which he is destined to bestow in the future. I would be happy, on entering the Corps Legislatif, to be able to be associated with the measures he will take to reestablish order, base authority on solid foundations, and strengthen the general prosperity. I will support his government frankly, faithfully, and without any mental reservations.[5]

This lifetime member of the Party of Order kept the favor of the new rulers of France for about six years. Then the imperial bureaucrats decided that he was still too attached to the Orleanists. His official support was withdrawn, and Pierre lost his seat in the election of 1857. Two years later, at the age of sixty-one, he died. He left behind a daughter from a first marriage and two sons, sixteen-year-old Anatole and fifteen-year-old Paul, from his second marriage.

Paul Leroy-Beaulieu was born in Saumur in 1843 while his father was subprefect there.[6] His mother, Marguerite Laurence de Sainte Chapelle, was the second wife of Pierre Leroy-Beaulieu. Her father had been an *intendant militaire* (that is, an officer in the administrative services of the army), an officer of the Légion d'Honneur, and a Chevalier de Saint-Louis. That is practically all we know about her except that she was an extremely devout Catholic who moved permanently to Rome a few years after the death of her husband. Her inheritance and those of her sons enabled them all to live comfortably if not luxuriously.[7]

Throughout their youth the brothers Leroy-Beaulieu were sur-

rounded by prosperity, comfort, and respect, but their relatives expected them to climb even higher. Therefore, they were given the
best education possible. The first glimpse we get of Paul and Anatole's lives is at the Lycée Bonaparte, one of the elite secondary
schools of Paris. Their names appeared on the lists of prize winners
"an incalculable number" of times. In school assemblies "it was
always a Leroy-Beaulieu who was called to the tribune."[8] Given
the competitive nature of education in French *lycées*, these successes
must have resulted from a combination of application, academic intelligence, and acceptance of their family's expectations.

In fact, we have one particularly valuable confirmation of young
Paul's conformity to the values of his milieu. In a letter he wrote
at the age of seventeen to his half-sister, he commented:

> Everyone has his caprices; my brother's is collecting books and graphics,
> and collecting languages in his memory; that is undoubtedly an innocent
> pleasure. As for me, what is my caprice? I do not know, unless it is
> not to have any at all, to follow those of others, and to give myself
> up to those that surround me; or, rather, I am mistaken, mine is to
> work. I recently read that all men of merit are naturally lazy, so I am
> excluded from their number; too bad. I will not be stupid enough to
> become lazy just to become meritorious.[9]

Hard intellectual labor offered him more pleasure than idleness or
leisure. Already during his adolescence he had committed himself
to the value that remained the chief tenet of his ethical creed
throughout his life: work.

Paul and Anatole's performances in school seem to demonstrate
that they were dutiful sons, but both showed a degree of independence in their choice of careers. The question of a profession arose
for Paul after he had completed his law degree in Paris and had
spent the school year of 1864–1865 attending some courses in philosophy at the universities of Bonn and Berlin in Germany. The law
degree was the usual preliminary to obtaining a post in public administration, and members of the family wanted the brothers to
follow their late father's footsteps into a secure, prestigious career
in the bureaucracy. Both of them, nevertheless, insisted on choosing
their own directions. Anatole attempted, for a while, to make a
name for himself in the world of literature by publishing poems
and a novel. Apparently he had a healthy inheritance that permitted
him to persevere for some years despite a lack of success. After
more than a decade, however, he turned to the social sciences and

won a reputation that endures to this day as a student of Czarist Russia. Paul, in contrast, "right away took up the study of political economy and never quit it."[10] More exactly, he launched into that profession whose members the French call "publicistes" and whose meaning is only partially captured by the terms journalist and columnist. He sought to publish articles on topics related to agriculture and business. As a commentator on public affairs, Paul could hope to supplement his less opulent inheritance and take some significant steps towards higher status.

Though we do not know just how strong his relatives' pressure was, Paul Leroy-Beaulieu's decision not to become a bureaucrat hints at a strength of character. His singleness of purpose, his way of life in Paris, the amount of work he accomplished in a short time, and the values his publications expressed and defended tempt me to speak of him as an inner-directed personality. For some years he lunched with one or more friends in the same cafe in Paris, discussing "the economic and social topics which impassioned them." Years later one of them recalled, "I remember that no matter how animated our conversation or how attractive the prospect of a stroll after the meal, Paul Leroy-Beaulieu, though free from any professional engagement, took out his watch every day at the same hour and, lunch hardly finished, returned to his desk to work." The aspiring publicist amused himself solely with English novels and occasionally with the theater.[11] It is easy to picture these solemn Frenchmen in their early twenties dressed in the sober colors and severe costume of those of good family in the modern industrial age. Either unconsciously or quite intentionally they symbolized their allegiance to the austere ethic we associate with Puritanism and Capitalism. Puritanical devotion to a professional calling gripped no one more firmly than it did Paul Leroy-Beaulieu. His material inheritance and social-cultural heritage placed him close enough to the summit of French society that he could hope to attain it in his own lifetime if he exerted enough effort.

The key social and political developments of the 1860s in France were the end of the authoritarian stage of the Second Empire, the progress of economic modernization in France, and the revival of working-class and Socialist agitation. A survey of these developments and of the responses by Liberal leaders will help us grasp the meaning of the young Leroy-Beaulieu's views as he began to address current conditions and controversies.

Paul Leroy-Beaulieu became a publicist at a politically favorable moment for a scion of an Orleanist family. By 1865 Napoleon III had begun the process of liberalizing the political system of the Second Empire. Between 1865 and 1867 a series of laws gave the opposition members of the parliament greater freedom to debate government policy and to address public opinion through a press newly liberated from harassment and censorship. Periodicals seized the opportunity for critical examination of French life, and after 1867 dissenters also gained the right to hold public meetings to stir up opposition to the Empire. At the end of 1869 the emperor took another major step, permitting the erstwhile Liberal Republican deputy, Emile Ollivier, to form a majority cabinet made up of a coalition of centrists in the legislature. When the new government took office at the beginning of 1870, the country seemed on the brink of becoming a constitutional monarchy. Hitherto dedicated Liberal followers of the Orleans family were ready to transfer their allegiance to the emerging Liberal Empire.[12]

The Orleanists' attitudes toward the Bonapartist regime had begun shifting earlier. Many of them had reluctantly accepted the imposition of an authoritarian government in December 1851 because they were fearful about the outcome of the election scheduled for 1852. But after the new regime crushed the radical forces, the religious and foreign policies of the Second Empire led Liberals of all stripes into opposition to the government.[13] Nevertheless, by 1859 or 1860 leading Orleanist Liberals were ready to sacrifice their adherence to the Orleans family. Victor de Broglie, a Catholic Liberal and Orleanist notable, distributed in 1861 a few copies of his *Vue sur le Gouvernement de la France*, in which he stated frankly that the form of the political regime mattered far less than its commitment to parliamentary, constitutional government. Even a republic would be acceptable, he suggested, if it had a president and senate who could limit the impact of universal suffrage and thus preserve property, individual economic freedoms, and the influence of the "enlightened" classes.[14]

The Liberal orientation is illustrated by the attitude of the *Revue des Deux Mondes* toward the Second Empire. The founder and editor of the *Revue*, François Buloz, accepted the seizure of power by Louis-Napoleon as a guarantee of security, stability, and order. Still Buloz and his political chroniclers did not give up their attachment to mid-nineteenth-century Liberal viewpoints. One political commentator, Forcade, expressed this outlook in his warnings against "the exaggeration of expenditures, the thoughtless impulsion given to public works, . . . and the absence of coordinated views in the direction of our political economy." In the same article he stated a key Liberal tenet, warning that "There is no good financial governance at all without political liberty, outside of complete and rigorous control by representative assemblies and by the vigilant polemics of a free press."[15]

These statements show that this kind of French Liberalism had in common with its contemporary counterpart across the channel a strong desire for "cheap government." The Empire could hardly win the hearts of Buloz and his collaborators on this count. But the *Revue* did not automatically reject the Bonapartist dynasty. As Buloz wrote in a letter of June 1869 to Charles de Mazade, the political chronicler of the journal at that time, "we have finally neither any preference nor any antipathy for or against any political form, . . . we judge them all in proportion to the services they can render to liberty."[16] One important work published in 1868 gives us a measure of how far the political outlook of the heirs of Orleanism moved, especially after the emperor began to reestablish political freedoms. The book was *La France Nouvelle*, and the author was Lucien Prévost-Paradol, a young Liberal publicist. Although not yet forty, Prévost-Paradol was already a leading journalist and a major spokesman for mainstream Liberalism. His achievement was the adaptation of Orleanist Liberalism to the new circumstances of the day: the entrenchment of universal manhood suffrage and the liberalization of the imperial government. Unlike Guizot, Liberals of Prévost-Paradol's stripe accepted Tocqueville's thesis that the coming of democracy was inevitable. To them, democracy meant the existence of a powerful lower house of the legislature, elected by all the adult males of France. Once the original authoritarian constitution of the imperial system was replaced, Prévost-Paradol expected the once-weak lower house would become more and more influential. As with de Broglie in 1861, the crucial question for Prévost-Paradol was how to limit the power of this democratic branch of government. *La France Nouvelle* presupposes the continuation of a strong, monarchical executive as one barrier to "excessive" democratization and called for a strong, indirectly chosen second house of the legislature, which would be able to check the power of the legislators chosen by universal suffrage. As a final protection against rule by the people, Prévost-Paradol turned to a proposal popularized by Tocqueville and embraced by Guizot after his fall from power: the decentralization of the government. Finally, Prévost-Paradol welcomed the evolution of the regime and announced his support for it. In doing so he spoke for the new generation of the Liberal camp and helped to solidify their outlook.[17]

Economically the Second Empire was a crucial period in the modernization of France. Laws in 1863 and 1867 ended the elaborate and time-consuming procedure for forming limited-liability companies and permitted the almost unrestricted formation of business corporations. These measures meant that entrepreneurs could more easily assemble large amounts of capital and thus create giant enterprises that would enable the French to expand industrial production at a very rapid pace.[18] At least as dramatic was the movement toward free trade with other countries. This goal was dear to the Liberal economist Michel Chevalier, who had rallied to the new regime immediately after the coup of 1851. By the end of the 1850s he persuaded the emperor that the protectionist tariff system hindered the country's economic growth. In 1860 Chevalier succeeded in negotiating a commercial treaty between France and Britain that liberalized trade between the two nations. Similar treaties with other European lands followed. Staunch Liberal politicians such as Adolphe Thiers, still dedicated protectionists, detested the change, but Liberal economists had been fighting for it for decades.[19]

The "Social Question," namely what to do about the misery of the poor and the dissatisfaction of workers, entered a new stage as a result of the political evolution of the Second Empire. At the same time that Napoleon III began to make gestures toward the Liberal opposition, he endeavored to appeal anew to French workers through reforms favoring labor unions. In 1864 the government repealed the French Revolutionary legislation, the le Chapelier law, which forbade workers to form "coalitions." This important emancipation of the working class was followed in 1867 by legislation that permitted public political meetings, a measure strongly desired by both Liberals and workers. Despite the continuation of some restrictions, radical reformers and labor leaders took full advantage of the new opportunity for organization and for mass appeals.[20]

Universal manhood suffrage dictated the emperor's actions on behalf of the workers. In the late 1860s, as parliamentary elections increased the number of opponents of the regime, Napoleon hoped to obtain the allegiance of the artisans and the growing number of industrial workers. But it soon became evident that the regime's actions had been too limited to achieve their purpose. The Republican opposition won a majority of votes in the urban centers in the 1869 legislative election, and a wave of strikes between 1868 and 1870 demonstrated that the working class remained as discontented as it had been during the July Monarchy.[21] Napoleon's gestures toward the workers had heightened the urgency of the Social Question rather than solving it.

At the time of these transformations, what did it mean to be an economic journalist? What place did the study of economics have in the life of the mind of France, and what place did French economists have in the public affairs of their country? To understand Leroy-Beaulieu's thought we must look more closely at Liberalism in France, especially as it took shape in the aftermath of the French Revolution.

While the Classical Liberals of the eighteenth century were reformers who fought for a basic transformation of the Old Regime, the leading Liberals of the Restoration, July Monarchy, and Second Empire sought to prevent any significant modification of the modern regime created between 1789 and 1815. Therefore, the dominant Liberalism of this period was a defensive Liberalism.[22] Soon after the Revolution of 1830 and the creation of the July Monarchy, these Liberals constructed a strong intellectual establishment. Under the leadership of François Guizot, Orleanist Liberals took control of the French university system. The government entrusted the direction of higher education and, above all, the teaching of philosophy to Victor Cousin, who trained a generation of "Spiritualist" disciples to propagate a moderate Liberal outlook. Moreover, in the mid-1830s Guizot brought about the revival of a branch of the Institut de France set up during the Revolution and suppressed by Napoleon: the Académie des Sciences Morales et Politiques.[23] Since the academicians themselves elected new members, the Académie became the stronghold of the establishment. So did the Collège de France, whose professors also decided by vote who would succeed to vacant chairs. As a result, the Orleanist Liberals obtained an influence over French intellectual life that lasted long after the fall of the July Monarchy.[24]

Eminent figures among the professional economists, a new group of specialists, were also admitted into these two centers of the Liberal intellectual establishments, the Institut and the Collège de France.

Led largely by Joseph Garnier (1813–1881), Liberal economists founded the Société d'Economie Politique in 1840 and in 1842 began to publish the *Journal des Economistes*, which remained the sole prestigious journal in the field until 1887. In all their endeavors they had the support of the Guillaumin publishing house.[25]

Early in the nineteenth century Jean-Baptiste Say enunciated the principles to which established economists still adhered during the Second Empire. Say was a transitional figure between aggressive Liberals who attacked the Old Regime and defensive ones who sought to protect the Liberal social-political institutions whose existence the Revolution and Napoleon had consecrated. Writing in the aftermath of Napoleon's reimposition of mercantilism, Say denounced current government policies, yet he also helped to lay the basis for an economics that resisted alterations of free-enterprise Capitalism. Reviving the viewpoint of the Physiocrats, Say portrayed nature in terms of the clear-cut operation of a machine. The principles that accounted for the functioning of a self-regulating economy governed by market forces were "natural laws" that human beings could not set aside without causing breakdowns of production and unnecessary misery. Say and his successors first used this conception to promote laissez-faire and then adapted it to refute the reform program of dissident economists like Sismonde de Sismondi and the radical proposals of Utopian Socialists.[26]

The orthodox economists, as they were sometimes called, united most strongly on two issues: free trade and peace. They promoted the view that the wealth of nations would expand faster if all barriers to international commerce were removed. Their dedication to free trade was linked to their desire for world peace. From the early 1800s, beginning as early as Benjamin Constant and Henri de Saint-Simon, French publicists had proclaimed the imminent end of the warlike military era that had existed since earliest times. War, they declared, made no sense in the present age in which people were ever more devoted to industry and commerce. The abolition of barriers to the circulation of goods among nations, they insisted, would speed the coming of the era of peace because the prosperity of all peoples would come to depend upon peaceful international exchanges. This doctrine became an integral part of the outlook of the established economists. Even during the generation of armed conflict that began in Europe with the Crimean War they held fast to their faith that the growth of production and trade would lead to amity among nations.[27]

Despite their agreement over fundamentals, the Liberal economists of the mid-nineteenth century had a real if restricted range of differences of opinion.[28] They engaged in considerable controversy over what we might call technical questions, such as the impact of paper currency, the operation of the gold standard, the financing of railroads, and the regulation of credit. However, they agreed on basic ideological points. There were only minor differences over method, since all the economists held fast to the Ricardian deductive approach, "the good old dogmatic method," as Anselme Batbie characterized it.[29] Only a few members of the group called for supplementing deductive reasoning with empirical study. One major debate did occur over the "iron laws" of population and wages. Part of the establishment held fast to the formulations of T. R. Malthus and David Ricardo while a growing number disputed the reasoning of the two English thinkers. The former group may have regarded themselves as the more scientific since the motivations of the revisionists were almost openly ideological. The latter recognized that the iron laws implied that the economic interests of social-economic classes were irremediably opposed, and, therefore, they feared that the Malthusian and Ricardian teachings would have a radicalizing impact on the lower classes. Above all, they disliked Ricardo's analysis of the natural forces governing the distribution of wealth because it indicated that the gains of any social class—landowners, workers, or capitalists—came at the expense of the other classes.[30] The leading thinker of the "optimists," as the revisionists came to be called, was Frédéric Bastiat (1801–1850) who in the late 1840s formulated an eloquent battery of arguments defending his belief in the existence of a natural harmony of interests in society.[31]

On the theoretical and ideological levels perhaps the liveliest debate was over the proper role of the government. At least a few mid-nineteenth-century French Liberal economists rigidly insisted that government had only three functions to perform: preserving a country from external attack, preventing or punishing violence inside a country, and ensuring the fulfillment of private contracts. In fact, some went so far as to insist that governments should not even set up schools; education must be provided, they argued, by private individuals and associations. Probably most of the members of the Société d'Economie Politique were not so unbending. Although Charles Dunoyer (1786–1862) and Frédéric Bastiat held fast to laissez-faire, others, like Michel Chevalier, took a more positive attitude toward the state and had a more flexible version of the established doctrine.[32] With Dunoyer and Bastiat, Chevalier held that increasing production was society's prime need, and he supported the widest possible amount of freedom from government interference for entrepreneurs. Moreover, during the Revolution of 1848 he vigorously defended the existing economic institutions against Louis Blanc's criticisms. However, Chevalier believed that principles might have to be modified in practice because of circumstances, and he felt state agencies should be active in a number of areas of the economy, such as the provision of credit and vocational education. The urgent public need for education, good transportation, healthy cities, and honest stock transactions led most established economists to approve of a few, modest legislative measures. In general, however, they also sought to define a strict line beyond which legislators and bureaucrats would be forbidden to go. The debate was over whether any concession would weaken the line.[33]

This survey of the ideas of the main school of French economic thought in the nineteenth century shows why referring to this group of thinkers as "laissez-faire Liberals" or the "orthodox school," is an oversimplification. Instead we will use the term "Established Liberals" for the economists who gave their general allegiance to the heritage of Adam Smith and Jean-Baptiste Say, and for the politicians and political thinkers who sprang from the Orleanist heritage.

*I*t is difficult to gauge the influence of the Established Liberal economists, but the practical issues they studied grew in importance as the French economy developed. For decades intense public debate had gone on over such practical questions as the incidence of taxation, the proper organization of credit facilities, the advantages of free trade or of tariff protection, the desirability of gold, silver, or paper money, and the proper activity of the state with regard to railroad construction and operation. Since some economists saw a link between education and economic productivity, there was also discussion over whether the state should take the lead in providing schooling for the masses. Yet none of these issues were more pressing than working-class bitterness over low wages, long hours, poor working conditions, and the indignities workers suffered on and off the job.[34]

Literary figures, journalists, historians, professors of philosophy, professional philosophers, alumni of the Ecole Polytechnique, and, of course, members of the administration proposed solutions for the Social Question, as well as for other current economic topics. Sometimes the small group of professional economists seems merely to be a beleaguered fraction of the learned and literary world. Moreover, these specialists faced considerable resistance to their expert judgments, as their educated and influential contemporaries were often skeptical of the value of economic theory. Even fellow Liberals, like the political journalist Lucien Prévost-Paradol, denigrated their views.[35] The Bonapartists themselves must have been rather hostile to the established economists, since the regime had an interventionist bias.[36] Furthermore, the Société d'Economie Politique and the Académie des Sciences Morales et Politiques were tainted with Orleanism, and many of the economists must have been or have appeared to be members of the opposition to the imperial regime. As a consequence their access to official circles may have been limited.

Because they lacked support from official circles, the economists faced obstacles even in disseminating their views. Until 1864 the only economics courses regularly given in Paris were one or two at the Collège de France and one each at the Conservatoire des Arts et Métiers and at the Ecole des Ponts et Chaussées. There was no university teaching of economics at all. When the minister of education finally authorized a chair at the Faculty of Law in Paris, the government sent police spies to the lecture on the day the course opened.[37] The economists possibly spoke mainly to each other, through periodicals of limited circulation such as the *Journal des Débats*, and to a few like-minded Orleanist notables and major businessmen.

However, several aspects of the economists' situation could attract ambitious and intellectually inclined persons into their ranks. One benefit was financial. As members of the intellectual establishment, the economists helped control access to lucrative rewards and posts. Those coopted by election into the Institut received a handsome annual stipend. The Institut also gave sizable monetary prizes for manuscripts submitted in the competitions it sponsored every year. Furthermore, by the mid-1860s the economists could provide an aspirant with considerable opportunity for publication and public notice. The Société d'Economie Politique and its journal received the sponsorship of the important Guillaumin publishing company, which also brought out many of the books in the field. Aspiring economists had to conform to the orthodox views, however, since the Liberal establishment could prevent a candidate who opposed their viewpoints from being chosen for a chair in economics or from placing articles in the *Revue des Deux Mondes* or the *Journal des Débats*.

By the mid-1860s the Liberal economists were emerging from their narrow corner of French public life. As their field of study grew in importance, the public lectures and the Institut's prize competitions boosted their efforts to get publicity and to disseminate their ideas. The liberalization of the regime also assisted them. As Orleanists played a larger role in public life, the economists had more of a chance to be heard. And despite the intellectual limitations of established economics, the discipline had the outstanding advantage of offering the only complete explanation (other than the socialist doctrines regarded with intense hostility by most propertied French people) of the processes of production, exchange, commerce, and distribution. Finally, the handful of individuals who were making economics their profession were in intimate contact with influential literary figures, journalists, historians, professors of philosophy, alumni of the technical schools, and even important administrators. Some of these prominent individuals joined the Société d'Economie Politique, and members of this society formed an important segment of the Académie des Sciences Morales et Politiques.[38]

The comprehensiveness and coherence of the established Liberal system, with its relatively modest variations, explains another attraction of a career in the nascent economics profession. The establishment economists spoke and wrote with an enormous confidence in the validity of their statements. Since the time of Condorcet, if not since that of Montesquieu, thinkers had aspired to create a "science of society" as firmly based on natural laws as the physics of Newton. Economists often proclaimed that the founders of their discipline had uncovered the natural laws that regulated the production and distribution of riches. Palmade describes them as "full of assurance that they possessed a definitive truth" and quotes as typical the confident claim of Hippolyte Passy that "today political economy is a completed science" whose "fundamental principles are safe from any real attack."[39] In an age troubled over the decline of certainties, self-assured economists presented their discipline as a system with a concept of human nature, a view of the purpose of life, a sense of the meaning of history, and a set of prescriptions for the structure and operation of government, society, and the economy.

We can see, therefore, why Paul Leroy-Beaulieu might have wanted to enter the circle of the established economists. His Orleanist background gave him entry. He saw the opportunity for a career devoted to research and writing. And despite the limited influence that these specialists had exercised in the past, the ever-growing attention to questions of business and finance and the liberalization of political life in France gave reason to believe that more economists would become figures of great importance, just as Michel Chevalier had already become a key adviser to Louis-Napoleon Bonaparte.

Paul Leroy-Beaulieu began working as a publicist in 1865, at the age of twenty-two, soon after returning from his year of study in Germany. He contributed articles to *La Revue Nationale*, a journal whose leading figure, the Orleanist Liberal Edouard Laboulaye, was then considered the leading disciple of Alexis de Tocqueville.[40] At approximately the same time he began work on a manuscript for an Académie prize competition that sought the best treatise on "the influence exercised upon the level of wages by the moral and intellectual state of manual workers." Leroy-Beaulieu won that prize in 1867, and his work was published the following year. Between then and 1870 he wrote four more award-winning essays. In addition he made use of the library the Minister of War "put at his disposal" to do research on the economic consequences of recent European wars.[41] Out of this research came a series of letters on the losses of men and capital in recent wars and overseas expeditions, which appeared in January 1868 in *Le Temps*, the important republican newspaper in Paris. Later that year Leroy-Beaulieu published articles based on those letters in *La Revue Nationale* and *La Revue Contemporaine*. He then expanded these essays into a full-scale study, *Recherches Economiques, Historiques et Statistiques sur les Guerres Contemporaines, 1853–1866.*[42]

Leroy-Beaulieu's first prize-winning manuscript brought him to the attention of the Established Liberal economists of the Académie des Sciences Morales et Politiques. The writing of *Guerres Contemporaines* undoubtedly strengthened the connection. An abridged version of this work became the first publication of the newly formed French branch of the International League for Peace, which had among its leaders a number of Established Liberal notables. Michel Chevalier was a vice president of the organization, and Joseph Garnier, the leading figure in the Société d'Economie Politique, was one of the signers of the founding declaration. The secretary-general was Frédéric Passy, who ten years later would be one of Leroy-Beaulieu's rivals for membership in the Académie.[43] In associating with these figures, Leroy-Beaulieu signaled his adherence to that version of Liberalism denounced by critics as "cosmopolitan." The relationship between Chevalier and Leroy-Beaulieu may have begun as a result of the League's sponsorship of the latter's antiwar research.

Several months after his lengthy pamphlet appeared, Leroy-Beaulieu reaped a major reward for his hard labor, as François Buloz invited him to become a regular contributor to the *Revue des Deux Mondes*.[44] The invitation is in itself evidence of the aspiring publicist's location in the spectrum of French opinion of that day, for the *Revue* was directed at an economically elite audience. As the most recent historian of the bimonthly declared, "Buloz, in order to keep a free hand, deliberately limited himself to a rich and economically comfortable clientele, the only ones capable of buying a publication whose price was so high (the subscription cost fifty francs per year)."[45] In adding Leroy-Beaulieu to his staff, Buloz expected correctly that the young author would defend the cause of liberty as Established Liberals understood it.

In 1869 Leroy-Beaulieu began a remarkably fruitful period as a writer. That year he completed three articles for Buloz, one on the problem of fraudulent issues of stocks and two on agricultural enterprise. In the spring of 1870 he contributed a series of four long articles to the *Revue*, under the general title of "La Question Ouvrière au XIXe Siècle." In the competitions he entered, Leroy-Beaulieu achieved unprecedented success: in 1870 the Académie awarded the prize to each of the four treatises he had submitted. No one else had ever won so many prizes in the Académie contests, and no one ever surpassed this record.[46] The twenty-seven-year-old economist had completed his apprenticeship with a whole series of master works of impressive scope and promise.

Leroy-Beaulieu capped his successes with a brilliant marriage. On May 3, 1870, he married Cordelia Michel Chevalier, the daughter of Michel Chevalier, the economist, adviser to the Emperor, and Imperial Senator. The wedding took place in the chapel of the Senate, and the guests included senators, deputies, members of the Institut and of the Conseil d'Etat, the minister of commerce, and the British ambassador. This union, according to René Stourm, introduced Leroy-Beaulieu "into a sphere of talents, notoriety, and social position that immediately stamped him with the character of a man who had arrived or who was close to doing so."[47] Leroy-Beaulieu's fortune was a relatively modest 500,000 francs, but Cordelia brought substantial financial resources into the marriage because her father, also partly because of an advantageous marriage, had become a wealthy man.[48] Stourm, therefore, is quite justified in referring to this event as Leroy-Beaulieu's arrival at a higher social position. The marriage made Leroy-Beaulieu even more of a representative figure of the French Grande Bourgeoisie, since his social advancement followed from a typical combination of attributes: a good background (with the requisite ancestry, education, and manners), remarkable if not original achievements in intellectual life, and a marriage into a rich and prestigious family. The acceptability of Leroy-Beaulieu's views, nevertheless, may have been the key ingredient enabling him to move from the edges of the Grande Bourgeoisie into its ranks.

3
The Journeyman Publicist

■ By the middle of 1870 Leroy-Beaulieu had produced a series of impressive works, and he was on the brink of becoming a master publicist. An examination of the treatises and articles of his years as an apprentice and journeyman author demonstrates the scope of his interests and provides a portrait of a representative Established Liberal mind at the end of the Second Empire. This portrait will help us measure the trauma Established Liberals suffered as a result of the war and civil strife of 1870-1871.

Work and workers were the subject of Paul Leroy-Beaulieu's first book, *De L'Etat Moral et Intellectuel des Populations Ouvrières et de Son Influence sur le Taux des Salaires*. Submitted to the Académie in 1867 and published the following year, the study prescribed a solution for the Social Question. The young author confidently insisted that education by itself would raise the moral level of the working class, and that improved morality and knowledge would in turn bring about increases in production. As a result, wages would go up and the economic grievances of workers would disappear. In the course of his survey Leroy-Beaulieu took stands on a number of controversial matters: the determinants of wages, the impact of unions and strikes, and the role of government in education. In every case, he advanced the answers favored by those Established Liberals who held most closely to the laissez-faire position. There is nothing original in *L'Etat Moral*, as Hippolyte Passy recognized when he reported on the contest at a meeting of the Académie. Yet its derivative character was by no means held against it. "The author," the older economist commented, "has taken from every known source of information; from every one he has taken numerous insights."[1]

Leroy-Beaulieu's second major publication, *Guerres Contemporaines* (1869), was devoted exclusively to foreign policy. Based on the ideology of peace that many mid-nineteenth-century Liberals had embraced, *Guerres Contemporaines* combines a mild commendation of the development of nation-states with a hint of internationalism. Leroy-Beaulieu expressed at most a moderate endorsement of nationalism, acknowledging that peace would not come to Europe unless each nationality became an independent nation, but he severely criticized European schools for teaching a narrow patriotism, for glorifying war, and for keeping alive old antagonisms between nations.[2]

Packed with statistics and tables that showed the cost of recent wars in lives and resources, *Guerres Contemporaines* surveys colonial expeditions, primarily those by France, as well as conflicts on the continent of Europe. A year later, Leroy-Beaulieu submitted to the Académie a lengthy treatise on all aspects of colonization. Probably one reason why the subject attracted him was that it involved a wide range of topics in economics and administration: "the appropriation of land, the relations between capital and labor, taxation; . . . the communal regime, the role of the administration, of the individual, of the commune, and of the state." The study raised political and even religious and philosophical questions, he declared.[3] The competition gave him an opportunity to test his grasp of his own specialty and the wide range of his knowledge. Eventually published under the title of *De la Colonisation chez les Peuples Modernes*, the manuscript contains a long historical section that argues that colonies organized under the mercantilist system fail to prosper or realize their productive potential. Thus the study endorses free trade, a favorite cause of Established Liberal economists.

Another of the prize treatises of 1870, *L'Administration Locale en France et en Angleterre*, concentrates on France's internal politics. The study is not as much a contrast between the institutions of local government in France and England as it is a dissertation on the differing spirit of government in the two countries. The main thesis of the treatise is that French vitality and stability had declined because excessive centralization had stifled the initiative of individual Frenchmen.[4]

As important as political concerns were to Leroy-Beaulieu, the

Social Question dominated his attention throughout the climactic years of the Second Empire. Among the four treatises he sent to the Académie that year was *Le Travail des Femmes au XIXe Siècle*, his second long investigation of the condition of workers. *Le Travail des Femmes* is similar but superior to *L'Etat Moral et Intellectuel des Populations Ouvrières*. Again Leroy-Beaulieu synthesized published sources rather than interviewing business owners and workers. Yet in this study he chose relevant material and presented it in a supremely concise and well-arranged fashion. Present-day social historians might still find it useful. Among its valuable features are careful accounts of several experiments—both in the United States and in France—in providing women with working conditions compatible with their being homemakers and mothers.[5]

While *L'Etat Moral et Intellectuel des Populations Ouvrières* seeks mainly to identify the faults of wage earners, *Le Travail des Femmes* is aimed at the reformers who wanted to save the family and raise men's wages by preventing women from working outside the home. Excluding women from employment in industry, Leroy-Beaulieu countered, strikes a blow against human liberty since women are not minors but adults.[6]

At the same time as he was garnering a prize for this work, he also contributed four articles to the *Revue des Deux Mondes*. They appeared in the spring of 1870 under the title of "La Question Ouvrière au XIXe Siècle." These articles were his last publication before the outbreak of war with Prussia. Whereas *Le Travail des Femmes* dealt with one aspect of the Social Question, "La Question Ouvrière" addressed the issue in all its amplitude. With the exception of a chapter in *Le Travail des Femmes* on the role of the state, these articles also contain Leroy-Beaulieu's most ideological writing before the war. Again inspired by his indignation with reformers, the series attacked those who proposed cooperation, profit sharing, and unions as solutions to the Social Question. Leroy-Beaulieu critiqued Socialism and strike activity while defending Capitalism and the social hierarchy.

The perspective of "La Question Ouvrière" is slightly grimmer than that of *L'Etat Moral et Intellectuel des Populations Ouvrières*. The earlier work had a fairly optimistic tone. Still Leroy-Beaulieu characterized the Social Question as a virtual civil war between the working class and the rich and warned that, as a result, the nation was close to two noxious eventualities: revolution or government intervention in economic affairs.[7] By the spring of 1870 he was more apprehensive. While he celebrated the excellence of existing social and economic institutions, he feared that social revolution was imminent because the masses were ignorant of that excellence. He was particularly distressed over the threat of the disruption of industry by Socialist-inspired labor unions and strikes. He further worried that the "conservatives," with whom he apparently identified himself, would respond with repression and thus make the problem worse.[8]

"La Question Ouvrière" is marked by a strong sense of the fragility of modern Liberal society. In one article Leroy-Beaulieu remarked that employers were haunted by an awareness of how easy it would be to damage the powerful but delicate modern economic system.[9] At another point he used similar rhetoric in stating,

> The constitution of our society is delicate, susceptible, impressionable precisely because of its perfection. To the highest degree it needs internal peace and concord. . . . It seems that a grain of sand would suffice to stop the extraordinarily fine and mobile drive wheels whose arrangement and harmony has produced our marvelous civilization.[10]

There could hardly be a more eloquent statement of the insecurity that haunted those who invested in and owned the factories, mines, large agricultural estates, and banks of nineteenth-century France and of the West in general.

All Leroy-Beaulieu's early writings focused on the debates and uncertainties of the time. Only his treatise on colonization came close to being a general theoretical work, but its underlying concern was the reform of the French colonial system. Whatever the subject, Leroy-Beaulieu promoted the political, social, and economic views of Established Liberalism. Among his recurring themes were an idealization of self-government, an approval of parliaments and constitutions, a belief in gradual progress, a dedication to internationalism and peace, the defense of individualism and free trade, and the assertion of the preeminence of production among social values. Leroy-Beaulieu also expressed some general notions about human nature that are central to his thought, and a few passages in his early writings suggest his conception of the ideal society. To convey the essentials of Leroy-Beaulieu's thought, we will summarize his ideas on each of these topics, pointing out the class bias of this ideology and its ambivalence with regard to the principle of laissez-faire.

*W*ith the notable exception of Lucien Prévost-Paradol, Established Liberals advocated the same internationalist perspective that the International League for Peace promoted. The publication of Leroy-Beaulieu's *Guerres Contemporaines* by this organization verifies that the Established Liberals recognized his adherence to their ideology of peace. The book rests on the theory that Benjamin Constant, Henri de Saint-Simon, and Auguste Comte helped diffuse. Leroy-Beaulieu divides history and society into the same two periods these thinkers had discerned: the dark and benighted period of monarchy and war and the newly emerging period of industry and peace. Sharing the hopefulness of his predecessors, Leroy-Beaulieu asserted that Europe had finally entered a commercial and industrial age that made war an anachronism. Industry, aided by political democracy and education, would rapidly end the age of war.

Despite this optimistic analysis, Leroy-Beaulieu was distressed because the earlier political forms and mores had not completely disappeared. The surviving monarchical and aristocratic societies, he wrote, retained a capacity for causing trouble. We can see that the young publicist shared fully the Established Liberal hostility to authoritarian regimes. But he may have been more enthusiastic than his Liberal elders about a democratic political regime. To speed the coming of the new era of peace Leroy-Beaulieu urged that "all great questions that touch society be submitted to universal suffrage for decision."[11]

However, in his most extended treatment of government, *L'Administration Locale en France et en Angleterre*, very little of a democratic perspective emerges. Instead Leroy-Beaulieu advocated conventional liberal political positions and class government. This preference underlies his proposal that French government be improved by building upon the country's two generations of experience with the Conseils Généraux of the departments. He wanted the Conseil Généraux to acquire administrative functions and freedom of action at the expense of the agents of the central government, the prefects. Since the councils had already taken root in the life and habits of the country, and since the councilors had long acquired the respect of the people of the provinces, he claimed that increasing their powers would not be a radical innovation but would instead be part of a natural process of growth.[12] This seemingly straightforward proposition actually concealed a class-based bias. The Conseillers Généraux were unpaid. Consequently, they came overwhelmingly from the class of big property owners, the only group who could afford to give voluntary service. To strengthen the councils, therefore, was to strengthen the political power of the social stratum with which Leroy-Beaulieu identified.

Nevertheless, Leroy-Beaulieu treasured political liberty. Among his most revealing statements is one that he made almost casually in his treatise on local government. The goal of every civilized people, he proclaimed, is to achieve "self-government," a phrase he wrote in English.[13] This formula reveals his basic political value; his entire book can be read as derived from his belief in the value of self-government. However, his view retains an important ambivalence. What he admired about local administration in Britain was that the elites did most of the administering while the masses followed their guidance with deference. The greater participation he recommended for the masses was apparently limited to the exercise of the vote. Universal suffrage, for Leroy-Beaulieu, was the institution that enabled a country to claim it is fully self-governing. Political offices, nevertheless, should go to those able to serve without pay. Under those circumstances the role of bureaucracy would decline and political freedom would exist, yet without a threat to "social stability."[14] While still elitist in orientation, this analysis was a subtle attack on the authoritarian character of the Second Empire and an appeal for further evolution toward a parliamentary, constitutional system of government.

Forms of government, however, interested Leroy-Beaulieu less than other areas of contemporary life in which he more firmly supported the status quo, vigorously opposing alterations of the economic and social systems with the defensive tone typical of Established Liberalism. Constantly he marshaled arguments to show that the existing class hierarchy, the wage system, and ownership institutions are natural, inevitable, and final products of the historical evolution from barbarism to civilization. Particularly preoccupied with the question of how to reward work, since critics insisted that the wage system itself condemns laborers to poverty, he mobilized economic theory to defend that crucial institution from attack. His basic argument was that wages are determined by natural laws, not by human volition. With characteristically decisive language he declared that "it has been and remains *incontestable* that the level of wages is not arbitrary."[15] Instead that level "is a natural phenomenon" and thereby is subject to natural law. Since a law, he pointed out (citing Montesquieu), is "a necessary relationship that results from the nature of things," wages simply cannot be improved by "the violence of the masses or by the interference of the government." "Coalitions" of workers, therefore, could never succeed in bringing about an increase in wages or a reduction of work hours.[16] In effect, Leroy-Beaulieu argued for a productivity theory of wages, paying tribute to Bastiat as the originator of the idea that remuneration is based on services rather than on the need for subsistence.

Part of the intellectual weaponry Leroy-Beaulieu aimed at proponents of radical change was a conception of history dominated by a conviction that major change could occur only gradually. Each of the published treatises of 1870 combines history and doctrine. Not surprisingly, he saw history as the story of progress. Unquestioningly following the lead of Guizot and others, he asserted that, due to the deeply rooted nature of habits and institutions, society cannot be reshaped at will and that progress can result only from very modest, very gradual alterations in current ways. This historical doctrine enabled Leroy-Beaulieu to indict reformist proposals for rapid and wide-ranging institutional changes.[17]

Leroy-Beaulieu's major defense of the existing society was an argument for the natural superiority of the class that he alternately called "the bourgeoisie" or "the middle classes." He devoted half of a long article to describing the indispensable economic functions only the bourgeoisie can perform. In explaining why cooperatives, especially producer cooperatives, usually failed, Leroy-Beaulieu began with the premise that human beings are naturally undisciplined and lazy. Managers of modern industry, he pointed out, must have energy, a sense of order, discipline, foresight, and, above all, "the spirit of enterprise, the motive spring of all civilization." Bourgeois families create such men out of undisciplined raw material because they provide their children with traditions of work, frugality, and initiative. Working-class families, on the other hand, cannot do so because of their ignorance of the conditions for success in business.[18] The functional differentiation led to a natural hierarchy of social classes. Since this champion of the modern regime approved social mobility, he could claim that his position was not a defense of a society of classes.[19]

At the heart of Leroy-Beaulieu's outlook on life is a hostile conception of the state. At the outset of his career he was so opposed to government activity that he looked to private, voluntary associations to provide schools for working-class children.[20] He joined such Liberals as Tocqueville in arguing for freedom of association, but he subordinated this positive demand to a laissez-faire attack on government. In 1870 he vehemently rejected the claim by social reformers that the state is a superior being charged with shaping and guiding the development of society. Reformers, he argued, overlook the possibility that "society might be a complete, spontaneous, and independent being, the product and result of the action of individual forces, having within itself its own motor and law of development."[21] A great deal of his worldview is packed into this short statement, but the essential point is his conviction that the spontaneous action of individuals produces the development of society. Consequently, there is no need to rely upon political authorities as the motive force. Furthermore, Leroy-Beaulieu found it absurd to treat the state as a "superior being" above society, omniscient, omnipotent, and thus able to regulate properly the economic life of individuals. "Far from being above society," he proclaimed, "the State is the product, the delegation, the agent" of the group. Far from being infallible, as reformers asserted, the state "manifests a fallibility that is so frequent and so dangerous that it is vital to take as many precautions against its whims and intrusions as possible. Far from having an infinite responsibility, the state has limited and special functions that are clearly delimited by *natural law*. . . . These functions are solely those that would be badly performed by individuals."[22]

Leroy-Beaulieu applied these skeptical principles mainly to the defense of an unregulated labor market. Natural law, "the only real base of positive law," was for him the source of every person's right to offer himself or herself for hire. Infringe this inherent "right to work" and all law is undermined. Leroy-Beaulieu warned further that "Any trespass by the state beyond its limits leads by necessity to further encroachments"; once any concession is made "it becomes impossible to fix a stopping point."[23]

Despite these attacks on reformers and state intervention, Leroy-Beaulieu's treatise on local government, also written around 1870, makes it clear that he had developed a more nuanced, or perhaps an ambivalent, attitude toward the state. While he argued against a big, powerful state organization, resting his case in part on the harm he saw the French bureaucracy inflicting on the spirit of individual initiative and responsibility, he had become relatively moderate compared to Bastiat or Hippolyte Passy, who insisted that government's sole rightful functions are to ensure justice and to prevent attacks on the nation or on lives and property. Leroy-Beaulieu accepted that government rather than private enterprise had to take responsibility for most land transport, and he changed his mind about the role of government in education. A country needs a good system of education, he held in *L'Administration Locale*, since instruction advances prosperity and counters perverse instincts that lead people to threaten social stability. To drive the point home he quoted from Jules Simon: "The people which has the best schools is the preeminent people; if it is not today, it will be tomorrow." Instruction was so vital, therefore, that the state had to take the lead in this area.[24] Leroy-Beaulieu thus moved away from a strict laissez-faire position, but his continued hostility to the central government shows that he did so reluctantly. In his fundamental view of the state he remained firmly within the spectrum of Established Liberal thought.

In his comments on the state and society Leroy-Beaulieu reflected the individualist conception of liberty that was central to Established Liberal doctrine. *Liberty* was a term he constantly invoked in his attacks on the state, and he gave it two meanings. Liberty existed, he declared in *L'Etat Moral*, "in so far as no obstacle opposes itself to the march of each person in his natural path and prevents him from the most profitable use of his faculties."[25] More specifically, though, liberty meant freedom of contract and freedom from government. An especially eloquent defense of liberty in this sense appeared in *Le Travail des Femmes*. The key chapter of that work culminates in an apostrophe to individual liberty:

> This inviolable individual liberty carries with it the right to choose one's own line of conduct, to decide when and how to work, to make any usage of one's hands and brain—even if it be harmful. There are those who claim that if everyone or an entire class made a pernicious use of liberty, that would harm society as a whole. No matter! The state never has the right to intervene when the individual remains in his realm using his own liberty and does not directly and overtly violate the liberty of someone else.[26]

There could hardly be a more uncompromising statement of the rugged individualist conception of liberty.

One aspect of Leroy-Beaulieu's individualism deserves special emphasis. This trait emerged most forcefully in *Le Travail des Femmes* where he attacked the reformers' principle that the family is the basic unit of society. Leroy-Beaulieu forcefully insisted in response that in a modern "civilized" society the individual is in fact and in law the element from which society is made. The primacy of groups such as the family is a characteristic of barbaric societies. If laws established the family as primary, no one would be able to live alone and independently, and the state would also have to find family units for those without natural ones.[27] These words remind us that the Liberal movement advocated individualism not only in economic affairs but also with regard to social relationships. While nineteenth-century Liberals were deeply committed to liberating the individual from the bureaucratic tutelage of the state, many also wanted to emancipate individuals from authoritarian family arrangements.

While liberty for private initiative had the highest priority for Leroy-Beaulieu, he also stressed two other closely related values: work and productivity. An underlying theme in his first book was that "there are relative duties and there are absolute duties; one of the absolute duties is the obligation to work."[28] He tied this admonition to the standard Established Liberal contention that an increase in production is society's greatest need. If workers would not take Mondays off; if they would not pilfer from their employers; if they would not be careless with raw materials, wood, and coal—then production would go up without any additional investment and there would be more earnings to distribute among the workers themselves. In short, laborers wanting higher wages should work harder and produce more.

When Leroy-Beaulieu next addressed how to end the social conflict between workers and the bourgeoisie, in his 1870 *Revue* articles, there was one notable change from the views expressed in *L'Etat Moral* and one notable continuity. By 1870 he had given up the search for panaceas and no longer believed that education could transform the Working Class. The recent legalization of public meetings had enabled him to hear working-class leaders firsthand, and he discovered that despite their education they still thundered demagogic provocations to their audiences.[29] On the other hand, he held fast to the other side of his formula for ending working-class discontent: his claim that ever-increasing production would automatically raise the standard of living of the poor and end the threat of social revolution.

Throughout his works we find passages which indicate that Leroy-Beaulieu had a conception of an ideal society.[30] One part of this vision can be discerned in his descriptions of the factory regime he wanted to see established. Leroy-Beaulieu envisioned a hierarchical society based on private property and devoted to unremitting toil, one in which workers would be zealous in producing high-quality goods and furthering their firm's prosperity. Since their morale would be good and their conduct honest, "subordination" would not be "the effect of fear and necessity but of respect and deference."[31] But subordination would remain. Toward the end of *L'Etat Moral*, Leroy-Beaulieu drew a picture of factory hands so dedicated to their tasks that they would be constantly innovating and inventing.[32] Social harmony would exist because all classes would see the truth of political economy's maxim that the interests of "industrialists and workers, producers and consumers, are all identical" (*solidaires*).[33] This insistence on a basic, even obvious, harmony of interests among landowners, employers, and workers was a distinguishing mark of Established Liberalism, and Leroy-Beaulieu repeated the arguments his forerunners had developed to support this assertion.[34]

*T*he reports on the prize competitions confirm that Established Liberals immediately recognized Leroy-Beaulieu as one of their own. The first report, lauding Leroy-Beaulieu's essay on the moral and intellectual condition of workers, was delivered by Hippolyte Passy, one of the most distinguished representatives of the extreme laissez-faire wing of Established Liberalism. A leading economist and member of parliament during the July Monarchy, he had even served that grand-bourgeois regime as minister of finance. His perspective comes through clearly in his critical comments on the other monograph submitted for the competition. Passy disliked the somberness of its description of working-class conditions and protested that it used terms like "proletarian" that could provoke "upsetting irritations" in the ranks of the workers.[35] Moreover, he objected to the hints that French society was divided into classes since, as he complacently reminded his audience of *académiciens*, the French Revolution had abolished such divisions.[36] With regard to Leroy-Beaulieu's work, Passy was happy that it took the side of the optimistic political economists of his country against the Malthusian doctrine.[37] Other than mentioning a few minor faults, Passy had nothing but praise for the victorious manuscript.[38]

The report on the prize competition on local government also shows the harmony between Leroy-Beaulieu's views and those of the academicians. Cauchy, the commentator, stated his agreement with the monograph's main contentions. While not "going as far as the author to say that we, among all peoples, are the one most attached to our comforts and least attached to our liberties," Cauchy did agree that the French had a "natural disposition" to rely too much on the state. He certainly approved of the proposal to widen the functions of the Conseils Généraux, and like Leroy-Beaulieu he saw in Britain the example of the happy impact of self-government on a country's prosperity.[39] Both the book and the commentary reflect the Anglophilia generally prevalent in French Established Liberal thought. We should note, however, that most French political forces of the time, not only liberals, agreed on the need for decentralization.[40]

When the prize jury considered the manuscripts that related to women workers, they found quite a contrast between Leroy-Beaulieu's treatise and the other submission. The competing manuscript illustrates the reformist position Leroy-Beaulieu and the Established Liberals of the Académie found totally objectionable. The unnamed author proposed to eliminate middlemen from French commercial life, using the four billion francs they earned each year to ameliorate the work situation of women. "One guesses the rest," the commentator said with mild sarcasm; "it is always a golden age that is in sight; the theme is an ancient one."[41] This well-meaning idealist, he pointed out, had ignored the framework set by the economists of the Académie for the contest, for the writers were supposed to discuss the "improvements that could be accomplished in the situation of working women without giving too profound a shock to customs, mores, and traditions."[42]

In contrast, Leroy-Beaulieu's treatise amply fulfilled the conditions, exhibiting "an accuracy of view worthy of the greatest praise."[43] Perhaps the main virtue the committee found in his three-hundred-page treatise was that it argued against a diminution of the available amount of "manual laborers with all the incalculable moral consequences and material damage (*préjudices matériels*) that would bring."[44] These words reveal without equivocation that the well-to-do landowners and investors who dominated the Institut intended to give their prizes only to those who championed the maintenance of a large supply of workers seeking to sell their services in the market.

*I*t would be an injustice to attribute Leroy-Beaulieu's successes simply to his adoption of the capitalist outlook of those who judged the competitions. His works were clearly written, well-organized, informative, and persuasive. They build a strong case for the ideas they defend. Nevertheless, as we have seen, his early works also show that from the outset Leroy-Beaulieu was committed to Established Liberalism. He adhered closely to Liberal principles of free trade and individualism. He said entrepreneurs should have the maximum of free rein compatible with ensuring investors some protection from stock fraud. He considered any regulation of the labor market an infringement on the natural rights of persons seeking employment. He unequivocally shared Established Liberalism's suspicion of the state, although by 1870 he had moved slightly away from the laissez-faire wing of that school of thought. In common with such Liberal predecessors as J.-B. Say and Guizot, he divided humankind into two groups—the able, moral, and disciplined and the unintelligent, dissolute, and shortsighted—in a way that reinforced class-based distinctions. Like other Established Liberal economists he believed increasing wealth through increased productivity was the best way to resolve the class conflicts of the time.

Unquestionably the young Leroy-Beaulieu's chief preoccupation was the social conflict between owners and laborers. The imminent danger of social upheaval inspired him to write three long studies of the working class in just four years, always defending the existing social hierarchy and especially the position of the "bourgeoisie-middle classes." Identifying with the whole of that broad category in French society and championing their cause quite openly, he made no attempt to conceal the class base of his ideological arguments.

One striking aspect of Leroy-Beaulieu's early writing is the confidence with which he stated his ideas. Free from self-doubt, he wrote as one who believed the truth was known and needed simply to be sufficiently propagated so that everything might be well. However, as we saw in his changing views of the state, not even this stalwart believer was entirely impervious to experiences that caused him to shift positions, at least within the spectrum of the Established Liberal ideology. One potential source of further change was buried in his earliest work, *L'Etat Moral*, in which he commented on the need of human beings to be active.[45] For others this notion led eventually to a revision of the Liberal doctrine of human nature, a break from the fundamental Liberal conviction that the threat of want and the promise of riches are the only forces that can motivate a basically lazy human race to make the earth fruitful.

While, therefore, the young publicist held the views typical of his mentors and colleagues in the Liberal establishment, and while he shared their complacent sense of certainty, in mid-1870 there remained the possibility that his ideas might evolve toward less orthodox or settled positions. Usually, however, some dramatic event is required to motivate a thinker toward extensive reevaluation. Soon after the last of the series on "La Question Ouvrière" appeared in the *Revue des Deux Mondes*, such an event occurred, as the French were shaken by the dual cataclysm of defeat by Prussia and an insurrection in Paris. The Franco-Prussian War and the Commune had a significant impact on the outlook of many thinkers in the unhappy country. The impact of these blows on Leroy-Beaulieu and other Established Liberals is our next concern.

4

Leroy-Beaulieu during the War and the Conservative Republic

■ The relatively secure world Leroy-Beaulieu had known since childhood was rocked by the military defeats and insurrections of 1870 and 1871 and by the fall of the Second Empire. After these storms public life remained strained in the country as a result of an impassioned struggle over what regime would replace the Bonapartist system. Since right-wing and centrist groups controlled the government until the end of 1877 and shaped the new constitution in 1875, the period from 1871 through 1877 is often called the epoch of the Conservative Republic. In this political environment Leroy-Beaulieu turned his attention to topics he had not previously discussed, as well as reconsidering older issues like the Social Question in a new context.

Nevertheless, the years between 1870 and 1877 do not mark a distinct period in Leroy-Beaulieu's life. The war and the insurrection in Paris barely interrupted his professional progress. Neither the shocks of the early 1870s nor the domestic conflicts of the Conservative Republic produced deep or extensive alterations in his outlook and feelings. These events perturbed Leroy-Beaulieu but did not disorient him, so that his writings in this period remain compatible with his early views. There is only one significant new attitude: a moderate nationalism, as, along with other Established Liberals, he became deeply concerned about national power and France's future. Otherwise his prewar and postwar endeavors form a unity.

The French generally were overwhelmed by the violence that began in the summer of 1870. Established Liberals must have felt particularly distressed about the turn of events. Judging from the words of Charles de Mazade, political commentator for the *Revue des Deux Mondes*, 1870 began auspiciously from the Established Liberal point of view. At the end of December 1869 the emperor, by asking the Liberal journalist Emile Ollivier to form a cabinet supported by a majority of deputies, "consecrated the intervention of parliament in the direction of public affairs."[1] Few anticipated that war with Prussia would break out by midsummer or that it would lead to the rapid defeat of French arms and the overthrow of the imperial regime. Even though the conservatives and moderates of the provinces quickly rallied behind the republican-dominated Government of National Defense, the final admission of defeat came just four months after the beginning of hostilities. When the government organized an election of a new National Assembly in January 1871, the republicans suddenly found themselves in a minority. Then in late March, with no time to recover from the shock of defeat, the loss of Alsace-Lorraine, and the imposition of an immense war indemnity of five billion francs, the French plunged into the bloody civil strife of the Commune in Paris. The Communards in turn went down to defeat in May after they executed hostages and set fire to public buildings. The final tragic act of 1870–1871 saw the execution of thousands of Communards by government firing squads. All these dreadful events occurred in little more than a year.

The bimonthly *Revue des Deux Mondes* chronicles Established Liberals' dismay over these events. As one calamity succeeded another, Frenchmen sometimes feared they were witnessing the annihilation of their country.[2] Liberals of the stripe associated with the *Revue des Deux Mondes* must have felt impotent during the fighting with Prussia because the Government of National Defense shut them out from posts of importance. The results of the election in January 1871 gave them some satisfaction, while the May victory by the new national authorities over the Commune was hailed with relief.[3]

Since Leroy-Beaulieu wrote articles on the state of France before and after each crisis, we can trace his reactions to the upheavals of 1870–1871. In late August 1870, a few days before the surrender of the emperor and his army at Sedan, Leroy-Beaulieu praised the French people for their bravery, dedication to their homeland, and fortitude. But he displayed no hostility toward the Germans. Instead he wrote admiringly of their industrious and progressive spirit.[4] In the early stages of the war, while the threat from outside kindled Leroy-Beaulieu's feelings for his country, he continued to be a peace-loving Liberal who prayed that European peoples would experience "a peace that will not be a truce."[5] When Leroy-Beaulieu's tone became bitter two months after the end of the war, he directed his ire at his fellow countrymen, not the foreigner. France, in his judgment, had performed miserably because of "the vices of our national character, of our administrative system and of our governmental traditions."[6] After the government had crushed the Commune, Leroy-Beaulieu recorded that he had felt as if he had been passing through "a moment when the country seems to be in dissolution."[7] Nevertheless, he did not give in to panic at the time of the insurrection in Paris. During the struggle with the Commune, the National Assembly passed a law that gave local self-government to cities with populations under 20,000, but refused to permit larger cities to choose their mayors. Leroy-Beaulieu considered the reform an utterly inadequate gesture toward decentralization.[8]

Leroy-Beaulieu's distress about the performance of the wartime government generally parallels the assessments in his earlier writings. However, a partisan note in his analysis of the defeat by Prussia gives us a new insight into his class identification. The Radical Republicans, he charged, had put politics before the war effort. They had selected "new men"—Parisian journalists and lawyers belonging to the advanced republican party—as prefects rather than those who had solid places and associations in the provinces. In other words, his protest was that the Liberal bourgeoisie had been passed over.[9] Another writer for the *Revue des Deux Mondes*, Elme Caro, stated the same grievance in even stronger terms.[10]

All in all Leroy-Beaulieu seems to have maintained a kind of equanimity during the crises that began with the outbreak of war with Prussia. Nationalism was a new theme in his writings, yet both during and immediately after the war he voiced his concern for France more quietly than most of his countrymen. Apparently he remained in the provinces during the conflicts of 1870–1871, and his absence from Paris during the suspense and suffering of the siege and civil war may have shielded him from the sense of devastation others felt. For whatever reason, the French army's defeat produced no sense of personal humiliation in him as it did in other French intellectuals. Nor did he share the vengeful hatred for the Communards expressed by many French writers and political leaders. This moderation remained characteristic of Leroy-Beaulieu's thought throughout the period of the Conservative Republic.

The restoration of peace and the reestablishment of the central government's authority in May 1871 hardly brought an end to the difficult times that faced France. From the point of view of big property owners, the quiescence of the working class, deprived of many of its leaders by the crushing of the Commune and by the legal repression that lasted until 1879, was a positive change. But otherwise France's situation was disquieting. The disorganization of the French army and the veiled threats of Prince von Bismarck created a fear of renewed conflict with Germany. War damage had to be repaired and new fortifications and a new army had to be assembled. Parts of the nation were occupied by German troops, and only after paying its huge war indemnity in 1872 was France freed from the distressing presence of its conquerors. The new government needed to raise large amounts of money, from a nation whose economy had already suffered from the fighting. As President Adolphe Thiers, his cabinet, and the National Assembly wrestled with the difficulties, they also engaged in a struggle over the constitution.

The political struggle would go on for most of the decade, but economic recovery from the war came more quickly than anyone expected. A flood of hidden savings came forth when the government sought loans to pay off the indemnity, making possible a much more rapid liberation of the occupied territories than either the French or the Germans had anticipated. Within a short time factories and instruments of production resumed their previous advances. The years of the Conservative Republic saw an enormous growth in the number of steamships; the great age of business concentration began; and department stores, an important novelty in distribution, grew in size and number.[11] The people and institutions of France manifested a surprising vigor, and for several years it seemed as if the country might be spared the business crisis that struck the West in 1873. Nevertheless, economic problems caused by phylloxera and foreign competition brought uneasiness.

Despite the victory over the Commune, the possessing classes feared that conspirators and rebels might still cause trouble. To prevent unrest the National Assembly turned to the policy of repression against which Leroy-Beaulieu had warned early in 1870. The legislators chose to crush such working-class movements as the First International and to prevent their revival. Throughout the 1870s special military courts prosecuted individuals accused of participating in the Commune, and newspapers that defended the rebels were taken to court.[12] Some Established Liberals did propose other responses to the discontent of the masses beside suppressing it by means of the law and the army. Some business and political leaders supported the imposition of an income tax—albeit a nonprogressive one—as a means of demonstrating to the masses that the affluent would make sacrifices to help the country recover from the financial damage inflicted by the war. In addition, some Established Liberals supported strengthening the legal protection of women and children employed in industry.[13]

The intellectual context changed because internationalism and the ideology of peace were among the main casualties of the Franco-Prussian War. In January 1871 the historian Fustel de Coulanges could still use the old language of the ideology of peace, in speaking about the battle of the "*esprit de conquête*" against the "*esprit de travail*," and he could still echo the old charge that sovereigns and ministers plunged peace-loving peoples into the "evils and furors" of wars. Yet his perspective had shifted, since he now saw the conflict between the two spirits as "eternal," not one that would pass away with the development of material civilization.[14] The reaction against the old hopes and illusions grew as the months passed, so that by May the influential Liberal de Mazade was indicting "international cosmopolitanism" as one of the forces that "had enfeebled the sense of *la patrie*" and the moral sense of the French.[15] Similarly, in January 1871 Elme Caro, a renowned professor of philosophy, celebrated the decline of egoism and the reawakening of "the idea of *la patrie*" that had resulted from the war.[16] This striking statement by a prominent Liberal exemplified the newfound nationalism that pervaded the group with whom Leroy-Beaulieu was associated.

Love of country, a sense of humiliation, and a desire to create a better defense led journalists, scholars, and political leaders to ask why the country had been so badly prepared for war and why its military forces had performed so poorly. A number of thinkers, like Leroy-Beaulieu in his articles of March 1871, attributed the country's woes to the frivolity and superficiality of the French. The issue immediately became entangled with the question of whether to maintain the newly created republic or restore a king. Republican leaders blamed the Bonapartist monarchy for having weakened the moral fiber of France. For republicans like Jules Ferry and Léon Gambetta the revitalization of the country depended, above all, upon preserving the republican regime that had been proclaimed on September 4, 1870. From the right and center of the political spectrum came far different analyses and prescriptions, all of them strongly influenced by the insurrection of the Commune as well as the defeat by Prussia. Ernest Renan and Hippolyte Taine argued that mediocrity had sapped France's moral strength, and, in turn, blamed democratization—that is, universal suffrage and the increase of social equality—for that mediocrity. Symptomatic of the impact of the Commune was the angry panic of Hippolyte Taine, which led him to begin his famous study of the French Revolution. There he placed the responsibility for France's decadence on the masses and radical intellectuals, and he warned that a republic would further undermine the soundness of the country.[17]

Divisions among the centrists further complicated the struggle over the constitution. The main split was between the Centre Droite, which favored the restoration of a strong monarchical executive combined with a strong parliament, and the Centre Gauche, which favored a republic with a strong president and a Senate. A smaller group, the Constitutionnels, moved back and forth between the other two depending upon the issues and circumstances of the moment.[18] The leaders of these three groups all came from the same social strata—the Grande Bourgeoisie and the nobility connected to the Grande Bourgeoisie. Although they seemed to have the same fundamental ideology, throughout the 1870s they failed to form a long-lasting alliance. According to Jean Bouvier, their divisions were probably due to the differing intensity of fear the Commune aroused in them. Despite the savage destruction of the Commune, many among the propertied classes still worried about revolutionary conspiracies. As universal suffrage began to be a significant force in French political life, some well-to-do bourgeois Liberals and a number of intellectuals moved to the far right wing of Liberal thought or even gave up their former Liberalism in favor of authoritarian solutions to social unrest. Organized as the Centre Droite, they cooperated with ideological Conservatives and reactionaries in an effort to restore a strong royal executive, a step they considered essential as a guarantee of social stability.[19]

The Liberals of the *Revue des Deux Mondes* resisted this movement to the right. Regarding the republic and universal suffrage
as accomplished facts that they could turn to their own ends, these
Liberals became stalwarts of the Centre Gauche, the party composed largely of individuals who recovered more quickly from the
fear engendered by the uprising of 1871. They were confident that
a properly constituted republic could preserve social order. Furthermore, they suspected that a monarchical restoration could not be
achieved because of the internal disagreements among the
monarchists—or even worse, as Buloz believed, that such a restoration would set off a revolution by the republicans. These moderately
hopeful Liberals sought to establish a stable Conservative Republic.
They wanted a regime that would permit universal suffrage but
would limit its impact by means of a strong presidency and a Senate
elected by a restricted suffrage.[20] This program, of course, was the
one such Established Liberal oracles as Lucien Prévost-Paradol had
recommended during the 1860s (see Chapter 2 above).

De Mazade used his political column in the *Revue des Deux
Mondes* to support the Centre Gauche program, and Joseph Garnier
took the same line in his columns for the *Journal des Economistes*.
In the middle of 1871, after the Commune had been crushed and
the treaty of peace had been signed with the new German Empire,
de Mazade began to state ideas that would become constant themes
of the *Revue*: the need to bend all energies to the revitalization of
the country, and the absolute necessity to end the divisive conflicts
over the form of the regime. De Mazade voiced the aspirations of
the Center Gauche for a government that would move ahead to reor-
ganize the country's finances and military forces and to promote
the conditions for industrial and financial prosperity.[21] The constitutional question, however, could not be banished from the heart of
French politics. More than any other issue it dominated the public
life of the country after 1871. The Centre Gauche eventually prevailed because the Constitutionnels, the group which floated between the two centers and usually voted with the Centre Droite,
supported the passage of the constitutional laws favored by the Centre Gauche in 1875.

Whatever institutions of government they desired, the survivors
and heirs of the Orleanist establishment also obtained a renewed
share of public offices. As officials of the discredited Bonapartist
regime were eliminated from political life, the highest ministerial
and administrative posts became open to the Liberal elites again,

after a hiatus of more than twenty years. Adolphe Thiers, president of the republic from 1871 to mid-1873, was a former prime minister during the July Monarchy, and numerous Established Liberals, including the economists Anselme Batbie and Joseph Garnier, achieved election to the National Assembly.[22] In the mid-1870s the *Revue* and the Grande Bourgeoisie seemed to be on the winning side.

*W*ith the coming of the Conservative Republic, Leroy-Beaulieu resumed his rapid march forward in his professional life. He continued to contribute substantial articles to the *Revue des Deux Mondes*, and beginning in June 1871 he wrote regularly for the *Journal des Débats*. Six months later he obtained an important academic post, becoming one of the first faculty members at the new Ecole Libre des Sciences Politiques. Founded by the economist Emile Boutmy with the support of Hippolyte Taine, the school included on its staff such luminaries or future luminaries as Paul Janet, Emile Levasseur, and Albert Sorel. In January 1872 Sorel, destined to be recognized as a great historian of European diplomacy, gave the first lecture; Leroy-Beaulieu, speaking on the English income tax, gave the second. The Ecole Libre would quickly become the main training ground for the administrative elite of the French state.[23]

Boutmy's frank explanation of the purpose of the Ecole Libre shows that, in joining its faculty, Leroy-Beaulieu took another major step toward becoming a spokesman for the interests of the Grande Bourgeoisie:

> The classes with established positions (*situations acquises*) face the risk in their turn of being excluded from political life (*le pays légal*) from which they once excluded the majority. . . . Legal privilege no longer exists, and democratization will not be reversed. Constrained to submit to the right of numbers, the elevated classes can only preserve their political hegemony through invoking the right of ability. It is necessary that, behind the crumbling walls of their prerogatives and traditions, the rising tide of democracy should run up against a second rampart composed of superiority, of resplendently useful merit, of abilities that the people would be foolish to deprive themselves of.[24]

As his contribution to the cause of buttressing the political importance of the "elevated classes," Leroy-Beaulieu taught a vital subject, public finance. In the curriculum vitae that Leroy-Beaulieu supplied in 1878 to the Académie des Sciences Morales et Politiques,

he claimed that the course had been an innovation in French education, and he admitted, "I was rather inexperienced in these questions." To his satisfaction, he said the classes had "succeeded beyond
his expectations."[25]

Less than a year and a half after taking his first teaching post,
Leroy-Beaulieu acquired the forum from which he undoubtedly
hoped to wield a widespread influence, *L'Economiste Français*. Leroy-
Beaulieu may have taken the initiative in 1872 in promoting the
journal, but the government authorized publication only in 1873,
after a Catholic Monarchist, Adalbert Frout de Fontpertuis, became
the administrator of the proposed periodical.[26] Established finally
by a corporation of two hundred fifty industrialists and merchants,
the first issue appeared in April 1873. Published weekly, the journal
was devoted to economic affairs of particular interest to big businessmen in France. In introducing the first issue, Leroy-Beaulieu
openly avowed his intention to advance the interests of the major
industrialists and merchants who engaged in international trade. The
publishers dedicated the magazine "to the moral and material regen-
eration of France," but above all it planned to be "a center of information and a center of action" for interests that "do not enjoy fair
representation that can make the public and the government listen
to their wishes." These interests were factory owners and big merchants, whom the new editor praised because they were "practical"
rather than theoretical men.[27]

The first issues, which proved to be typical, included articles
on the national budget, foreign and domestic loans, foreign trade
problems and opportunities, the Social Question, and the entire
range of industrial and political economic concerns of the late nineteenth century. Then came pages of tables crowded with figures
that traced the weekly course of production, trade, and stock market
transactions. Considerable space was devoted to economic and financial conditions in other countries and regions of the world. According to one of Leroy-Beaulieu's obituaries, he directed every
department of *L'Economiste Français*, and nearly every week until
his death in 1916 he wrote an extensive lead article. Within a short
time after its appearance the shareholders were apparently so satisfied
with the journal's direction and tone that they allowed Leroy-
Beaulieu to treat it as if it were his own exclusive property.[28]

As Leroy-Beaulieu expanded his journalistic endeavors and began
a teaching career, he was also preparing his prize treatises and prewar articles for publication in book form. Two books appeared in

1872: *L'Administration Locale en France et en Angleterre* and *La Question Ouvrière au XIXe Siècle*. *Le Travail des Femmes au XIXe Siècle* came out in 1873, and the fourth work, the massive *De la Colonisation chez les Peuples Modernes*, was issued in 1874. All but one of these works were published by Guillaumin, the firm so intimately connected with Established Liberal economists. None of these books contain any important revisions, since Leroy-Beaulieu was undoubtedly devoting his energies mainly to his weekly business periodical and to his teaching.

Until the mid-1870s Leroy-Beaulieu continued to comment on a wide variety of public concerns. He participated in the debate over why the debacles of 1870–1871 had happened and how to rehabilitate the wounded country. He addressed the sources of French military weakness and started to write on education, connecting educational reform with the recovery of national grandeur. "If France wishes to reconquer her rank in the world, if she wishes to fight on an equal footing with Germany, England and America, . . . it is necessary that the teaching at all levels of our educational institutions be more substantial, more lively, more modern," he stated.[29] For a short while he wrote often about the needs and demands of workers. He also joined in the struggle over the system of administration, demanding further measures of decentralization.

Then the range of Leroy-Beaulieu's writings narrowed considerably after he began writing his weekly column for *L'Economiste Français*. References to the war and the Commune disappeared. So did concern for the Social Question—understandably, in view of the leaderless and demoralized condition of French working-class movements at that time. In 1875, in his only discussion of workers during that year, Leroy-Beaulieu concluded that French workers had given up their utopian dreams of immediate change, had turned against state intervention, and had even become critical of strikes.[30] As early as 1874, when he published his prewar treatise on colonization, he was already concentrating on government finance and on the needs of French industry and commerce. Although he wrote occasionally on business organization, the gold standard, railroads, education, and demography, Leroy-Beaulieu became a specialist on the national budget and taxation. Throughout the 1870s he spoke with increasing authority on how the government should meet its financial needs. When he finally brought out an entirely new book in 1877, it was a *Traité de la Science des Finances*, a two-volume work based on his lectures at the Ecole Libre. This book confirmed his position as a leading expert on the national budget and taxation.

Perhaps the relative tranquillity of French society after 1873 encouraged him to narrow his concerns. On the other hand, the sense of national military helplessness made even optimistic and fortunate French citizens anxious. And stormy debates over the constitution continued even after the passage of the 1875 constitutional laws that promised some stability for the republic. The struggle went on as the unhappy monarchists, reinforced by resurgent Bonapartists, fought back in the parliament and in the country with a verbal ferocity fortunately unmatched by deeds.

Leroy-Beaulieu remained reticent about constitutional questions. All that the prefect of police could report in early 1873, when Leroy-Beaulieu was seeking authorization for *L'Economiste Français*, was that the economist's "political opinions do not seem to be hostile to our present institutions."[31] He never stated his own political allegiances openly, and *L'Economiste Français*, in contrast to the *Revue des Deux Mondes*, was committed to political neutrality.[32] Nevertheless, a few brief comments he made in the mid-1870s clarify his political position. In 1874 he expressed admiration for the United States because American politics centered on administrative and economic questions. Europeans in general, he complained, wasted their energies in squabbles with other nations and quarrels over their internal constitutions.[33] At the height of the struggles over the future shape of the French government and society, Leroy-Beaulieu insisted that there were no great political questions to settle. In an article in *L'Economiste Français* in March 1876 he emphasized that, with the constitutional laws already passed and the distribution of powers and the form of suffrage fixed, politicians should be devoting their efforts to advancing "the permanent interests" of any nation: the economy, education, and national defense. As for the religious questions that occupied political attention at that time, he complained that those sources of division ought simply to be avoided.[34] Plainly, Leroy-Beaulieu experienced the same impatience over the constitutional conflicts as Buloz and de Mazade. His annoyance with the struggle over the form of government, his optimism with regard to the Social Question, and the similarity of his language to that of Buloz and de Mazade suggest that he was very close to those ex-Orleanist Liberals of the Centre Gauche. It is not surprising that, after he began running for the Chamber of Deputies in 1878, his opponents consistently identified him as a member of the Centre Gauche.[35]

At any rate, Leroy-Beaulieu's publications in the mid- and late 1870s concentrated heavily on the needs of the economy or, more precisely, on the interests of a particular group of producers and merchants. So favorable was Leroy-Beaulieu toward big business that in 1875 he defended the growth of business concentration. As so often, he used the criteria of efficiency and productivity to justify the replacement of small shops by department stores.[36] Invariably he promoted the goals of one segment of the business community: exporters and importers. In contrast, his consistent opposition to favors for the railroads and his demand that the national debt be lowered shows his indifference to the interests of financiers and middle-class *rentiers*.[37]

Leroy-Beaulieu's position on taxes and tariffs is another prime example of his bias in favor of industrialists and merchants engaged in foreign trade. Already in 1871 he had joined the battle against Thiers's demand for higher tariffs. Above all, he combated the president's request for duties on raw materials and instead recommended an income tax to meet the government's financial needs.[38] His *Traité des Finances* of 1877 carried on this fight. Although that book criticized tariffs, calling them taxes on consumers, it presented primarily a productivist argument for freedom of international commerce. The main disadvantage of tariffs, Leroy-Beaulieu stated, rehearsing the standard Liberal arguments that dated back to Adam Smith, is that they prevent an efficient employment of labor and capital.[39]

As in 1871 Leroy-Beaulieu advocated an income tax as the means to raise revenues. Although he once called it a "brutal tax," he supported it because he wanted to find an alternative to the protective tariffs that would more directly harm businesses engaged in international trade.[40] Despite the fears of Thiers and others that an income tax would be used to redistribute wealth through expropriation of large fortunes, Leroy-Beaulieu accepted this levy, as long as it was proportional and not progressive.[41] In the *Traité*, as in his earlier articles, Leroy-Beaulieu strongly opposed the use of the income tax to diminish social inequality.[42] Recognizing, nevertheless, that the system of taxation was unfair to low-income groups, Leroy-Beaulieu urged exempting poor wage-earners from the income tax.[43]

One notable feature in Leroy-Beaulieu's discussion of the progressive tax is the absence of any sign of anxiety about the outcome of the debate. His comments are general and his argumentation sparse. At this early point in the Third Republic he may have felt he was dealing with a purely intellectual issue since there was no chance that the moderate National Assembly would impose a fiscal system contrary to the interests of the well-to-do. Especially in 1876 and 1877 he could feel reassured, because the election of 1876 and political necessity had made the Centre Gauche the leading group in the parliament and the government.

Nevertheless, Leroy-Beaulieu had reason to be disturbed by political affairs both in Europe and in his own country in 1877. France's right-wing president, Patrice MacMahon, sparked a crisis in May by provoking the resignation of the cabinet of Jules Simon, and that crisis continued until October 1877 when the republicans won a decisive victory in the election of a new Chamber of Deputies. There was also the threat that other European powers would be drawn into the war between Russia and Turkey that had broken out in April. Economic conditions in France began to deteriorate noticeably as the depression that had begun in Central Europe and the United States in 1873 finally made itself felt in France. The equanimity Leroy-Beaulieu had shown for years began to crumble under the strain that would become worse during the next few years.

On the personal level, though, 1877 was a good year. Leroy-Beaulieu took a successful first step toward a political career when he was elected to replace his father-in-law, whose declining health forced him to relinquish his membership in the Conseils Généraux of the Herault. Even though he soon found the council's work petty and boring, he and his family must have hoped that he would soon follow other Established Liberals into the parliament.[44] There was good reason to expect such an outcome. The Established Liberals allied to the Centre Gauche still seemed in 1877 to be an indispensable part of the republican coalition, and Leroy-Beaulieu was well on his way to being a nationally prominent figure among Established Liberals. His work on *L'Economiste Français* and the *Journal des Débats* made him a widely known figure, and his *Traité de la Science des Finances* won him renewed plaudits at the Académie des Sciences Morales et Politiques.[45]

But the *Traité de la Science des Finances* was published just before another transformation in France, the shift from a republic dominated by the right and center to one controlled by dedicated republicans. Around 1880, partly because of this change, Leroy-Beaulieu's outlook shifted dramatically. Consequently, it is helpful to sum up the extent of the movement of his views and characteristics at the end of 1877. Although we have to recognize that Leroy-Beaulieu's mind and feelings were touched by the crises of 1870–1871, we must guard against exaggerating the extent and depth of the new convictions he stated.

Leroy-Beaulieu's attitudes toward war, peace, and national strength are a major case in point. Before the Franco-Prussian War Leroy-Beaulieu was unconcerned about military power, and he seemed confident that Europe was heading toward a peaceful future. Experience diminished his hope that an age of commerce was replacing the earlier age of conquest. This chastening led Leroy-Beaulieu to consider other aspects of social life from the perspective of their relation to military power. To a degree he turned away from his prewar attitude toward the enlargement of a country's territory and population. In February 1873 he commented that "in the future as in the past the power and influence of a people will be proportionate to the quantity of territory it will be able to occupy, exploit, and civilize in countries that are now barbarous."[46] Despite this reevaluation Leroy-Beaulieu did not make national expansion a main theme of his writings during the Conservative Republic. Throughout these years he mentioned expansion only a few times, and only in the vaguest terms. As an article of 1873 on commercial education demonstrates, he stressed the growth of foreign commerce, not expansion of colonies, as the way to spread French influence in the world.[47] In addition, his 1877 treatise shows that he still hoped for a future that would be relatively free from war. That is, he accepted the necessity of current military spending, but he also reminded his readers that just a generation of peace would set France's financial house in order. "Peace," he wrote in the conclusion to the first volume, "is the indispensable condition of all fiscal reforms."[48] In sum, while Leroy-Beaulieu gave up his utopian expectations about world peace, he held fast to his basic values and hopes for international life.

Nationalist feelings are also a novel aspect of Leroy-Beaulieu's writings after 1870, but during the era of the Conservative Republic he was far from becoming a rabid nationalist. The publicist's new anxiety over national power and grandeur was mixed with other considerations, and often he seemed to be using patriotic appeals to gain support for the economic programs he favored. Sometimes his appeals for the restoration of France's international status seem to support his efforts to promote the interests of French business-men. There are instances where his patriotism was still cool enough for him to make use of it in his propaganda for his favored economic policies.[49] Unlike his compatriots who dreamed of revenge on the Germans, Leroy-Beaulieu was only a moderate nationalist through-out most of the 1870s.

A similar pattern of development took place in Leroy-Beaulieu's thought about the state. His increased sense of identification with his country combined with new realism about international affairs led Leroy-Beaulieu to accept more activity by the state. As his previ-ous indifference toward France's relatively low birth rate gave way to a fear that his country was endangering its security through lack of fecundity, Leroy-Beaulieu was ready to invoke the power of the state to promote population growth. So in 1874 he advocated gov-ernment programs, including the promotion of settlement in colo-nies, to stimulate the growth of large families.[50] In 1877, returning to the topic after three years of preoccupation with budgets and taxation, he went still further. He recognized that the prime source of the stagnant birth rate was the fear that a large family would be a handicap in the struggle for status. The individual interest, he concluded, had become opposed to the general interest, and the only way to reconcile the two was for government to encourage more births through tax relief and aid to education.[51] The danger of war, more than any other factor, prevented Liberals such as Leroy-Beaulieu from striving to reduce the size and influence of the centralized state.[52]

Leroy-Beaulieu's study of public finance reinforced his acceptance of state activity moderately greater than that approved by the strict-est Established Liberals. As in his articles and treatises of 1869 and 1870, Leroy-Beaulieu struggled during the mid-1870s to avoid a doctrinaire hostility toward the state. Linking his analysis of public expenditures to practical experience rather than to abstract principle, in the *Traité des Finances* of 1877 he actually widened his earlier list of legitimate state functions. The growth of budgets, he con-ceded, resulted from the fact that civilized societies demanded more services from the public authorities.[53]

By no means, however, had Leroy-Beaulieu become a champion of wide-ranging state intervention in economic life. In his 1870 trea-tise on local government Leroy-Beaulieu had voiced the moderate position among Established Liberals, concluding that laissez-faire was not the correct rule for delimiting the operation of state authorities; yet he also held on to the long-standing Liberal distrust of the state. Despite his admission that civilized societies need more government he rejected many specific government activities. For example, he counterbalanced his approval of public forests with an admonition that the state should own farmland only for the sake of operating model farms. Furthermore, he added, these establishments should be sold as soon as the surrounding agriculturalists had learned from them.[54] Commenting on government run industries, Leroy-Beaulieu insisted that "incontestably the state in general is a bad industrialist." All mines, foundries, salt pans, and even railroads, therefore, should be privately owned. And he never even hinted that the government might have a role to play in the solution of the Social Question. The "general rule," in sum, was that "we must not uselessly complicate the functions of the state." A more specific criterion for appropriate state involvement eluded him.[55] To put the matter another way, he continued the difficult act of balancing an ingrained dislike of an active state with the lessons he learned after 1867.

When Leroy-Beaulieu analyzed the sources of his country's internal problems, his positions shifted on occasion. Immediately after the Franco-Prussian War and the Commune he was quite critical of the French elites. In the angry conclusion he added in 1872 to *La Question Ouvrière au XIXe Siècle* the economist-turned-moralist described how the upper classes paraded their frivolity, idleness, addiction to liquor, and easy morals on the boulevards of Paris, and he asked how the workers could fail to imitate this bad example. Nor did he exempt the bourgeoisie from his indictment. "The whole society," he fumed, "not just one or another fraction of it, is sick."[56] In the same section of the book he showed a newfound sympathy with the grievances of workers. When he started his career, as every page in *L'Etat Moral* testifies, he was insensitive to workers' experiences. By 1870 he had tried to achieve greater understanding and thus was more able to comprehend the near-religious enthusiasm of men and women at socialist meetings. He grasped that the lives of working-class people had an emptiness that socialist doctrines were filling. He also recognized that some workers wanted every personal desire sacrificed to the need for class solidarity because they felt they were involved in a desperate struggle with the capitalists.[57] In the remarks he added to *La Question Ouvrière* in 1872 Leroy-Beaulieu went further, pointing out that some employers in the factories and mines imposed unfair fines and regulations. While each individual abuse was relatively trivial, in the aggregate they were exasperating, frustrating, and damaging.[58] In addition, he spoke of workers' desperate need for security, an aspect of working-class existence he had overlooked in the 1860s.[59] In 1875 he commented on how difficult it was for members of the bourgeoisie to learn the realities of workers' lives and beliefs; this statement indicates his awareness of the need to see life from the point of view of others.[60] And two years later, in the *Traité de la Science des Finances*, he stated in an almost offhand remark, "The ideal of life is not uninterrupted, forced labor or a constant mental agitation and exertion; the ideal is the augmentation of leisure devoted to calm intellectual occupations and moral enjoyments."[61]

Yet he failed to follow up these potentially fertile insights. After 1872 his writings contained no further negative comments about the bourgeoisie, and he did not print another word about the insecurity faced by the working class. Having stated these crucial problems, he never explored their nature or meaning. Nor did he fundamentally change his prewar analysis of what was wrong with France. Like others in his milieu, he still believed that the unwieldy administration and the faulty French character were the factors most responsible for the country's economic failings and military weakness. In the long run, however, this indictment did not produce any significant change in his proposals for national policy. And his recognition in 1877 that work is not the ultimate value was an isolated thought that played no role in his weekly commentaries for *L'Economiste Français*.

The explanation for this neglect may be found in Leroy-Beaulieu's thought processes. Priding himself as a cold and impartial student of society, Leroy-Beaulieu cultivated in the name of objectivity a detached habit of mind that often hinders an individual from entering empathetically into the lives and minds of other people. With the few exceptions listed here, he was unable to see that the lower classes' view of life might have some validity. He failed to overcome the barriers he himself recognized were obstacles to understanding the working class.

Every solution that Leroy-Beaulieu proposed for the Social Question shows that he held firmly to moderate Established Liberal positions. Although he described the sickness of his society in desperate terms, he still prescribed the nonpolitical remedies Established Liberals had favored for decades. To create better housing he

recommended private philanthropic initiatives.[62] The injustices of
the factory, he asserted, could be cured not by legislative but by
moral actions, such as the censure of public opinion and "a great
spirit of conciliation, a real honesty, simplicity and frankness, . . .
balms that little by little can calm the angers."[63] He urged vigilance
against that ineffectual and harmful weapon, legislation.[64] Leroy-
Beaulieu argued in effect that the advance of justice depended upon
self-imposed moral reformation. The rich had to relearn that
the proper usage of wealth was not for conspicuous consumption
but for good works and for job-creating investments.[65] On the
other hand, he reasserted, bourgeois reformers had to stop casting
doubt on the validity of the current social and economic regimes.
Although he reiterated his faith in the power of time and increased production to close the wounds of division and eliminate
the scars of conflict, he ended *La Question Ouvrière* by exhorting the
bourgeoisie to come together to present a solid front to the Working Class.[66] Resistance to change, combined with philanthropy
and economic growth, comprised his basic solution to social unrest.

Leroy-Beaulieu's ardent prewar support for the capitalist system
became even more evident after the Franco-Prussian War and the
Commune, because he took on the task of promoting the interests
of big businesses heavily engaged in international trade. His only
unexpected policy recommendation was his advocacy of an income
tax, and this exception is easily explained in view of the government's urgent need to raise additional funds after the war. French
capitalists engaged in foreign commerce unquestionably preferred
an income tax over tariffs as a means of avoiding the fiscal disaster
that seemed to threaten the country as a result of the Franco-Prussian
War. Thus, even when Leroy-Beaulieu called for higher taxes on
the well-to-do, he was looking at the world as a self-conscious member of the bourgeoisie. He never concealed this identification, or
his intent to defend this group's interests.

Leroy-Beaulieu remained vague with regard to the boundaries
of this social stratum, using the terms "bourgeoisie" and "classes
moyennes" interchangeably. But this vagueness reflects his tendency, while recognizing the existence of separate levels within the
bourgeoisie, to stress the unity of the class rather than its heterogene-
ity. That outlook could mean that into the 1870s he did not identify
himself specifically as a member of the Grande Bourgeoisie. On

the other hand, he may have sought to obscure the competition for position and power between the Grande Bourgeoisie and the middle level of French society. His imprecise, generalized sense of class identification must have come under greater pressure during the Conservative Republic as the advanced republicans increasingly mobilized truly middle-class Frenchmen in an assault on the citadels of power the ex-Orleanist bourgeoisie had once again occupied.

Every one of Leroy-Beaulieu's ideas would have been welcomed among the Orleanist Liberals of the July Monarchy—with the exception of some of his sneers at monarchy itself. Whether in war or in peace, he shared almost without deviation the reactions and outlook of his social and intellectual milieu. His postwar writings, like his earliest works, show no signs of uncertainty or doubt, no sense that life might be a difficult puzzle. Politically his espousal of "self-government" was hardly radical even in the context of the Second Empire, and after the fall of the empire he was as content with the institutions of the Conservative Republic as were the authorized columnists of Liberalism who wrote for the *Revue des Deux Mondes* and for the *Journal des Economistes.* If the disillusionment he experienced during the crises of 1870–1871 had continued, it might have combined with his work on government finance to move him away from the certainties of the Established Liberal position. That did not happen, and his work recovered the character of his earliest writings. He continued to align himself quite closely with that shade of Established Liberal thought that approved entirely of the existing social hierarchy, saw no faults in the free-enterprise market system, and accepted only modest state regulation of social-economic life. The few brief signs that he might become open to a slightly modified view of the working class and its demands soon disappeared.

These considerations might indicate that the war and the Commune had only a superficial influence on Leroy-Beaulieu's deeply rooted views. However, that turbulent year sharpened his awareness of the fragility of society. Early in 1872, when the National Assembly outlawed the International Association of Working Men, Leroy-Beaulieu ridiculed the notion that the Commune had been the result of a conspiratorial organization. In *La Question Ouvrière* he had argued that in normal times socialist organizations had too few resources to be dangerous unless they allied themselves with the "Jacobin," that is, the extremist republican, parties.[67] Consequently, he counseled the deputies:

Destroy the International if you can; but if the circumstances which followed the siege of Paris reproduce themselves, you can take it as assured that the catastrophes of March 18 and of the Commune will be renewed. All your wisdom and efforts should be bent toward preventing the reappearance of the material and moral conditions in which France and Paris were placed last Spring.[68]

Despite the indignation he shared with other propertied Frenchmen against the Communards, he continued to insist, as he had in the spring of 1870, that coercion would not end the danger of revolution. The true dangers to social stability, he warned repeatedly, were war, military defeat, and the resulting disorganization of political authority.[69] Under changed conditions between 1879 and the mid-1880s, this lesson would become the most significant conclusion Leroy-Beaulieu retained from the period of the Conservative Republic.

5
The Turning Point

Experiences and Reactions of the Late
1870s and Early 1880s

■ Between 1877 and 1880 the concurrent appearance of domestic, economic, and international crises created a gloomy outlook
for France. In 1877 war between Russia and Turkey threatened the
peace of all of Europe, and late in the same year depression threatened to undermine France's prosperity. The next few years of hard
times also saw the revival of working-class militancy. From Leroy-
Beaulieu's point of view, the dramatic alteration of the political situation inside France was another serious disappointment. The constitutional conflict between the monarchists and the republicans came
to a head in 1877, and the republicans won a series of parliamentary
and electoral victories in 1877, 1878, and 1879 that pushed the centrist and conservative forces out of power. The new leaders made
major changes in the country's administrative personnel and unleashed an anticlerical campaign that exacerbated deep divisions
among the French. This stretch of time, crowded with unexpected
and sometimes dangerous events also saw the emergence of influential critiques of Liberal orthodoxies. All these developments aroused
the indignation of Established Liberals and members of the Grande
Bourgeoisie, Leroy-Beaulieu among them. As a new period in the
history of the Third Republic—the Republic of the Republicans—
began, Leroy-Beaulieu reached a number of turning points in his
activities and ideas.

*W*hile crisis and change marked France's existence, Leroy-Beaulieu continued to achieve success and honors. In the late 1870s he was one of the founding members of the Association pour la Défense de la Liberté Commerciale, a group created by major businessmen and leading politicians to defend the system of free trade against a growing protectionist movement.[1] In 1878 he was elected to the Académie des Sciences Morales et Politiques. For a number of years he was the youngest member of that body.[2] The death of his father-in-law, Michel Chevalier, in November 1879 led to another distinction: he succeeded Chevalier as professor of political economy at the Collège de France. This chair was the most prestigious academic post in France for an economist.[3]

At the time of his election to the Institut and the Collège de France, Leroy-Beaulieu had published five books, but his most impressive work was still ahead of him. Between 1881 and 1889 he produced four more volumes and issued a major revision of *De la Colonisation chez les Peuples Modernes*. These publications were in addition to his weekly articles for *L'Economiste Français* and his columns for the *Journal des Débats*. Despite all this activity as author and editor, he nevertheless took an active part in the discussions of the Académie and the Société d'Economie Politique.

To think of Leroy-Beaulieu solely as a professor and a journalist during this period of his life would be a mistake. In the 1870s he had been a capitalist landowner who also received shares—above all, shares in the Suez Canal Company—as part of Cordelia Michel Chevalier's dowry.[4] After the death of Michel Chevalier, he became a large-scale businessman. While continuing to manage the farms he had inherited from his father in Normandy, he also began to supervise Montplaisir, the much larger domain in the Midi that had belonged to his father-in-law. After the French conquered Tunisia in 1881 he acquired a share in a sizable vineyard in the protectorate and also became a shareholder and a director in railroad and phosphate enterprises there. In addition, since 1870 he had been investing in "both worlds," i.e., Europe and the Americas.[5] During the 1880s he apparently purchased land in the Rocquefort region, and he eventually became president of the Caves du Rocquefort, the company that made the famous cheese.[6] These business activities crowned his upward ascension in the social hierarchy. By the mid-1880s his fortune and his professional positions put him incontestably in the elite Grand Bourgeois class.

Leroy-Beaulieu's appearance and manner during these most successful years of his career suggest he knew he had arrived. Photographs, obituaries, and a portrait by the noted painter, Carolus Duran, give us a good idea of his appearance and manner. In his mid and late thirties he had a fairly slim and very erect figure and a ruddy face that reflected the good health that helped him to do the prodigious amount of work he turned out. In keeping with the fashion of the late nineteenth century, Leroy-Beaulieu wore a very full and flowing beard. The blue eyes of the Norman economist contrasted in a striking manner with his abundance of black hair. His friend René Stourm later recalled that his expression was both friendly and reserved, and that in both youth and age "a certain solemnity presided over his movements."[7] Another biographer, apparently a younger man who had not been close to Leroy-Beaulieu, wrote frankly of his rather cold and forbidding manner.[8] Marcel Proust captured the essence of the man in a typically apt phrase when he referred to "the severe and Assyrian profile of Leroy-Beaulieu."[9] Despite his successes, Leroy-Beaulieu may not have been very comfortable with other human beings.[10] His stiffness with people may explain why success evaded this journalist-professor-landowner-capitalist in one area: national political life. Beginning in 1878 in a by-election, he persistently attempted to enter the Chamber of Deputies. In 1881, 1883, 1885, and 1889 he again contested the seat for the district of Lodève where Montplaisir was located. However, he never gained an uncontested victory. When he was reported as the victor by a narrow margin in 1889, the hostile Chamber of Deputies decided after a parliamentary inquiry that a new election should take place. In this contest, in 1890, Leroy-Beaulieu was defeated, and he did not run again. The lively and extroverted people of the Midi may not have taken to the reserved Norman, whose intellectual nature and personal characteristics may have prevented him from overcoming the hostility of the idealistic republicans and compensating for the declining influence of the local notables who favored his candidacy. However, after he won a seat on the Conseil Général in 1877, he was reelected for many years.[11] The correspondence between Paul and his wife indicates that *she* was the political animal in the family. Early in his career as a *conseiller général* he complained about the inanity and boredom of the post, but his wife's letters are full of zest for the electoral battles, in which she probably served as the prime manager.[12]

Leroy-Beaulieu's candidacies give us considerable information about his political commitments, in contrast to the dearth of material on the previous years of his life. One local newspaper says that he ran in his first election as a "moderate republican" while other sources called him an independent or a "constitutional" candidate.[13] These designations indicate that he accepted the regime installed in 1875. Yet as early as 1880 a republican newspaper had singled him out as a right-winger. Displeased by his nomination for the chair of political economy at the Collège de France, the *Nouveau Journal* declared that "for ten years the distinguished economist has unceasingly used his credit to infest France with functionaries and business executives imbued with the worst sentiments of reaction and clericalism."[14] Indeed in 1885 he ran for the Chamber of Deputies on the list assembled by the monarchist forces, and the republicans who controlled the Chamber in 1889 certainly viewed him as an enemy. Even so, although Leroy-Beaulieu became a part of the opposition to the new leadership of the republic, he shunned the monarchist cause. As we review Established Liberals' reactions to the events of this period, we will see that Leroy-Beaulieu remained in the Centre Gauche current during the Republic of the Republicans.

Shocks, relief, and renewed shocks characterized the experience of the Established Liberals from the late 1870s through the early 1880s. Their anxieties started in spring 1877 with the outbreak of fighting between Russia and Turkey. Joseph Garnier expressed these feelings when he deplored the new war as opening a period of "crimes and miseries," decline of civilization, and exacerbation of the economic crisis then spreading around the world. He worried that the war would not remain localized.[15] Mourning the suffering and death wreaked by the battles, sieges, bombardments, and destruction of villages, Garnier wondered indignantly at the end of the conflict whether "the worst peace is not preferable to the best war."[16] The threat of another Europe-wide conflict reminded him and other Established Liberals of just how fragile peace could be.

The international crisis abated by the end of the year, only to be replaced by an economic one. When depression struck the world in 1873, France suffered some economic dislocations. Yet French business and commerce revived and flourished for several years. During the spring of 1877 the editor of the *Journal des Economistes* wrote happily that "France is still, among all the countries of the continent, the one where business is going best, where taxes are most easily collected, and where the populace has the least anxiety."[17] The economic situation then deteriorated quickly, and in December the monthly meeting of the Société d'Economie Politique took up the question of "The Causes of the Current Crisis." The economists did not agree on the causes of the depression, and although they all believed in depending on the "natural course of things," they were uncomfortable because the so-called natural forces no longer seemed to be doing their job of restoring equilibrium.[18]

Adding to the uneasiness of the Liberals was the revival of working class militancy as expressed in strikes and Socialism. During the years of repression that followed, the Commune workers had been cautious, but the political changes that began in October 1877 made them bold once again. The *Journal des Economistes* first noticed the renewal of strike activity in the middle of 1878. Toward the end of 1879 the journal published a report about a congress of trade unionists in Marseilles in which a pioneer French Marxist, Jules Guesde, gained a hearing just a year after a similar congress had rejected the views of its Socialist delegates. According to one reporter, "not one original or new idea had been set forth at the congress," but "never before, even in the conventions of the International, had anyone said so uncompromisingly that it was necessary to take over private property and collectivize it."[19] The workers' congress of 1879 was an augury of renewed activity. By 1880 they had fully recovered from the effects of the intimidation, and over the next two years they battered factories and mines with a wave of strikes. The directing classes fought back with firings, strikebreakers, police and troops.[20] The turbulence revived the Social Question with all its dilemmas.

At this juncture Established Liberal defenses of the existing social and economic arrangements came under increasing intellectual challenge. In the late 1850s and the 1860s nonsocialist thinkers in France, such as Charles Dupont-White, Léon Walras, and Charles Renouvier, launched a search for alternatives to the predominant forms of both Liberalism and Socialism.[21] Their influence was slow to be felt, however. A more powerful assault came from a number of thinkers in Germany who held important university chairs and who had high reputations as scholars. Though this group of Germans is often divided into the Historical School of Economics and the unfortunately named "Socialists of the Chair," actually many of them partook of both strands of thought. The historical approach was a relativistic outlook that rejected the deductive method and belief in universal natural law that had characterized Liberal economics since J.-B. Say and David Ricardo. Those identified as Socialists of the Chair developed arguments to vindicate the capacity of the state organization to act efficiently in the economic sphere, and they insisted that the state had a vital role in bringing about progress. At least one prominent member of this group, Lujo Brentano, also praised trade unions for their useful role in the economy. Criticizing Liberalism as excessively individualistic, the Socialists of the Chair were probably the first important group of academic thinkers to recommend old-age pensions and unemployment benefits, which they saw as measures that would wean workers away from the socialist movement.[22] In the early 1870s, while Leroy-Beaulieu was publishing his *Question Ouvrière au XIXe Siècle* and starting *L'Economiste Français*, the historical and reformist outlook had one important promoter in France: the Belgian-born economist Emile de Laveleye, an intellectual of European standing. In 1878 the established French economists were angered to discover that the recently appointed instructor of political economy at the Paris school of law, Paul Cauwès (1843–1917), was disseminating the new doctrines to his students. By 1881, after several more university chairs of political economy had been set up, there was at least one more dissident, Charles Gide (1847–1932) who would soon have a wide audience for his ably written texts. The Established Liberals had lost their academic monopoly, and they quickly found themselves on the defensive on a front they had previously dominated.[23]

Cauwès's *Précis d'Economie Politique*, the first important French expression of the new outlook, came out in installments in 1878 and 1879, amidst the crises and transformations we have been tracing, and a second edition was published in 1880. Although the work was rather badly organized and inconsistently argued, it provided the first alternative in France to dogmatic antistatist and free-trade approaches. Cauwès challenged the older school head-on from the beginning. In the preface of the first edition he scornfully dismissed laissez-faire, "the favorite formula" of the "Anglo-French economists," and celebrated the "salutary reaction that is going on against this limitless doctrinairism."[24] He charged that the old ideas exposed society's "flank" to Socialist attacks by providing Proudhon and Marx with the intellectual weapons they used to attack "capital."[25] After hurling these charges, the author stated in the introductory chapters that economics was incomplete as a science; that the historical method and relativism of German economists was superior to the Anglo-French school's belief in natural law and the abstract deductive method; and that protectionism rather than free trade was the correct policy for France. Further, he wrote that the state as well as the individual should have a role in the improvement of society.[26] The nation as a whole, Cauwès stressed, is as real and as significant as the individual. As a consequence government must promote economic development for the sake of military strength and national independence and must use tariffs to encourage investment in vital areas that short-sighted investors might neglect.[27] Above all, he insisted that the state has an obligation, required both by the need to resolve the Social Question and by the demands of justice, to intervene in the distribution of wealth by supporting workers' efforts to improve their wages.[28] The combination of humanitarianism, nationalism, and protectionism made Cauwès's doctrine an appealing rival to Established Liberalism, competing for the allegiance of France's middle classes.

While the news from the intellectual front looked grim for the Established Liberals, the political situation shifted back and forth. After the election of 1876 produced a republican majority with a seemingly strong Centre Gauche component, the chroniclers of the *Revue des Deux Mondes* and the *Journal des Economistes* looked hopefully toward the future. But the "Seize Mai" crisis of 1877, the six-month effort launched by President MacMahon and the duc de Broglie to overturn the electoral decision of the preceding year, turned the Established Liberals' satisfaction into distress. They protested that the MacMahon-Broglie government violated the norms of parliamentary rule, and they applauded when the right went down to defeat in the elections of October 1877.[29] The Senatorial elections of January, the subsequent resignation of Marshal MacMahon, and the election of a republican elder, Jules Grévy, as head of state, put the republicans in charge of the entire government. The Established Liberal intellectuals were initially delighted with these developments, largely because the Centre Gauche provided the prime ministers and other important cabinet figures for 1878 and much of 1879.[30]

This rejoicing was mixed with concern, however, since many of the Centre Gauche goals differed widely from those of the other republican groups. The former favored the free-trade treaties of the 1860s while a large body of Opportunist and Left Republicans endorsed protectionism. Although the Centre Gauche went along with a limited purge of those administrators who had actively supported the May 16 action, many other republicans were eager to go much further. They wanted to rid the judiciary, as well as the government bureaus, of recent converts to republicanism and to replace them with men who had given long and faithful service to the republican cause. Another dispute raged over policy toward the Catholic Church and, above all, over the role of the clergy in education. Advanced republicans considered Catholic priests and monks to be the most dangerous enemies of modern intellectual and political freedoms, but many in the Centre Gauche saw the Church as an indispensable ally in the struggle for social stability (by which they meant the preservation of the existing social hierarchy).[31]

The struggle for power between the republican factions broke into the open late in 1879. In the months that followed the senatorial election in 1879 the committed republicans realized that they no longer needed the republican converts of the Centre Gauche to form a parliamentary majority. Thus they insisted on a ministry headed by and dominated by leaders of their own stripe, and they began to implement their full program. Anticlerical legislation proposed by the Opportunists and the Left Republicans and supported fervently by the Radicals became the battlefield that confirmed the supremacy of the advanced republicans. Within two years, largely because of this issue, the Centre Gauche had lost its former prominence in republican cabinets, and from then on its leaders generally found themselves excluded from ministerial office.[32] They were thus impotent when the new masters of the republic intensified the purge of prefects, judges, and other officials whose loyalty to the regime was doubtful. The *nouvelles couches sociales* (new social strata), whose rise had been signaled in Léon Gambetta's speeches in the early 1870s, seemed on the point of dominating every aspect of the country's government.[33]

The republican victors' interventionist bent added to the frustration and fury of Established Liberals. The orthodox economists worried about proposals for state action aimed at ameliorating the living and working conditions of the working class.[34] Contributors to the *Revue des Deux Mondes*, meanwhile, identified the chief sin of the advanced republicans as their policy of exclusion.[35] As early as February 1879 de Mazade began reminding his readers that the republic owed its establishment to the moderation of Thiers. The legacy the republican party should receive from that first president of the Third Republic, de Mazade stated, was "to divest itself of its past exclusiveness in order to adapt itself to French society's mores, interests, and need for security." The new regime had won out because it protected "les intérêts libéraux," "tous les intérêts serieux."[36] These euphemisms designated the long-established possessors of landed and industrial property and the long-entrenched holders of high administrative and judicial office. In May 1880 he burst out: "Exclude, always exclude, that is the first and last word of the political program of certain republicans."[37] His disgust came through still more clearly in an account of a speaking tour by Léon Gambetta in March 1881. As elections approached, de Mazade fulminated, Gambetta made his appeals to "traveling salesmen, wine-shop proprietors, receivers for bankrupt firms (syndics de toutes les industries), and petty clerks in the stores." The aggravation was largely that of former Orleanists who had converted to republicanism and who then saw their social inferiors shutting them out from the prestigious public offices they had barely regained.[38]

Leroy-Beaulieu's writings during and after the transition from the Conservative Republic to the Republic of the Republicans reveal the same frustration, rooted in the same class feeling, as that expressed by de Mazade. But the economist devoted his attention to the economic crisis and the challenges from workers, Socialists, and reform-minded intellectuals as well as to the shift of political influence away from the Grande Bourgeoisie. Rather abruptly, therefore, he turned away from the study of government finance and became once more the multifaceted thinker he had been before the Third Republic. He wrote more frequently on the population question, a topic intimately related to his concerns with foreign affairs and national power. Old interests such as the Social Question, the role of the state, and war and foreign policy reappeared in his articles. These subjects, together with his comments on economic woes, crowded out the discussions of railroads, taxes, and loans that had been his main interests during the Conservative Republic.

The growing economic crisis clearly weighed heavily on Leroy-Beaulieu's mind once he recognized that France would not escape the worldwide business downturn. For several years he ignored the troubled state of the world's economy. When he finally wrote on the depression in May 1877, he gloomily commented that the crisis might actually end the long period of rapidly expanding production and trade that had begun with the application of steam power to manufacturing. Since 1840, he pointed out, Europeans had fully equipped their countries with the most essential industries and communications. In fact, too many investors had entered the iron, steel, and textile industries. Leroy-Beaulieu declared that "the present business crisis has a more permanent and disquieting character than the preceding ones" because it arose from a general readjustment of the pattern of production.[39] Three years later, in 1880, this pessimism had lifted considerably, and Leroy-Beaulieu judged that "this crisis is much more superficial, much more local, much more specialized than is claimed." By mid-1880 he was ready to announce that "diverse symptoms" showed that the depression was coming to an end.[40] In the interim, however, his confidence in the future of capitalism had been shaken.[41]

Leroy-Beaulieu was even more discouraged by the new political scene. Repeatedly throughout the 1880s he castigated the new masters of the Third Republic for their religious and the personnel policies. Although Paul, unlike his Liberal Catholic brother, Anatole, was a secularist, he shared Established Liberals' indignation about the anticlerical measures pursued after 1879.[42] Yet this grievance was less important than his dismay at the displacement of members of the old elite from the administration. Although he did not write any lengthy commentary on the situation, various phrases and passages show his resentment. In 1882 he expressed bitterness over the purge of the Grande Bourgeoisie, calling on the new leaders to "reenter the way traced for them by M. Thiers" and to govern "without sectarian spirit, seeking the support of all social strata." The next year he characterized the majority of political leaders in scathing and class-conscious terms:

> Until now we have been governed by minor lawyers and unimportant barristers from the provinces, and it is difficult to believe we can descend a degree in the scale of government capacity. It has been the wisdom of Nerac and Beziers which has ruled our destinies.[43]

And a year later he explained the new "invasion" of government in economic affairs as the consequence of universal suffrage, which had given power to the "so-called 'nouvelles couches,'" the middle-class representatives who aspired to a leading role in political life.[44]

These statements not only testify to Leroy-Beaulieu's strong sense of the superiority of the Grande Bourgeoisie but also suggest that the political battles had sharpened his sense of class identity. By 1881, at the latest, Leroy-Beaulieu ceased to see himself as part of a broad bourgeoisie or middle class, instead locating himself specifically within that superior stratum, the Grande Bourgeoisie. His bitterness was a lament that the elite class was being elbowed out of political dominance by people it considered inferior. In this regard he completely shared the feelings of de Mazade and other Liberals who wrote for the *Revue des Deux Mondes*. And, as his exclusion from the Chamber of Deputies shows, Leroy-Beaulieu was one member of the Grande Bourgeoisie who suffered personally from the determination of the advanced republicans to push lukewarm republicans out of the center of public affairs.

Soon after the advanced republicans took control Leroy-Beaulieu also began to complain about the impact of the political shift on the Social Question. The speeches and programs of the republican left, particularly those of the Radicals, aroused his ire, because he was convinced that they fueled the renewed working-class discontent. He believed that the nonsocialist politicians' constant cries for reform and their attacks on capitalists heightened the passions of the working class and made them feel justified in turning to Socialism.[45]

Leroy-Beaulieu was in effect returning to his apprehensions of the 1860s; indeed he may have been more worried about the future in the early 1880s than he had been during the closing years of the Second Empire. Since he believed by the early 1870s that the most radical wing of a radical movement eventually comes to dominate that movement—a lesson drawn from the French Revolution— he feared the eventual triumph of the Radicals.[46] And by 1881 he was complaining that universal suffrage had turned the country into an "unreflecting democracy," thus bringing the republican firebrands near to power and threatening to strangle individual liberty.[47]

In 1885, Leroy-Beaulieu ruefully observed that the new schools of social-economic thought were winning the battle for the minds of the opinion leaders of society. Believing that reformist versions of socialism would not succeed as "antidotes to revolutionary socialism," he lamented, "It is toward these first two socialisms that the majority of the minds in the political world and the scientific sphere are inclining. The defenders of economic truth and economic liberty are far from numerous in Europe today."[48] He agreed entirely with the opinion of Guy de Molinari, who had succeeded Joseph Garnier as editor of the *Journal des Economistes*, that philanthropically motivated legislators would do more damage to the economy than could the militant movements of the working class.[49] Refusing to give up the fight for "truth" and "liberty," Leroy-Beaulieu redoubled his efforts in the struggle against thinkers he considered "sophists" and "dupes."

The impact of political and economic change on Leroy-Beaulieu's convictions is vividly illustrated by his new position on an income tax. Before the advanced republicans took over the parliament and cabinets, Leroy-Beaulieu had advocated an income tax modeled on the British system, preferring this step to the tariffs and indirect taxes proposed by Adolphe Thiers in 1871. As late as 1879 the second edition of the *Traité des Finances* repeated the first edition's statement that "the tax on incomes merits introduction in France."[50] Just two years later, in his *Essai sur la Répartition des Richesses et sur la Tendance à une Moindre Inégalité*, he reversed this stand,[51] and the 1883 edition of the *Traité des Finances* also contained a disclaimer of his former opinion. As his colleague René Stourm later explained, Leroy-Beaulieu would not have argued in favor of the tax in the 1870s if he had foreseen how quickly France would become an "unchecked" democracy.[52] Leroy-Beaulieu was now concerned primarily by the threat that the new distribution of political power posed to the wealth and status of the Grande Bourgeoisie with whom he fully and unequivocally identified.

*L*eroy-Beaulieu's position on the political spectrum also shifted as his class consciousness sharpened. When he first ran for the Chamber of Deputies in 1878, he supported the new republic, but with some reservations, as shown by his decision to run as a "constitutional" or independent candidate. A strongly republican newspaper in his home region, the *Indépendant de Lodève*, defined the meaning of that affiliation in a hostile but illuminating fashion in an April 1878 article entitled "Les Faux Dévots Republicains." The Constitutionnels, the newspaper stated, were "former liberal Orleanists, disdainful of the Republic . . . but enemies of the Empire which formerly had chased them out of places and . . . [who] from being lackeys have made themselves masters."[53] Predictably, this newspaper attacked Leroy-Beaulieu bitterly. He certainly had the support of proclerical, antirepublican groups in his district, including the openly antirepublican newspaper *L'Echo de Lodève*. However, his first electoral poster, issued in late June 1878, reveals his effort to appeal to republicans as well as conservatives. He assured republican voters, "I am not to the slightest degree hostile to the existing institutions. I give them my sincere adhesion, desiring only that they function in an orderly and peaceful fashion." However, he went on to separate himself unequivocally from the advanced republicans and the Radicals by declaring, "The best policy is the policy of moderation, . . . that which does not alarm either property or religion."[54]

A letter he wrote to his wife on November 16, 1879, provides further information about where he saw himself in the political spectrum. Commenting on a newspaper notice that said he would present himself in a future election as a republican candidate, he stated: "That's what I am, in effect, although with an odd moderation about which it would not be useful to say anything at this time."[55] What did he mean? It seems likely that he did not wish to express his reservations too strongly for fear of alienating voters who were fully committed to the republican regime. Certainly he showed no sympathy, even privately, for the monarchist cause. "All the pretenders," he growled to Cordelia in April 1880, "are inept, and the best course is to attempt to accommodate to the republic and to attempt to make it more moderate."[56] Like Centre Gauche politicians he supported the republican form of government because he saw this regime as the only practical one at the time—not because he believed the republican system was the only good form of government.[57]

When Leroy-Beaulieu ran in 1878, 1881, and 1883, he confronted opponents who were not simply republicans but members of the Radical Party. His rival in 1878 and 1881 was Eugène Arrazat whose positions were consistently Radical: amnesty for imprisoned and exiled Communards, secular education, freedom of divorce, separation of church and state, suppression of existing laws limiting freedom of the press, restriction of the legal workday to ten hours, and protection of railroad workers against unreasonable dismissal.[58] Arrazat's anticlericalism and his belief in state intervention, stands typical of France's radical republicans, ran counter to everything Leroy-Beaulieu wanted for French society. To Leroy-Beaulieu the radicals were a horrible species of destroyers who endangered the very existence of civilization.

The radicals in turn detested Leroy-Beaulieu. When Arrazat died in office, the prefect of the Hérault, Auguste Galtier, resigned in order to become the radical republican candidate. In one of his electoral posters he warned that Leroy-Beaulieu, the "Orleanist candidate," was an implacable adversary of the arrondissement's interests because he was a free trader.[59] This indictment was gentle compared to the comments of *L'Indépendant de Lodève*. On the eve of the voting in 1883 this newspaper portrayed him as surrounded by the men of the "Seize Mai" and other reactionaries "united for the moment through hate of the Republic." The editors excerpted a biting article by Paul de Cassagnac, the uncompromising Bonapartist, in which he characterized Leroy-Beaulieu as "neither fish nor fowl" and as "a disguised republican, one of those *centres gauches* without opinions, without principles, always in the train of the victor whoever he might be."[60] Several days later, after Leroy-Beaulieu outpolled Galtier and forced a runoff, the tone became even more nasty.[61] An anonymous pamphlet satirizing Leroy-Beaulieu's pretensions christened him "Colladent," a term from the Greek best translated as "Diarrhea Mouth."[62]

What aroused the fury of the Radicals—aside from Leroy-Beaulieu's near victories in a series of elections? Although he resolutely presented himself as a republican candidate, in all his campaigns his main backing came from the antirepublican, proclerical notables of the department and their mouthpiece, *L'Echo de Lodève*. This extremely conservative newspaper viewed a parliamentary regime as a guarantee of political crisis.[63] The day before MacMahon dismissed the republican cabinet of Jules Simon, an editorial angrily condemned the republicans because "they demand that the arsonists of Paris and the assassins of hostages be recalled from New Caledonia while they refrain from expressing regrets for the victims of the Commune."[64] The editors' fury was especially aroused by threats to the Catholic Church. For this newspaper "free thinker" was an insulting epithet, and its editorial columns roundly assailed Gambetta for his anti-Catholic statements.[65] On the brink of the October 1877 election the *Echo* warned that a radical victory would mean European war. A week later it declared frankly, "Revolution never founds anything; it always destroys."[66]

Originally this newspaper gave only qualified support to Leroy-Beaulieu. When he first ran for the Chamber in 1878, the *Echo* also approved the candidacy of Charles Delpon de Vissec, whom it called a pure monarchist. It reasoned that the presence of three candidates would assure a runoff and "the check of M. Arrazat and the defeat of the radical ideas that he personifies." However, after Delpon de Vissec withdrew and Arrazat won, the *Echo* deplored the unwillingness of the monarchist conservatives to vote for Leroy-Beaulieu, who was a conservative although not a monarchist.[67] For this newspaper the election of a Centre Gauche candidate would still have been a victory.

Even though committed monarchists at first hesitated to vote

for even as right-wing a republican as Leroy-Beaulieu, their programs had much in common. While he constantly appeared before
his district as a republican candidate, like the monarchist conservatives he detested the Radicals for their attacks on the Catholic
Church, their demands for the separation of church and state, and
their outlook on foreign policy. According to his circular of 1881,
the program of "the partisans of the radical republic . . . is made
up only of destructive measures: suppression of the Senate, . . .
suppression of the Presidency of the Republic," and elimination of
public funding for organized religions.[68] Furthermore, beginning
with the election of 1881 his programs and speeches included lively
attacks on the existing Opportunist governments. He complained
that the Opportunists wasted taxpayer money, particularly on the
senseless expenditures of the Freycinet Plan of public works. In
addition, in comments whose significance will become more apparent when we look at his adoption of the policy of imperialism,
in 1881 and 1883 he warned about the failures of republican foreign
policy that had increased the danger of war.[69] Almost nothing distinguished Leroy-Beaulieu from those just to the right of him, the
still somewhat liberal adherents of the old Centre Droite, and beginning with the election of 1881 the old-style monarchical conservatives seemed able to tolerate him.

Given their common enemies and frequent agreements, Leroy-
Beaulieu's participation in 1885 on the monarchist and conservative
electoral slate is hardly startling, even though he appears to have
maintained his moderate and resigned republicanism. The election
of 1885 was an odd one. The Bourbon pretender, the Comte de
Chambord, had been rigid in his ideology, which was close to that
of the Conservatism of the early nineteenth century. His death in
1883 left the Comte de Paris, a member of the moderate Orleans
family, as head of the monarchist cause. For the 1885 election the
Comte de Paris chose to minimize the question of the regime and
to stress issues around which right-wing republicans could rally.
Leroy-Beaulieu was among the individuals persuaded to join the conservative forces as a result of the Orleanist prince's desire to "re-
publicanize" his slates.[70] By this time candidates in such regions of
the Midi as the Hérault needed the support of moderate republicans
in order to win elections. Therefore, the monarchists would be more
likely to back a lukewarm supporter of the republican regime.[71]

There is no reason to believe that Leroy-Beaulieu saw the restoration of a monarchy as a practical alternative to the regime established

in the 1870s. Rather, he sought a revitalized "conservative" coalition, the alliance of the two "Centers" (Gauche and Droite) that
had not materialized in the years of the Conservative Republic.
Consequently, in his 1885 campaign speeches he took the same
stands as in the previous elections and emphasized the same issues.
On September 6, 1885, in his main campaign speech, he renewed
his former attacks on "the constantly growing deficit, the ruinous
adventures, useless wars, the foreign expeditions conducted with
the most deplorable incapacity, the mob of incompetents who
swarm" in the government. And he concluded with phrases that
must have stuck in the throats of his less republican supporters.
Calling for an end to "the arbitrary policies, the secret informers,
and the favoritism that are invading France more and more," he
proclaimed that "it was time that liberty, fraternity, and equality
should no longer be vain words and should begin to reign" in the
country.[72] Even in the 1885 campaign, Leroy-Beaulieu continued
to reaffirm his "strangely moderate" republicanism.

Nevertheless, Leroy-Beaulieu's collaboration with the monarchists signals a turning point in his orientation toward the public
life of his country. So great was his anger and dismay over the
direction the advanced republicans were taking in the 1880s that
he had become alienated from the type of republic they were creating. At the same time, however, he refused to join a new attempt
in 1889 to bring about a centrist coalition. Before the election of
1889 a group of French leaders—many of whom had been prominent
in the Centre Gauche faction—issued a call for the formation of a
new political grouping, "L'Union Libérale." Their program called
on all conservatives to accept the end of monarchy in France and
pinned its hopes mainly on winning popular support for a stronger
Senate that could check the body elected by universal suffrage, the
Chamber of Deputies.[73] Instead of accepting this program Leroy-
Beaulieu ran as an independent, proposing that legislation passed
by the Chamber of Deputies be resubmitted to voters in the form
of a referendum. In other words, he envisioned using universal suffrage to block the evils it produced.[74] It is tempting to imagine
that his aloofness from the Union Libérale was another manifestation of the contemptuous, isolated attitude that led him to characterize "nearly all of his colleagues at the Institut as 'imbeciles.'"[75] On
the other hand, he might have realized that it was chimerical for
a party to call upon the voters to reduce their own powers by increasing those of a legislative body, the Senate, chosen by restricted

suffrage. In any case, Leroy-Beaulieu's proposal for the use of referendums was an alternative means to the same end, weakening the power of the socially inferior politicians of the Chamber of Deputies. As it turned out, neither approach won approval, although the evidence does indicate that Leroy-Beaulieu actually had a small majority in the 1889 election and that the republicans maneuvered him out of the seat.

The maneuverings of the republican majority that deprived him of a place on the national political stage fed Leroy-Beaulieu's disgust with the recently established system of government. No longer would he extol universal suffrage, as he had done on several occasions in the 1860s and early 1870s. But another shift in his outlook reached a climax in 1882: he became a forthright, unhesitating advocate of colonial imperialism. The transformations of France and Europe that began in 1877 were largely responsible for this conversion. The connections will become clear as we trace his thoughts about empire from the 1860s through their culmination in 1882 in the second edition of *De la Colonisation chez les Peuples Modernes*.

6
The Path to Imperialism

Leroy-Beaulieu on Colonial Empire,
1869–1881

■ Since the 1930s or 1940s historians of imperialism have
been mainly responsible for keeping Paul Leroy-Beaulieu's name
alive primarily through their studies of his expansionist doctrine.
As early as 1870 Leroy-Beaulieu had a coherent position on the
organization of a colonial system, and by 1882 he had assembled
an elaborate set of justifications for the acquisition of a colonial empire. The doctrine as a whole was a remarkable achievement because
it was a Liberal imperialism. One key issue raised by Leroy-
Beaulieu's work, therefore, is how he reconciled Liberalism and imperialism. A related problem is his contribution to the development
of imperialist thought. Until recently most writers have assumed
that Liberals were uniformly hostile to imperialism until Leroy-
Beaulieu and others began to propagandize in favor of empire during
the 1870s.[1] However, Raoul Girardet's authoritative interpretation,
first published in 1972, has taught us that during the last years of
the Second Empire a number of prominent Liberals shaped a militant colonialist doctrine. Girardet holds that Leroy-Beaulieu derived
his ideas from these predecessors. Thus, the question of the economist's originality deserves our attention. In agreement with earlier
historians of imperialism, I will argue that Leroy-Beaulieu redefined
the term "colony" in a fashion that was crucial for the new doctrine
of the late nineteenth century. But, in addition, I will point out

that he synthesized justifications for imperialism into the brilliant form of a three-part argument.

Historians have overlooked a third important question about Leroy-Beaulieu's outlook: the problem of explanation. Should we accept Leroy-Beaulieu's arguments in favor of imperialism at face value as his reasons for favoring that policy, or are there hidden motivations? Marxists and other leftists have long insisted that imperialists concealed selfish economic designs beneath humanitarian and nationalist rationalizations.[2] Recently, on the other hand, historians have judged that Leroy-Beaulieu's desire for the greatness of his country was the dominant motivation behind his advocacy of expansion. That is, they have taken his own words seriously. The specialists, however, have paid too little attention to the timing of Leroy-Beaulieu's propaganda campaign. By following Leroy-Beaulieu's reactions to the events of the 1870s, we will discover that he became a fervent imperialist only around the beginning of 1880, soon after the establishment of the Republic of the Republicans. The interplay between his nationalist feelings, his fear of social upheaval, and his suspicion of republican foreign and domestic policy accounts for his transformation into a fervent imperialist.

Leroy-Beaulieu shaped his ideas about colonies in the context of the decline of the French colonial empire up to 1830 and the acquisition of territories in the mid-1800s whose value was doubtful. Before the Revolution of 1789 the French had lost Canada and the British had defeated their attempts to become the dominant power in India. As a result of the Napoleonic Wars, the nation lost the last of its valuable overseas possessions and was left with just three small plantation islands and a few trading post footholds on the coast of Africa. On the map of the world the great French empire had dwindled to a few dots; it was hardly an empire at all.[3] The abolition of the slave trade in 1815, the same year as Napoleon's great defeat, destroyed the prosperity of the sugar islands in the Caribbean and in the Indian Ocean, and to help them the government in the mother country discouraged the cultivation of the sugar beet in France; as a result, sugar prices rose and the colonies incurred the further dishonor of becoming burdens rather than supports to the French economy.[4] However, in the 1830s and 1840s French forces conquered Algeria, which was the one significant possession in the French overseas empire during Leroy-Beaulieu's youth. The mid-1860s, the years when Leroy-Beaulieu was beginning his career as a publicist, saw the French government seize portions of Indo-china, and enterprising colonial governors in West Africa pushed French control into the hinterlands beyond the small coastal stations. Since the new acquisitions were not fabulous lands of gold and spices, the growth of the empire attracted attention only fitfully.

Despite the insignificance of France's overseas territories into the mid–1800s, throughout the nineteenth century a number of publi-cists and political figures were troubled by the condition of their country's islands and trading posts. Among the controversial issues were the nature and organization of the dependencies, the subsidies for the sugar islands, and the status of slavery in the plantation is-lands. For economic and political experts, however, the colonial question went deeper. The purpose and structure of empire had been perfectly clear throughout most of the Old Regime: colonies were to serve the economic welfare of the mother country, and colo-nial governments were strictly subordinated to bureaucrats in Paris. This system of monopoly and control persisted into the nineteenth century. But as Liberal economists criticized the regulations and the dependencies became too poor to aid the French economy, the old justifications for colonies ceased to be persuasive, and some won-dered whether colonies served any purpose at all.[5]

The conquest of Algeria increased the dilemmas. Here was a land which did not fit into any of the established categories of over-seas possessions. As the French military pushed into the interior, instead of merely establishing trading posts on the Algerian coast, it confronted a large indigenous population with a civilization that differed radically from that of its conquerors. The French wondered if the Algerians could be assimilated into European and French cul-ture and mores. Some suggested that the Arabs were a nationality and should be treated as such. Among the policies considered was *refoulement*, the policy of relocating the native inhabitants deeper into the hinterland in order to provide land for immigrants. After the agents of the Second Empire began to acquire additional territor-ies in Africa and Asia, such as Senegal and Cochin China, the prob-lem of indigenous populations became even more perplexing. The Southeast Asian land was heavily populated, and European observ-ers believed the West African territories were uninhabitable by white settlers. The French experience of empire during the Constitutional Monarchy and the Second Empire was beset with discouragement and confusion.[6]

Beginning in the early years of the nineteenth century, those French political and intellectual leaders who were opposed to imperialism created an antiexpansionist ideology drawn largely from the work of Adam Smith. Jean-Baptiste Say began the systematization of this doctrine, and it was complete by the middle of the century. From *The Wealth of Nations* came the idea that trade under the typical colonial system hinders the growth of the productive powers of both parent country and colony. Free trade is no better, because under that system the colonizing nation obtains no tangible profit from the expense of founding settlements.[7] Colonies also drain badly needed capital from the homeland, through both the investments diverted to them and the increased taxes needed to pay for fortifications and fleets.[8] To this ideology Say added one much-repeated observation, which might be called the national character argument. Successful colonization, he asserted, requires colonists with youth, capital, and a wide knowledge of practical arts. With a jaundiced eye on his own country, he offered this barbed comment: "Nations where these qualities are rare and which are distinguished by social talents rather than by talents useful to society, are not the right ones to found colonies and do not succeed."[9]

As the conquests in North and West Africa and in Indochina proceeded, critics further protested that the French could not successfully colonize the new territories since they were already fully inhabited. According to Charles Ageron, during the Old Regime the dominant definition of the term "colony" treated an overseas dependency as a "ferme du commerce metropolitain," i.e., a subordinate trading partner whose wealth the possessing country exploited. Early in the nineteenth century this notion was replaced or supplemented by one that equated "colony" with "settlement." Another historian described this conception when he declared, "It may, I think, be said that so far colonization in its purest and classic form has generally been thought of in terms of a movement of peoples outward from a mother country into empty lands."[10] Almost every nineteenth-century writer on colonial questions that I have studied habitually associated the term "colony" with an image of settlers occupying and cultivating the soil. As a consequence, the prize possession of the British Empire, India, was denied this title.[11] The semantic point is important here since the definition implicitly assumes that the main value of a dependency is to provide land for emigrants from the mother country. The lands seized by the

French in the post-1815 period did not seem to be promising for settlement, thus, from the point of view of many contemporaries, the expansion was meaningless.

During the July Monarchy another side of French antiimperialism became evident: a preference for regaining territory and power on the European continent. Hippolyte Passy wanted to use Algiers as a counter in diplomacy: "There are men who said that is necessary to keep Algeria because we could cede it in compensation for other advantages. As for me, I will not hide it, I would willingly exchange Algiers for a hovel on the Rhine."[12] Amédée Desjobert, a leading opponent of overseas expansion in the Chamber of Deputies, expressed disgust over the lives lost in the conquest of Algeria and complained that the colonial policy prevented France from carrying on an energetic continental policy. "It is on the side of our land frontiers," he proclaimed, "that we ought to seek to extend our territory; our efforts ought to lead to the reconquest of Savoy and the departments of the Rhine."[13] Passy and Desjobert gave their intellectual allegiance to the Established Liberal economic teaching of their time, with its emphasis on the desirability of peace. Yet they were obviously nationalists as well, and for them building a colonial empire was incompatible with achieving nationalist goals.

A generation later, in the 1860s, nationalism led a few Liberals in the opposite direction, as they embraced the cause of colonial expansion and created a Liberal imperialist doctrine. Jules Duval, a Liberal economist influenced by Saint-Simonian and communitarian socialist thought, argued that a country derived economic benefits from colonization even when it did not maintain a monopoly of commerce with the colony. Other economists and journalists joined Duval in demanding "the regime of freedom" (i.e., economic freedom) for colonies.[14] Prévost-Paradol, in La Nouvelle France, also linked nationalism and imperialism. Foreseeing the coming age of giant powers—the British Empire, Tsarist Russia, and the United States—he contended there was only one means for France to retain "a place so substantial and tangible as to be worthy of our legitimate pride, a place still capable of commanding some deference from the peoples of the world and of surrounding the glorious name of old France with sufficient respect." That means was "to increase the weight of France in the world through augmenting the number of our country's citizens and, at the same time, the extent of her territory through the foundation of a powerful Mediterranean empire pivoting on Algeria."[15] A year after the publication of La Nouvelle

France, another Liberal journalist, Henri Verne, echoed these words. Writing in *Le Correspondant* on December 25, 1869, he called both for free trade and for the acquisition of new lands overseas as a means of strengthening France. Verne succinctly stated the themes of the new outlook:

> The moment has come for every true-hearted Frenchman to plead the cause of Algeria. . . . Time presses: Russia is marching with giant steps toward the conquest of Asia; Prussia has doubled its power, England is establishing itself throughout the oceans and seas. France has Algeria and, if she opens her eyes to her role, her share remains the best. She has before her the entire commerce of Central Africa, peopled with at least sixty million inhabitants, and numerous ports on the Mediterranean, the highroad to Suez.

Verne added that "to assure rapid and fecund development, above all we must have land and a liberal regime."[16] Even without a monopoly of commerce with its colonies, he insisted that France would reap the benefit of increased trade. This idea was central to the new Liberal imperialism. However, we need to note two other aspects of the ideas of such Liberal imperialists as Duval and Verne before we can appreciate the contribution of Leroy-Beaulieu. They conceived of colonization as settlement and saw the benefit of expansion in terms of increased trade for the colonizing power.

Another sign of Liberal concern about colonies in the late 1860s is that the Académie des Sciences Morales et Politiques offered a prize for a manuscript on the subject of modern colonial systems. Emile Levasseur, a distinguished economist, reported on the results early in 1870 and embraced many of the views of the prize essay.[17] The manuscript bore as an epigraph a statement by John Stuart Mill: "In the present state of the world . . . the foundation of colonies is the best affair in which the capital of an old and rich country should engage." Nevertheless, Levasseur did not take what we would call today an imperialist stand. He did not approve of exploiting possessions like India by means of capital investment rather than settlement. Instead he called upon France to develop the settlement colony because this was the type "that creates people made in the image of Europe and who in the future will be fit to propagate her civilization in the world."[18] Whether the prize winner shared this viewpoint is our next topic, for he was the young Leroy-Beaulieu.

Leroy-Beaulieu's works published before the Franco-Prussian War give only fragmentary evidence about his attitude toward overseas expansion. Nevertheless, he appears to have opposed the conquest of colonies. In *Guerres Contemporaines* Leroy-Beaulieu attacked wars of colonial conquest as fiercely as other kinds of aggression, and he pictured colonial territories in an unflattering manner. The mercantilists, he stated mockingly, had fought for "uninhabited and sometimes uninhabitable" continents, for sun-scorched, little islands, "lost almost without resources in the immensity of the ocean." He also commented ironically on the disorganization of the six provinces in Indochina recently acquired by the fleets of the Second Empire. He even ridiculed the notion that the Asian possessions could be called colonies, since the only French inhabitants there were a few administrators, military personnel, and Carmelite nuns living in cloisters, "all of whom die, more or less quickly, of fever."[19] The conquests, he insisted, were heavily motivated by French vanity, revealed by the way his countrymen were flattered by news that their country's flag was flying in the center of China. He concluded that the so-called colonies were "often nothing more than territories under military occupation" and condemned overseas expeditions as almost always unjust and unrealistic.[20]

Leroy-Beaulieu's only other statement about colonial affairs in these years occurred in an article that appeared just a few days before the battle of Sedan. In "Les ressources de la France et de la Prusse" he again expressed coolness toward overseas possessions. Most of the islands and coasts that could be inhabited by Europeans, he argued, are occupied. Furthermore, "in time of war colonies are more embarrassing than useful; they divert a part of the forces of the metropolitan country."[21]

In light of these negative statements it seems odd that Leroy-Beaulieu would write a monograph on "the colonial system of modern peoples" that was far from uniformly hostile to overseas dependencies. Although the original manuscript is no longer in the possession of the Académie, Levasseur's report on the prize competition stated plainly that the treatise "approves colonization without approving all colonies."[22] There seems to have been quite a contradiction in the outlook of the young publicist. But the contradiction is only apparent. Fortunately, Levasseur's summary, other reviews, and internal evidence prove that the first edition of *De la Colonisation chez les Peuples Modernes*, published in 1874, was almost identical to the prize manuscript.[23] Thus we can use that volume to reach conclusions about Leroy-Beaulieu's outlook before as well as shortly after the Franco-Prussian War.

Two motives are apparent in the book, which represents part of the French Liberals' effort to reform the nation's colonial system. First it attacked the *exclusif* (the parent country's attempt to monopolize colonial trade), as well as authoritarian rule over colonies. Leroy-Beaulieu wanted all the imperial powers to abolish the remnants of mercantile policies so as to increase the productive powers of the dependencies, and in turn world trade, at a faster rate. Second, the book urged the development of Algeria. As he remarked in his September 1870 article on the relative strength of France and Prussia, colonies in general deprive a nation of military power but Algeria, "forming an almost unique exception in the history of colonization, is for us an important aid in time of war."[24] When we read *De la Colonisation* with this statement in mind, we can see how the prize treatise of 1870 aimed above all at promoting the development of Algeria.

Since many historians of imperialism now stress the causal relationship between nationalism and French expansionism, it is significant that in the 1860s Leroy-Beaulieu did not share the fervent nationalism of Prévost-Paradol or Verne. While he recognized that peace would not come to Europe unless each nationality became an independent nation, he condemned the schools of the European countries because they taught a narrow patriotism, glorified war, and kept alive old hatreds. Connecting wars with the "excessive susceptibility of national self-love," he asked: "How much has it cost us, this exaggerated development of national pride?"[25] These are hardly the words of a nationalist. Leroy-Beaulieu did not deny the French right to dominate native Algerians, but neither was he a full-fledged imperialist as of 1870. While he may have dreamed vaguely in the 1860s of the spread of French influence and European civilization from France's North African foothold, he did not favor French conquest of additional territories. In 1879, when Leroy-Beaulieu declared that he had always been the partisan of the "penetration" of Africa, his memory was in error, at least insofar as that process entailed seizures of territory.[26]

*F*rance's humiliation in the war of 1870–1871 awoke mild nationalist feelings in Leroy-Beaulieu. Several times in the early 1870s he made favorable statements about the creation of a new empire, reflecting his distress at his country's weakness. Yet I believe he became an imperialist only in principle, not in practice. The articles he wrote after the Franco-Prussian War and his minimal revisions of the prize treatise on colonization indicate that he remained chiefly concerned with the development of Algeria and only slightly interested in the acquisition of additional overseas territories.

Unquestionably Leroy-Beaulieu acquired after the war a concern with preserving France's power. By February 1873, as noted already in Chapter 4, he openly accepted that the future power and place of his country would depend on the amount of uncivilized lands it would be able "to occupy, exploit and civilize."[27] Dedication to national grandeur also manifested itself, as we have seen, in the economist's new interest in population growth. In addition, he wrote frequently on the need to expand French interests and contacts abroad, and he complained that, despite the industriousness of the French, "We do not occupy upon the map of the world the place that our natural qualities ought to have given us; thus we allow others to dominate the markets of the Orient . . . our foreign markets are far from having the magnitude that we could give to them."[28]

*B*ased on such comments, some historians have concluded that Leroy-Beaulieu's nationalist preoccupation with population, territory and power transformed him into an imperialist before 1874, the publication date of the first edition of *De la Colonisation chez les Peuples Modernes*. According to Agnes Murphy, Leroy-Beaulieu launched his "real propaganda for a policy of imperialism" in 1872.[29] In an article of November 1872, she points out, he "noted the exodus of many Alsace-Lorrainers from their country," and in their misfortune he saw a ray of hope. These emigrants, he urged, should be directed toward Algeria, which he called "a practically unlimited field for the expansion of our race."[30] In the next few months he returned several times to the subject of France's colonies, sometimes discussing them as part of larger problems. For example, in a discussion of administrative reforms, he suggested the government attract Alsatians to Algeria.[31] Early in 1873 he noted, "We still have several scattered remnants of our once magnificent overseas domain. . . . It only remains for us to make them productive." In the same articles he went on to complain, in an analysis of French attitudes, "One of the great faults of our policy for almost two centuries has been to regard France as a purely continental and European country and to pay only a distracted attention to our distant possessions."[32] This opposition between "continentalist" and "colonialist" perspectives would later weigh heavily in Leroy-Beaulieu's thought.

At first glance these comments about territory, population, and overseas possessions appear to be incontrovertible examples of imperialist thinking. However, Leroy-Beaulieu did not proceed from the premises to the conclusions one might expect. Although he declared that a nation's strength would depend upon the extent of its colonial empire, the main theme of the 1873 article just quoted was that France should make its existing colonies more productive, not that it should pursue new ones. Furthermore, the same article also included an attack on the current government's commercial policies, in which the economist declared that those who wanted the colonies to prosper must prevent Thiers from damaging the merchant marine through his protectionist leanings.[33] This attack suggests that colonies were important to Leroy-Beaulieu primarily because of their connection to foreign trade. Not once did he propose that his country immediately set out to acquire new colonies. The disasters of 1870 and 1871 had led him closer to a fully imperialist position, but he had not yet taken the final step.

Nor did he take it in 1874, when he published *De la Colonisation chez les Peuples Modernes*. Experts disagree over whether the first edition of this book was primarily a scientific study or expansionist propaganda. Charles Ageron, however, has rightly observed that "In 1874 Leroy-Beaulieu did not propose overtly any colonial policy," although the economist "did conclude with an eulogy of colonization that had a very imperialist tone."[34] Despite the book's imperialist tinge, expansion was not one of its practical goals. Instead, as the following discussion of its contents will show, its purpose was the same as that of the original treatise: to justify a Liberal political and economic regime for existing colonies and to awaken enthusiasm for the development of Algeria.[35]

On the theoretical side, the treatise aimed at establishing the first principles—the "plan of conduct," or "body of precepts"—that should guide colonization. The bulk of the book is a historical survey of imperial regimes, whose purpose is to set forth the "means for bringing a colony to the highest degree of population, power, and riches."[36] Leroy-Beaulieu assumed that analyzing the experience of Europeans over several hundred years would enable his generation to establish universally valid rules for successful colonization.[37] Running through Leroy-Beaulieu's discussion of precepts, however, are two polemical purposes: the promotion of free trade and the reform of colonial administration. The historical section concluded that the old mercantilist system unquestionably hindered the rapid and healthy development of the resources of colonies. And Leroy-Beaulieu constantly directed fire at his favorite target, the French bureaucracy, charging it with mismanagement of France's overseas dependencies.[38] As in his articles on colonization in 1872 and 1873, he argued that successful and morally justifiable colonization required three policies: the establishment of free trade, the grant of self-government as soon as possible for settlers, and the promotion of a civilizing influence on native inhabitants. History, in other words, taught what Liberal economics had proven deductively.

In the first (and the smallest) part of the doctrinal section Leroy-Beaulieu discussed the economic advantages of empire, indicating that a country does not profit much from owning a colony. He accepted Adam Smith's notion that the virgin soil of underdeveloped lands makes labor and capital unusually productive, and he followed Smith and Mill in asserting that dynamically growing colonies stimulate the industry and commerce of the parent country. Yet he vitiated the effectiveness of the latter claim by damning the *exclusif* and by accepting the corollary of his Liberal predecessors that under a regime of free trade all countries could benefit equally from any nation's colonies.[39] With regard to emigration, he paraphrased one major theoretical objection, asking, "Is it good for a nation to have colonies? . . . The blood of which she deprives herself, does it not as a consequence weaken her?"[40] In response he contended that this "generating fact of colonization" neither hurts nor hinders the mother country. In contrast to both the Malthusians, who wanted emigration as a remedy to overpopulation, and the anti-Malthusians, who wanted numbers for the sake of national power, he stated that a moderate migration to colonies has little effect on the rate of population increase.[41] Therefore, neither from the point of view of trade nor from the perspective of population change do colonies make much difference to a parent country.

Leroy-Beaulieu's one claim of a significant economic gain from colonies is found in his response to the argument, made by Desjobert among others, that the export of capital is damaging to a country. To answer this objection, Leroy-Beaulieu distinguished three kinds of dependency: the settlement colony proper, the commercial colony, and the plantation colony. Settlement (or agricultural) colonies should only be undertaken by nations with potential for an abundant emigration. Commercial colonies (i.e., trading posts and

small maritime settlements) and plantation colonies do not need settlers, but they do need managers and capital. Hence this kind of
colony is the appropriate one for the old, capital-rich nations with
little population to spare.[42] Leroy-Beaulieu argued that the possession of commercial colonies is a considerable advantage, because this
type of colony provides insurance against business crises by giving
an outlet for the export of excess capital that could otherwise cause
a depression.[43] This argument would become one of the key points
in his mature doctrine of imperialism, but he placed little emphasis
on it in 1874. Surely he felt deeply about the economic benefits
of any course of action, but his case for the economic benefit of
colonization is weak. In fact, its weakness hints that his main concern was not for the profit of any particular nation but rather for
the development of Algeria and of the world's resources.

Significantly, despite his three-way typology, Leroy-Beaulieu
throughout the book discussed the subject of colonization as if only
one kind of colony existed, the settlement colony.[44] Still, the three
categories anticipated the epoch-making classifications he was to
make in 1882. Even in their 1874 form, the distinctions enabled
him to dispose of the objection, by such leaders as Guizot, that
France was unable to colonize because it had no surplus population.[45]

As a work of practical propaganda, the first edition of *De la Colonisation* aims above all at winning proselytes to the cause of Algeria.
While Leroy-Beaulieu asserted that the other colonies, despite their
lesser value, could be made prosperous through reforms, he called
Algeria "the largest field open to our colonizing activity and the
one which is easiest to make fecund."[46] In response to antiimperialist
criticisms he argued that the climate of Algeria is healthy for Europeans and that land could be made available for French settlers. The
colony had great promise, he said, provided that it was free from
excessive control by the French administration.[47]

Propaganda for expansion is almost totally absent from the 1874
edition of *De la Colonisation*. In six hundred pages *Leroy-Beaulieu
made only one statement about expansion.* That one statement, in a
section that appears to have been added to the original manuscript,
reads, "We are among those who believe that the future of France is
in great part in Africa and that, through linking Algeria with the
Senegal, we will come one day to dominate and civilize the entire
northwest of Africa."[48] But the book is almost devoid of appeals
to nationalism. Once Leroy-Beaulieu expressed his unhappiness

over the decline of France's grandeur,[49] and at the end of the book he seemed to be warning his country when he declared, "From any point of view, whether one considers prosperity and material power, political authority and influence, or whether one rises to the contemplation of intellectual grandeur, here is a proverb of incontestable truth: the nation which colonizes the most is the greatest nation; if it is not first today, it will be tomorrow."[50] Yet these words are not the theme of any part of the book. They appear only in the concluding three pages, and even the conclusion deals mainly with the impact of colonization upon intellectual, not political, greatness.

When Leroy-Beaulieu finished his treatise in 1870 and (for the most part) when he published it in 1874, the subject of colonization involved the problem of the moral vigor of the nation, the triumph of the Liberal regime in colonial life, and the development of the world's commerce. Furthermore, until Leroy-Beaulieu himself helped change the meaning of the term in the 1880s, he thought of colonization as settlement rather than conquest of additional lands. Whenever he used the term, he applied it exclusively to overseas lands already inhabited by Europeans. The terse and still rather vague approval of expansion in the first edition of De la Colonisation is far from a ringing cry in favor of imperialism. Leroy-Beaulieu was not ready to proceed from his prophecies about France's future to demands that his nation take up arms and begin the march outward from Algeria and Senegal.

These conclusions are confirmed by a series of three lead articles on colonies Leroy-Beaulieu wrote for his own magazine in August 1874.[51] For the most part the articles summarize the ideas discussed at length in De la Colonisation. One of them contains similarly vague, general statements, about expansion. Speaking of the importance of France's North African foothold as a means of ensuring its future grandeur, he stated, "In our opinion, if France is going to play in the future a great role in the world, it is less perhaps in Europe than in Africa." He continued, "Algeria in the north and Senegal in the west, these are two bases for civilizing operations."[52] But he did not explain what he meant by "civilizing operations." Even in the year in which he published De la Colonisation, Leroy-Beaulieu went no further than generalized speculations about imperial expansion.

Over the next few years a few of Leroy-Beaulieu's columns in the *Journal des Débats* coupled his nationalist interest with other broad statements about France's role in Africa. At the close of 1874 he wrote that France could avoid decadence because, among other factors, it had a splendid future in Africa.[53] A year later he restated the vision of a world of superpowers that Prévost-Paradol and Henri Verne had put forward in the late 1860s:

> When we consider what will be the different civilized nations in a hundred or even in fifty years, we see the United States occupying all of North America, with a population of a hundred million; England with Australia and her African and Asian colonies, increasing in each day in riches, in inhabitants, and in her civilization; Russia occupying and colonizing all north and central Asia, and reaching, perhaps, as far as the Bosporus, having a compact mass of more than one hundred fifty million inhabitants; finally, the Germans established in the midst of Europe and forming there a solid block of sixty or eighty million people.

Saddened by the contrast between France's past grandeur and her potential retreat into relative insignificance, he repeated the theme that his cherished colony, Algeria, and its extensions into the Sudan would enable France to remain the equal of the other great powers.[54] And in 1876 he wondered once more, "Will our beautiful language, once the instrument of so many cultured men, still be in vogue in a large part of the world? Will our customs, our ideas, even our products, be diffused throughout the globe and exercise some influence?" However, the article in which he posed this problem dealt with stagnation in French population growth rather than with overseas dependencies.[55]

These comments on the possible value of colonization remained infrequent during the four years after the publication of *De la Colonisation*. From mid-1874 to the end of 1878 Leroy-Beaulieu wrote very little on the topic and never made it the subject of his weekly lead commentaries for *L'Economiste Français*. The journal did not entirely neglect the cause, but other writers on the staff dealt with it; the editor was silent.[56] This reticence tells us that he was still not fully committed to the policy of acquiring a colonial empire. Despite his fears about the end of France's greatness, Leroy-Beaulieu merely flirted with the idea of expansion instead of embracing it passionately. Theoretically in favor of acquiring new colonies, he could not yet bring himself to accept the price—moral, perhaps, as well as pecuniary—that empire would cost.

A series of catalysts appears to have contributed to the transformation of Leroy-Beaulieu's stance: the outbreak of the Russo-Turkish War in 1877, the arrival of the depression in France in the same year, the revival of working–class and socialist agitation around 1879, and the capture of political power by the advanced republicans between 1877 and 1880. By early 1880 Leroy-Beaulieu had converted to a full-fledged imperialism and was completing his imperialist doctrine, the definitive version of which appeared with the second edition of *De la Colonisation chez les Peuples Modernes* in 1882.

When Leroy-Beaulieu broke his silence about overseas expansion, however, he did not immediately call for military expeditions into Indochina or the interior of Africa. Instead, in February 1878, he pressed France to intervene jointly with Britain in Egypt. The two European countries, moved by concern for bankers and bond holders, had taken control of Egypt's disordered finances; Leroy-Beaulieu urged them to go further and take over the government of Egypt. Broadly speaking this demand was imperialist, but it was not nationalist, and Leroy-Beaulieu still refrained from proposing that the French take exclusive control of any independent territories in Africa or Asia.

When Leroy-Beaulieu wrote on Egypt, he grouped his arguments for imperialism in three categories: humanitarian, economic, and political. This approach has been called the "Three Part Argument."[57] A quotation from his first article conveys both the three-part argument in general and the flavor of the humanitarian plea in particular. When he demanded intervention to keep the Egyptian ruler from abrogating changes in the country's financial system, he argued:

> In ensuring that the present reforms are not withdrawn some day, France and England are not defending only the interests of their merchants and capitalists; they do not safeguard merely their legitimate influence and their authority in the Orient; but still more they will render a service to humanity in general by ameliorating the destiny of the fellahs and by instituting a regular and legal order of things on the banks of the Nile.[58]

The humanitarian and economic justifications are unambiguous. What Leroy-Beaulieu meant by guarding "legitimate influence" is less clear here, but the political component of his argument is more prominent in an article he wrote seven months later. In that article he declared that England and France must exclude "enemy influences" from the vicinity of the Suez Canal, and he identified the enemy in question as Russia.[59] Although the unilateral occupation by the British ended Leroy-Beaulieu's campaign for intervention, the three-part approach persisted as he began consistently to present questions of expansion jointly in political, economic, and humanitarian terms.

While Leroy-Beaulieu was advocating intervention in Egypt, the depression provoked him to widen his economic case for the penetration of Africa. At the close of 1878 he suggested that undeveloped lands, such as those bordering Lakes Tanganyika and Chad, might prove to be a new Indies for a Europe that badly needed additional markets. But he also conceded that the economic blessings would not be realized for fifteen to fifty years. While he declared himself to be a *"great partisan of the exploration and even of the colonization of Asia and Africa,"* his rhetoric reveals that he was still not a fiery advocate of expansion.[60]

Evidently Leroy-Beaulieu was warming up because in February 1879 he elaborated further upon this solution for the depression. This article began with a reference to the "universal industrial distress" of Europe. Since short-sighted younger countries had been raising tariff barriers, he said, industrialists of the Old World would have to look to other lands for markets. Africa would free Europe from economic stagnation because, according to recent explorations, the interior of the continent was not a desert but a rich agricultural region. The continent, he commented, "offers herself to Europe, we do not say as a prey—a very bad word that renders our idea most incorrectly."[61] Shifting to his humanitarian argument, he said, France was called to bring civilization to the Sudan, an immense region that amounted to nearly a third of Africa.

Despite this call for expansion into the Sudan, Leroy-Beaulieu still held back from proposing that the French send armies into the area to establish direct rule over the Africans. "When we talk of colonization," he declared, "we do not mean . . . the conquest or peopling of central and middle Africa by Europeans: that would be a chimerical enterprise." Instead he called for the establishment of "a completely moral and civilizing influence through the creation of trading posts, roads, and ports." Once again he warned that developing the area would take a long time.[62] Apparently the depression led him close to an outright embrace of overseas expansion, but he stopped short of a full commitment, as is also shown by his continued reticence on the subject. The article was the only discussion of colonies that he contributed to *L'Economiste Français* in 1879.[63]

Leroy-Beaulieu's campaign for the acquisition of colonies finally began in earnest in May 1880, five months after the first cabinet composed exclusively of advanced republicans had taken office. That political change stimulated his fear that the government would pursue the policy of *continental* expansion that had long been a tradition in republican ranks. In other words, with aggression against other European nations looming as the possible alternative, colonialism became a more inviting policy. For a few years, as the direction of republican foreign policy remained ambiguous, Leroy-Beaulieu pressed for action in Tunisia, continued to treat the Sudan as a French preserve, and criticized the government for pusillanimity for not seizing Tonkin and thus opening a new market to French industry.[64] He suddenly became so dedicated to imperialism that, setting aside his usual devotion to fiscal economy, he implored his nation to have "in Senegal as in Algeria an enterprising policy; let us carry ourselves more and more forward without recoiling before a few expenses."[65] "Let us not fear throwing half a billion into the Transsaharan railroad," he cried out; "what is half a billion? It is three or four of our annual budget surpluses. Colonize, colonize, and what above all can we colonize if not the Sudan?"[66] However, he devoted his colonialist propaganda to advocating the annexation of Tunisia, the territory to which the cabinet of Jules Ferry approved in 1881 the expedition that launched France on a new career of empire building.

When Leroy-Beaulieu dropped all ambiguities and demanded forthrightly the annexation of overseas territories, he switched the emphasis of his propaganda from humanitarian and economic considerations to political ones. For the first time he appealed mainly to French nationalism and strategic concerns. He warned that France could not hold Algeria securely without subjecting the Tunisian tribes that made forays into Algeria, and he declared that the Regency would be a threat to France's North African possessions if it came under the control of another country.[67] Attempting to stir nationalist sentiments of the French, he emphasized that the Bey of Tunis had insulted France.[68] Leroy-Beaulieu pictured the issue as a test of French courage and described the Arabs as waiting to see if the French dared to take Tunisia in the face of English objections.[69] Despite these inflammatory statements, he still presented himself as "profoundly devoted to peace. . . . We speak such an uncompromising language [because] we know that humiliations are never the guarantee of a durable peace."[70]

Central to Leroy-Beaulieu's political case for imperialism is the stand he took in the debate that had long divided opponents and partisans of imperialism: the merits of a continental versus a colonial policy. In 1879 he had already described the penetration of Africa, in highly suggestive terms, as a "revanche" for France's disasters.[71] The import of this theme became clear in 1880 and 1881 when he contrasted the fruitfulness of the continental and colonial policies. In May 1880, in his first article that unequivocally embraced the imperialist cause, he stated that a main advantage of the colonial policy is its safety; in pursuing overseas expansion France "runs hardly any risks."[72] The next year he was even more specific. "The great historical fault of France," he charged, "is that for two centuries she preferred the continental policy to the colonial policy." France would be richer and more powerful if it had not been tempted into wars of expansion on the continent.[73]

In attacking the traditional foreign policy of the Republicans and its new ingredient, revenge for the defeat in 1870, Leroy-Beaulieu utilized one of his opponents' favorite ideas, the belief in a national mission. "Each people," he proclaimed, "who wishes to maintain its vitality must have a mission. What henceforth could be the mission of France?"[74] Formerly decentralization, education, and dynamic foreign trade had been his prescriptions for national health. Now he described the task of bringing civilization to the Africans of the Sudan as the salvation of his own country.[75]

Three years after Leroy-Beaulieu launched his open advocacy of colonial expansion, he published a revised version of *De la Colonisation chez les Peuples Modernes*. The original version of 1874 had been appreciated by the specialists, but it did not "notably attract attention in that period of disarray." The exhaustive, even longer second edition is noteworthy, on the other hand, because it reached a wide audience and had more influence than either the first edition or the later ones. By 1882 "public opinion was a little aroused from that systematic ignorance of colonial matters."[76] Leroy-Beaulieu's first edition may have made a major contribution to the revival of interest, but both he and the general public were undoubtedly influenced by reports of the overseas explorations that had become so important in the intervening years.

While a new climate of opinion greeted the second edition, the book's own qualities contributed heavily to its success. Retaining the bulk of the original treatise, with its virtues of clarity and systematic presentation, the 1882 edition added an eloquent preface and stirring arguments for the acquisition of new colonies. These changes, although not extensive, transformed the entire tone of the book. The second edition no longer confined itself merely to arguing for investment and governmental reform in existing colonies. Instead the author emphasized the internal resources of both claimed and unclaimed lands. Also, Leroy-Beaulieu repeatedly called for territorial expansion—in the preface, in new conclusions added to some of the chapters, in sentences and paragraphs inserted in the old text, and even in footnotes. "That which a colony needs above all," he proclaimed, "is space."[77] He spoke of current French possessions as empires and "embryos of territorial empires."[78] He hoped that France would dominate a fourth or even a third of Africa. As for Tonkin, the French must not hesitate "to occupy it militarily," and perhaps all of Annam as well.[79] These citations from the 1882 edition of *De la Colonisation* show how far Leroy-Beaulieu's thinking had traveled since the mid-1870s.

Leroy-Beaulieu now had a complete ideology of imperialism, comprised of a historical account of empire, Liberal lessons about imperial organization (both stated in the first edition), a revised typology of colonies, and an impressive set of political and nationalist arguments for imperialism. A careful dissection of the parts of the doctrine presented in the new edition exposes what elements of Leroy-Beaulieu's imperialist thought were original and what his sources were.

The starting point of Leroy-Beaulieu's thought is the idea that colonization somehow springs from the biological-physiological nature of human beings and society. Individuals and nations, he held, have an inherent drive to expand. Agnes Murphy paraphrases this idea as a belief in "a natural instinct which impels [a country] toward the unknown and the adventuresome."[80] This statement no doubt satisfied the common sense and common experience of the time, and it is still a respectable explanation for the mysterious phenomenon of empire building. However, whereas Leroy-Beaulieu saw emigration as purely a matter of biologically based urges, he saw colonization as an intentionally chosen policy. Consequently, he sought to justify the practice and, as well, to state rules that would make colonies successful.

The chief rule he promoted was the same one he defended in 1870 and 1874: the mother country should not seek to monopolize the trade of subject land. Commerce should naturally develop in the most efficient and fruitful path available. Leroy-Beaulieu did not turn his back on Liberal ideology but instead embraced it, holding illiberal policies responsible for every instance of poor economic performance by a colony.

One less traditional aspect of his propaganda is his answer to the antiimperialist charge that the French had no aptitude for colonization. Citing specific examples of French initiative from the previous two decades, Leroy-Beaulieu claimed just the reverse. In an obvious reference to the Suez Canal, he boasted: "The greatest projects of this time, as regards to public works, have been or are being carried out by Frenchmen." Recent French explorers had been as hardy as Chevalier de la Salle in the seventeenth century. What the French lacked but could acquire, he went on in a repetition of an old complaint, was perseverance and a systematic line of conduct.[81]

When Leroy-Beaulieu also took up the question of whether France had the resources for empire building, he made one of his most significant contributions to the imperialist cause. He altered the terms and definitions of his earlier typology of colonies and used the new conceptions to great effect. He combined two previous types, colonies of commerce and plantation colonies, into the new category of colonies of exploitation, and he distinguished this type from settlement colonies and from mixed colonies such as Algeria. The first change was the crucial one. By colonies of exploitation he meant dependencies that do not require settlement for their development but instead need investment and direction by a small group of European administrators. French imperialism would not be handicapped by the lack of settlers, he argued, because France had an excess of capital and could, therefore, establish colonies of exploitation. France's wealth similarly enabled the flowering of mixed colonies such as Algeria where only a small immigration from the parent country was required. Capital, he proclaimed in the preface, was "the true nerve of colonization." If only a quarter of the surplus funds in France went to her dependencies, "what splendid results would be obtained in twenty-five or thirty years!"[82]

Throughout the 1882 edition of *De la Colonisation* Leroy-Beaulieu strengthened considerably his economic justifications for empire building. Although the section on the material benefits obtainable from colonies was only slightly altered,[83] he described in more

fulsome terms the economic promise of the newly acquired territories and of the Sudan. He emphasized the resources waiting to be
tapped, the customers whose numbers made up for their poverty,
and the high interest to be gathered from investments in those
capital-starved areas.[84] The idea of "exploitation colonies" was
the most weighty economic argument, since this notion by itself
answers the common Liberal objection that colonization in combination with free trade would be unprofitable. This charge was the
most serious issue confronting a Liberal imperialist, and Leroy-
Beaulieu dealt with it masterfully.

Yet he also went beyond the issue of purely economic advantage,
writing that "to evaluate the advantages of colonies solely on the
basis of statistics of the commerce between them and the mother
country is to consider only a part, perhaps not the most important,
of the relations which have so many varied and happy effects."
Among the additional benefits he noted was the creation of jobs
for France's "liberal professions"—scientists, educators, doctors, and
technicians.[85] And "from the moral point of view," he remarked,
"there is an elevated pleasure in thinking that [one's] savings have
created faraway societies that add to the national grandeur, that con-
serve the honor, the language, mores and spirit of the fatherland."[86]
Here he again identified imperialism as the national mission that
would preserve the vitality of France.

Nationalist and political justifications for overseas expansion, almost completely absent from the original edition of De la Colonisation, are prominent in the second edition. Leroy-Beaulieu's preface
opens with an indictment of the continental policy and closes with
his rhetoric of national mission. He spoke ominously of France as
in danger of being eclipsed by the growth of huge powers. In the
face of giant Russia, of sixty million Germans supported by thirty
million Austrians, and of the widespread and numerous Anglo-
Saxon community, France would sink into insignificance and impo-
tence. Therefore, "for France colonization is a question of life and
death: France must become a great African power or she will be
a second class nation in Europe, counting about as much as Greece
or Rumania."[87] Leroy-Beaulieu underscored the importance of this
theme by returning to it in a long footnote that echoed the thoughts
expressed in the preface. He prophesied the day when the Russians,
Chinese, Anglo-Saxons, and Germans would be so numerous and
would have spread over so much territory that "the language, customs, tastes of these predominant peoples . . . would push back

and confine into narrow spaces the idioms, literature, and arts of peoples who do not have colonies." For France and other peoples—like the Scandinavians with their "solid qualities"—this would mean "obscurity and mediocrity." In sum, "the lessening of a people's relative rank in the world, the indefinite decline of her proportion of the world's population, is for a country almost the equivalent of disappearance." As before, he insisted that the continental policy had left the country diminished in prestige and territory, and that the French would experience further "rebuffs" unless they gave up their ambitions on the other side of the Rhine. The building of a great overseas empire, he continued, was "the only great enterprise destiny permits us."[88] Such arguments must have resonated strongly with those who recognized that Germany was militarily far stronger than France. Through these arguments Leroy-Beaulieu turned the doctrine of national mission away from its dangerous implications for foreign policy.

The 1882 edition of *De la Colonisation* presents what would have seemed impossible half a century earlier: a Liberal doctrine of imperialism. By linking colonization with the expansion of free trade, the disposal of surplus capital, and the solution of depressions, Leroy-Beaulieu argued persuasively that even under a Liberal regime colonies could serve an important purpose. Yet, although his writing was certainly skillful and penetrating, much of the argument repeated the ideas already developed by other Liberal publicists of the 1860s: Jules Duval, Prévost-Paradol, and Henri Verne. Leroy-Beaulieu's unique contribution was to redefine colonization so as to make it easier for convinced Liberals to embrace the imperialist cause. As we have seen, the standard definition of "colony" was a narrower one oriented to settlements until Leroy-Beaulieu developed the idea of colonies of exploitation. In addition, while he was not the first to reconcile Liberalism and imperialism, he provided a systematic, comprehensive, and coherent synthesis of his predecessors's views in the form of his three-part argument for imperialism.[89] And he presented his case boldly, breaking entirely with the tentative style of his rare comments before 1880.

What transmuted Leroy-Beaulieu's timid advocacy of overseas expansion into a reiterated cry for immediate action in North Africa, the Saharan region, and Indochina? His conversion coincides with rising interest in the African continent throughout Western Europe and with the adoption of imperialism by other influential Frenchmen.

Thus, to grasp his motivations, we must ask how the atmosphere was shifting in France and in Europe at this time. We have already noted briefly the impact of the Republicans' rise to power. We must consider the effect of international tensions around the time of the Russo-Turkish War, as well as other political, economic, and social developments that he viewed with dismay. A review of his comments on economic life and international developments, along with another look at his nationalism, shows that these factors predisposed Leroy-Beaulieu to embrace imperialism. Yet there are good reasons to conclude that the crucial factor may have been his fear of war and social upheaval, a fear reawakened and intensified in 1880 when the advanced republicans took over the government.

Leroy-Beaulieu's fundamental commitment to economic productivism, a central conviction for all Liberals, helped to justify imperialism. Productivism implied that the world's primary interest was the full development of all productive resources. Europeans had a right to compel the inhabitants of Africa and Asia to cultivate their fields, dig mines, and labor to bring forth riches because production was the primary duty of all humankind.[90] But this productivism was always part of Leroy-Beaulieu's outlook, so it does not explain his shift to aggressive imperialism.

Economic considerations in general do not explain his conversion, even though he began to call for colonial expansion soon after depression hit France. It is true that in 1877 the business crisis seemed so severe to him that he said the great era of Western economic growth had come to an end, and that in 1879 he hoped trade with Central Africa might restimulate the European economy. At that time he began suggesting that colonies would enrich the country as a result of the high returns from capital investments in them. On the other hand, as a number of historians have pointed out, most French investors and entrepreneurs were unenthusiastic about the economic prospects of the African and Asian lands that were coming under French control. In this case, therefore, Leroy-Beaulieu was not playing his usual role as a spokesman for the business community; instead he was seeking to persuade it that colonies made economic sense. His arguments seem designed to gain the support of groups that habitually measured the worth of a political policy in material terms. Even so, however, he felt constrained to admit that the material benefits of imperialism would come only after the passage of several decades. That admission is important evidence that, despite the depression, economic motives do not explain why the cause of imperial expansion rather abruptly became a priority for Leroy-Beaulieu.

The influence of international developments on Leroy-Beaulieu is easy to document. As we have already discovered, however, the Franco-Prussian War did not lead him to embrace decisively an active policy of imperialist conquest. The conflict of 1870–1871 caused him to move away from antiimperialism to a moderate approval of empire, but until the late 1870s he focused only on the more rapid development of Algeria, a territory the French already controlled. His advocacy of additional conquests came later and coincided with two other developments in the international sphere: the sudden growth of European interest in Africa and the Russo-Turkish War.

During the mid-1870s French-speaking intellectuals and politicians began to manifest a lively interest in the exploration and development of Africa.[91] In 1876 Leopold II of Belgium sponsored the international conference on the Congo that marked the beginning of his efforts to carve out a personal domain in that region. The adventurous journeys of Livingstone in tropical Africa attracted public attention to the region in the 1860s and 1870s, and in the last years of the 1870s other explorers led important expeditions into West Africa. Specialists debate whether the "scramble" for Africa began in 1879 or in 1881, but either date makes it plausible that Leroy-Beaulieu began his advocacy under the pressure of events.[92] The urgency of his appeals may reflect his sense that France had to move quickly or face the threat of being shut out from the partition of African territories. However, during the years in question, Leroy-Beaulieu never referred to a danger that other nations might beat France to all the desirable territories. Thus we can assume that the sudden outburst of imperialist activity around 1880 was not the main force impelling him to take the final step from theoretical approval of colonies to fervent support of expansion.

In contrast, the war between Russia and Turkey does appear to have pushed Leroy-Beaulieu toward imperialism indirectly, by way of stimulating his nationalist feelings. Even the Franco-Prussian War had not entirely destroyed his hope that Europe would experience "a peace that was not a truce" (see Chapter 4 above). But in 1877 this peace-loving intellectual came to understand fully the meaning of the international violence of the mid-nineteenth century.

Retaining the Liberal and Saint-Simonian language of his youth, but now denying that humanity had entered a new age, Leroy-Beaulieu admitted in a brilliant article on the war in the Balkans that "we are still in the dramatic period of the history of mankind: the taste for adventures, the passion for glory, the spirit of conquest are far from being dead."[93]

This realization may have aroused in Leroy-Beaulieu a poignant sense of the fragility of France's position in Europe and the world. Beginning in 1877 he wrote about the past and future greatness of France with a passion heretofore absent. "When one has been during ten centuries in the first rank of civilized nations," he confessed in an article on French population, "it is hard to see oneself slip insensibly into an inferior position." As before he urged population growth as a way to boost the nation's economic activity, but he also called it a source of national vitality and power: "a larger population growth would develop the spirit of enterprise, would render more active and vital many of today's inert personalities, and would give our country a greater diffusion and brilliance abroad and would maintain for our ancient French race a little of the prestige, power, and authority which she possessed in the past."[94]

This newfound depth of identification with his country had clear implications in relation to his conversion to imperialism. Even though he had stated in the early 1870s that a nation's power would depend upon the size of its territory and its population, in the late 1870s he stated this idea with greater fervor. In an 1879 article, for example, he declared, "One cannot disregard it: 37 million inhabitants and an area of 528,000 square kilometers are rather small for a great people."[95] Overseas expansion became the way for France to maintain its status as a world power. These nationalist feelings by themselves are sufficient to account for Leroy-Beaulieu's embrace of imperialism. However, while he began to express a fervent nationalism in 1877, he did not call for any specific imperialist activity until 1880. The chronology of his conversion, therefore, indicates some other influence played an essential role.

The coming to power of the advanced republicans seems to have been the final ingredient because it reawakened his fears of war and social revolution. To understand how this could be, we need to reconsider the outlook or, at least, the reputed outlook of advanced republicans on foreign policy. Léon Gambetta and Jules Ferry, the two republican leaders who were most responsible for launching

French imperialism in 1881, were well known as nationalists who desired to recover Alsace-Lorraine from German rule. Since the early 1870s Gambetta in particular had been associated in the public mind with the cause of revanche. As republicans who were finally in power by 1880, they "hoped to demonstrate the capacity of the Republic to conduct an impressive foreign policy"; as nationalists they wished to show that France was once again capable of forceful and successful military activity. Realizing that France could no longer seek to expand within Europe, they saw that conditions in the late 1870s made it possible for their country to reassert itself outside Europe.[96] To understand Leroy-Beaulieu's conversion to imperialism, however, we have to realize that Gambetta concealed his attitude from the public. For this reason, when Gambetta and the advanced republicans took power in France, Leroy-Beaulieu feared that they would provoke armed conflict with the Germans by seeking recovery of the Rhineland territories. Not for some years did Leroy-Beaulieu realize that the Opportunists, who controlled the ministries in the 1880s, had no intention of provoking Germany. Only in 1883 did he breathe a sigh of relief regarding France's relations to other Western nations:

> Although the political direction of France has not been for several years as moderate, as calm, and as stable as we would have liked, it is certain that one cannot, without bad faith, accuse the French government of seeking to exercise abroad any influence whatever that could be prejudicial to the institutions of other people.[97]

Before he reached that comforting conclusion, Leroy-Beaulieu's distrust of the new republican leadership had motivated his determined effort to redirect France's expansionist urges toward the acquisition of a larger overseas empire.

We have seen that his first insistent demands for a specific conquest appeared only five months after the advanced republicans gained exclusive control of the cabinet. Nor was this May 1880 article an isolated utterance, as was his vaguer plea of February 1879; rather, it was followed by numerous others in 1880 and 1881, and indeed his propaganda for empire never let up thereafter. Waiting in the wings, eager to displace relatively moderate figures like Ferry, were the Radicals who were even more identified by their countrymen with the continental policy and the cause of *revanche*.

Fearful that the republicans would bring further humiliations and sufferings on his land, Leroy-Beaulieu sought to protect France by focusing its ambitions on the non-Western world.

As the next chapter will show, Leroy-Beaulieu's class identification and the lessons he learned from the 1870–1871 crises also came into the picture around 1880, perhaps in a decisive way. He believed war with Germany would lead not only to defeat but also to social revolution. If the French did not discard the illusion of revenge, he warned, it would lead "to new reverses and new catastrophes." "The continental policy could only reserve frightful disasters for France."[98] While he did not specify the nature of the "frightful disasters" that would come about if the republic followed the continental policy, his writings recall those of 1871 and 1872 in which he stated that he feared war because of its possible social consequences for French society. He believed that socialist revolutionaries had only one chance to seize power in France: following a military defeat that would bring chaotic conditions like those that preceded the Commune.

In the light of Leroy-Beaulieu's concern about contemporary challenges to the social and economic standing of the Grande Bourgeoisie, we can see an alternative to the belief that Leroy-Beaulieu's imperialism was motivated by nationalism or economics. Since the fear of an upheaval of the existing social order was seldom far from his mind, it would be astonishing if his concern with the Social Question played no role in his conversion to imperialism. But his thought process was not the one historians usually cite in linking bourgeois fears with endorsement of imperialism. Usually, scholars point to the imperialists' hope that overseas territories would provide the new resources and jobs that would enable governments to satisfy the material demands of discontented workers.[99] Leroy-Beaulieu never mentioned such a possibility. Nevertheless, viewed in relation to his overriding preoccupations and in the context of contemporary events, Leroy-Beaulieu's imperialist writings after 1879 take on a social dimension. To me it appears that advocating imperialism was the best available tactic to reduce the threat of social revolution.

Other grand-bourgeois Liberal economists remained aloof from imperialists; for instance, Frédéric Passy, Leroy-Beaulieu's colleague and occasional rival, held to his early antiwar convictions and opposed colonial conquests. But this difference of opinion could be simply because these Liberals did not share Leroy-Beaulieu's expectations as to the consequences of a continental policy or his perceptions as to how the Established Liberals, while out of power, could most effectively work to prevent war with Germany. Undeniably Leroy-Beaulieu's fear of social revolution was only one factor among several that shaped his convictions. Yet the hypothesis—one hitherto ignored in the literature—that this was the primary motivating factor in his imperialism is supported by the fact that his most constantly reiterated argument for a colonial policy was the danger involved in the continental policy. This interpretation will appear even more plausible after we look at Leroy-Beaulieu's social thought in the 1880s and 1890s and see how again, as in the 1860s, he became preoccupied above all with the new threats he perceived to the position of the Grande Bourgeoisie.

7

The Mature Writings of Leroy-Beaulieu

■ The publication of the second edition of *De la Colonisation* came at the beginning of Leroy-Beaulieu's most productive period as a social thinker and writer. Along with a number of new editions of older works and two or three books of relatively minor importance, he completed three major new works in the 1880s. From articles written for the *Revue des Deux Mondes* and from lectures given at the Ecole Libre des Sciences Politiques and the Collège de France, Leroy-Beaulieu put together the *Essai sur la Répartition des Richesses et sur la Tendance à une Moindre Inégalité* (1881); *Le Collectivisme: Examen Critique du Nouveau Socialisme* (1884, with a second edition the following year); and *L'Etat Moderne et ses Fonctions* (published in 1889 and soon translated into English). Then in 1896 he capped his career with a massive, four-volume economics treatise, the *Traité Théorique et Pratique d'Economie Politique*. These works were his greatest achievements in his role as defender of the Liberal Regime. None of them, in my estimation, approaches the high level of creative and synthetic thought reached by *De la Colonisation*, but the *Traité d'Economie Politique* was the last in a line of monumental works by Liberal economists of the nineteenth century.

Leroy-Beaulieu's publications during the 1880s raised him to the summit of his profession in France, and he was as comfortable in his private life as he was successful on the intellectual scene. Despite repeated frustrations in his political endeavors, he settled into an enviable life as a large proprietor in the provinces and as a member of the learned high society of Paris. Nevertheless, he was far from fully happy with his world. Each of his extensive studies of the 1880s addresses events that distressed him: the intensification of the Social Question, the rise of new schools of social thought, and the dominance of French political life by the advanced republicans. Faced with these developments, the grand bourgeois Liberal felt again the apprehensiveness that marked his prewar writings on the foreign policy and social pronouncements of the republicans. The new treatises on distribution of wealth, socialism, and the state had a defensive character similar to his older discussions of the Social Question. And the economics treatise reveals him even more than before as the determined and able protector of capitalism and capitalists. In these works we see Leroy-Beaulieu coming into his own as an ideologist.

*A*round 1891 *La Grande Encyclopédie* declared that "In France M. Leroy-Beaulieu is the most honored representative of orthodox political economy and the most notable adversary of protectionist and collectivist theories."[1] His honorary positions testify to his preeminence. In 1887 he served as president of the Société d'Economie Sociale, an organization founded by Frédéric Le Play that sought to pacify working-class discontent by encouraging employers to adopt paternalism.[2] In 1893, at age fifty, he was elected president of the Académie des Sciences Morales et Politiques. Just after the turn of the century, two commentators on contemporary European economic thought singled out Leroy-Beaulieu as the leading figure of the "French School of Economics."[3] Within a few years he must have shared his position of eminence with such younger professors of economics as Charles Gide, whose textbooks, judging from their numerous editions, had a wider diffusion than the books of Leroy-Beaulieu. Yet during the 1890s, even before the publication of the *Traité d'Economie Politique*, Leroy-Beaulieu was probably the best-known French economist.

He maintained this position by keeping up the same intense pace of labor that had always occupied his days. He divided his time between his mansion on the fashionable Avenue du Bois de Boulogne (now Avenue Foch) and his country estate, Montplaisir. His acquaintances, visiting him at Montplaisir, were astonished by the unvarying regularity of his schedule. During the morning he took a walk to survey the activities on the estate, and then from 10 a.m. until 12:30 p.m. he retired to his study. After lunch and a second tour of his farms, he returned to his intellectual activities until evening. Dinner waited until he was done. René Stourm recounts that his every hour was "admirably regulated for the best employment of each day."[4] According to an English visitor, E. C. Bodley, he carried on the same kind of fixed routine in his mansion in Paris; Bodley wrote that "the grave economist" said he could do more work "among the smiling lawns which skirt the Bois de Boulogne" than he could in the country.[5] In Paris, although he hosted visiting European scholars and gave "lovely receptions to which the high society of Paris came in great numbers,"[6] work continued to be the main feature of his life. He embodied the same commitment to productivity as did his contemporary Frederick Taylor, the pioneer "efficiency engineer." Detesting the loss of time that could be used for output, Leroy-Beaulieu did not simply defend productivity and efficiency; he embodied these central values of modern civilization to an extraordinary degree.

Leroy-Beaulieu could not relax when he believed that Liberal values and the security of his social-economic class were under greater pressure than ever before. The French in the late nineteenth century had to deal with a complex economic scene. They saw the organization of economic interests on a nationwide basis; the rise of giant limited-liability corporations; the dependence of national power on economic affluence, education, and size of population; and constant reminders of the revolutionary potential of the working class. The new conditions pressured legislatures into repeated extensions of the state's social and economic activities. By the 1880s, few upheld the strict laissez-faire position.[7] On the intellectual front the threat to Liberal values grew as the number of writings defending large-scale government intervention in economic and social life multiplied each year, in France as in every Western nation. Liberal and paternalist governments alike passed or considered legislation to regulate workers' wages and hours and to provide them with some form of unemployment security and old-age pensions. And radical political figures advocated redistributive income tax systems to finance these schemes. Leroy-Beaulieu answered these challenges with a renewed prolonged effort to defend his class's values and position.

*I*deological defense is a foremost trait of the *Essai sur la Répartition des Richesses et sur la Tendance à une Moindre Inégalité*, which represented a recasting on a grander scale of ideas present in *L'Etat Moral et Intellectuel des Populations Ouvrières* and *La Question Ouvrière au*

XIXe Siècle. Like the two earlier works, *Répartition des Richesses* focused on the causes and cures of the Social Question, reconsidering working-class grievances and the immutability of the existing social hierarchy. The Social Question existed, he argued, largely because up to the mid-1800s industrial conditions had been very bad. Early industrial capitalism had passed through a difficult period of intense change and competition, when employers had exploited workers. However, Leroy-Beaulieu insisted that conditions had improved, thanks in part to the enlightened managers of the second half of the nineteenth century. Industry had become properly organized, and capitalists no longer squeezed the men and women who labored for them. But reformers and the working class had not yet awakened to the improvements. Instead they held on to past anger and resentment, demanding a reshaping of society that was unnecessary and unjustified since it derived from the memory of problems that no longer existed.[8]

In turning to solutions for the Social Question, Leroy-Beaulieu asserted, as in his early writings, that increased wages for workers depended on increased productivity. But he emphasized some novel forces that he said would lead to a gradual and irreversible diminution of inequality. Repeating a claim he first made in his articles on the depression that reached France in 1877, he insisted that interest rates and profits were entering a permanent decline while wages would continue their recent rise. On the basis of these new "facts" of social-economic existence, Leroy-Beaulieu concluded that the standard of living of wage earners would improve steadily and that the gap between them and those above them would close.[9] Consequently, there was no need for workers to have recourse to strikes, nor was there any need to ask the state to impose "artificial" arrangements—such as an income tax—to redistribute income.[10] On the other hand, Leroy-Beaulieu highlighted the idea that the reduction of differences in income and status did not mean the absolute end of inequality. Inequalities in income and status were rooted in the "nature of things," and therefore people would never be entirely on the same level.[11]

Even Leroy-Beaulieu's Established Liberal colleagues were skeptical about his contention that interest rates and profits would decline permanently. Nevertheless, they applauded his reprise of the old argument that social justice could be achieved without any alteration of contemporary institutions or the system of taxation.[12] But to whom was the argument addressed? *Répartition des Richesses* was a long, elaborate treatment of current economic developments, which few workers could afford or would want to read. The fact that Leroy-Beaulieu brought out a second edition of *La Question Ouvrière* at the same time, with its theme that the bourgeois reformers must join with the rest of the bourgeoisie to form a solid front to resist workers' demands, hints that *Répartition des Richesses* too was directed at the liberally educated bourgeoisie.

The next treatment of the Social Question, *Le Collectivisme*, is ostensibly an examination of the latest anticapitalist doctrines that had begun attracting a following among European workers and intellectuals. Actually, the analysis of the doctrines occupied far fewer lines than does a critical commentary that seeks to poke holes in the views of such advocates of the nationalization of land as Emile de Laveleye and Henry George and of such socialists as Karl Marx, Ferdinand Lassalle, and Albert Schaeffle.[13] Even more important, however, is the defense *Le Collectivisme* makes of a society based on private ownership, contractual relationships, free-market exchanges, and differences in wealth and social standing. While Leroy-Beaulieu wrote dozens of articles on behalf of the specific interests of large-scale entrepreneurs, in this 1884 publication we see him most openly as champion of capitalism and class society as a whole.

The defense of modern Liberal society rests partly on the contrast between capitalists and workers. The present social structure is justified because nature and upbringing produce two classes of human beings, one of them able, self-motivated, and highly disciplined and the other of limited abilities and weak character. For many reasons, the bourgeoisie develop the virtues necessary to make good in economic life, while members of the working class remain destined for subordinate roles. The bourgeoisie are characteristically hardworking and competent, with "an inherited sense of administration." Many of them are prepared for management positions by their families who have been directing businesses for generations. Because of generations of experience and training, members of all three levels of the bourgeoisie generally learn to exercise self-control, plan for the future, and make sacrifices for the sake of future benefits. On the other hand, workers are generally improvident, incompetent individuals who have had to sell their labor because they have failed to accumulate capital.[14] With the fervor of a fundamentalist clergyman, this puritanical and moralistic economist divided people into economic sheep and goats just as confidently as he had done fifteen years earlier and as Established Liberals had been doing for several generations. As a secular rather than a religious thinker, though, he spoke in terms of a natural, not a divine, right to wealth and status. The capitalist's rare gifts, he wrote, "have a decisive action upon the prosperity of nations," and his right to proportionally higher remuneration "derives from the natural order of things; it is a true law of society." The progress of economic life depends upon the capitalist's intellectual labor, which is superior to "gross manual labor" and will not be done unless it is rewarded very well. No artificial arrangements (i.e., reforms) can change the situation.[15] This portion of the book basically restated the adulatory description of the bourgeoisie that had appeared in *La Question Ouvrière.*

Drawing from Nassau Senior, an early nineteenth-century English economist, Leroy-Beaulieu further asserted that investors deserve their high incomes and respected position because their capital comes from accepting the pain of "abstinence"—that is, the self-denying refusal to use their incomes for personal consumption. Nor is this their only sacrifice: they also face the difficulties involved in buying machinery and raw materials, supervising work and construction, selling products, and running the risks connected with business enterprises. Thus their profits are a just reward for their efforts in organizing and operating enterprises that provide work for others.[16] None of these ideas were new, but they acquired a vividness and freshness from the verve with which they were presented.

Le Collectivisme does contain one characteristic largely absent from Leroy-Beaulieu's previous works: angry, denigrating, intensely ironic dissections of his opponents' ideas. Although, in the preface of the 1885 edition, he called his critique "*loyal et courtois*" and "without hate or animosity against persons," he set a tone of derisive superiority by saying he had shown "indulgence and commiseration" to "people who had allowed themselves to be seduced by chimeras."[17] Throughout the book he termed the new collectivists "superficial," "sophists," and "fools" (*sots*). At no point did he grant the validity of any opposing idea, nor did he ever signal an area of doubt that required further inquiry or reflection.

In *L'Etat Moderne*, Leroy-Beaulieu turned his polemic to contemporary, nonsocialist champions of the expanding state. Socialism he still regarded as only a very long-range threat; he wrote that the immediate danger came from the state and from those who saw legislation as the prime engine of reform and progress. For the past fifteen years, he protested, the state had begun to interfere "in a swarm of tasks and services from which it had hitherto abstained." So he aimed at defining the proper functions of the state and at drawing lines beyond which public authorities should not go.[18] *L'Etat Moderne*, in consequence, is the economist's most sustained effort at political thought and his most definitive statement on government and self-government.

L'Etat Moderne begins with a sketch of the origins and initial functions of the state. In the tradition that dates back to Liberal social-contract theories of the seventeenth century, Leroy-Beaulieu argued that society is prior to the state in time and superior to the state in character. Large-scale human associations appeared first, followed only afterward by separate state institutions. In each large, independent community, the state eventually received exclusive possession of two powers: the monopoly over coercion or legitimate violence in the community, and the right to take a part of everyone's production as a means to support the government. In other words, Leroy-Beaulieu shared the view, widespread among nineteenth-century Liberals, that the state is basically an agency of coercion and constraint. Furthermore, he emphasized that there was always a definite division of labor between the political and social institutions. The former simply provided military defense against external enemies, protection against evildoers, and mediation of disputes within a country. All other functions—such as economic activities, education, and science—were performed by private individuals and the private, noncoercive associations that make up society. The distinction between state and society and between their "natural" areas of competence implied that the state should be confined to its original sphere of action. This schematic, abstract, and genetic account led Leroy-Beaulieu to conclude that the natural and appropriate functions of the state are the ones it was created to perform: defense and internal security.[19] Seemingly, therefore, he wound up in the rigid position he had already characterized in 1870 and 1877 as untenable.

This contrast between state and society, like the similar contrast made by eighteenth-century Liberals such as Tom Paine and his sneering tone, conveys an intense deprecation of political institutions. Leroy-Beaulieu treated the state as an inferior, somewhat contemptible part of civilization, and he was no less contemptuous of those in the late nineteenth century who praised the state as a source of solutions for social and economic problems. Leroy-Beaulieu scornfully described these interventionists as idolaters, gripped by the illusion that routine-bound, sluggish bureaucracies could guide a society along beneficial paths.[20]

Nevertheless, the book soon moves away from a narrow conception of the modern state, since Leroy-Beaulieu accepted that the state must now do more than provide defense against outside aggression and security from crime inside the nation. The state should and can regulate conditions of work for the "weak." By requiring corporations to publicize aspects of their financial condition, state agencies also have a role to play in preventing stock frauds.[21] Public authorities should help promote population growth and provide public works such as ports to aid the development of colonial dependencies. Throughout *L'Etat Moderne* Leroy-Beaulieu acknowledged that the state should actively participate in the amelioration of society.

These concessions to state intervention were far from modest for their time, and they placed Leroy-Beaulieu in a theoretical and practical difficulty. Without the strict rule of laissez-faire, which set an unambiguous line beyond which government was not supposed to go, Leroy-Beaulieu had no principle which could disallow totally the kinds of intervention he disliked. He confessed that "it is impossible theoretically [i.e., by a priori classifications] to arrive at a fixed demarcation between the sphere of the State and that of voluntary associations and individuals; the two spheres often interpenetrate and shift ground."[22] Yet he wanted desperately to limit as far as possible what public authorities could do. To achieve this goal he relied on a variety of strategies. First, he said, the contribution of national officials must be auxiliary to that of private individuals and voluntary associations.[23] Second, he dealt on a case-by-case basis with such interventions as government-operated railroads, assistance to the poor, old-age pensions, workers' compensation, and the regulation of hours and working conditions. Invariably he pointed up the inconveniences, inequities, or inconsistencies in enacted or proposed legislation covering these areas of economic life.[24]

Moreover, Leroy-Beaulieu repeatedly resurrected *homo economicus*, whom he had buried earlier in the book, in order to present the standard Liberal argument that the activity of public officials threatens to crush the will and energy of individuals.[25] Wherever and whenever the authorities step in, he insisted, they promote routine and waste. Despite his efforts to move away from a totally individualist conception of society, Leroy-Beaulieu stressed that every great advance by humanity has been the result of efforts by individuals or voluntary associations. States are incapable of bring-ing anything fresh into existence, he proclaimed; a coercive organi-zation inherently lacks the spontaneity and flexibility required for inventiveness. Bureaucrats are either ignorant of society's real needs or unable to find the proper means to meet those needs. Whenever they seek to move people to action, they know only the stifling methods of command and coercion. Their orientation, training, and purpose rob them of the imagination needed to discover new proce-dures, ideas, and instruments. Public officials should wait for the private sphere, the true creative force in the development of civiliza-tion, to find solutions, some of which the state might subsequently codify by making laws. The state's proper contribution to social progress is thus limited to "conservation" and "generalization."[26]

The state's inherent faults, Leroy-Beaulieu went on, were multi-plied immensely under the new parliamentary and democratic re-gimes. This argument had already been prefigured in a key passage in *Le Collectivisme*, in which Leroy-Beaulieu explained why a mod-ern state could not successfully manage a nation's agriculture:

> The more we move away from the absolutism of ancient times, the more we engage ourselves in the parliamentary system, in democracy, in elected government offices with short terms, the more the State be-comes unfit for the new functions that some want it to undertake. This State is no longer a permanent being representing the entire nation; it is nothing more than a party in power defending with very little scruple the interests of a majority that is weakly established and changeable. . . . The modern parliamentary and democratic state is essentially a partial and negligent administrator. It is so by nature: its vices are not transitory.[27]

In *L'Etat Moderne* he expanded on this critique, drawing on those thinkers of the early 1800s who were generally hostile to the French Revolution, the rise of capitalism, and the creation of Liberal society—a group of individuals often called reactionaries, though I believe it is most accurate historically and ideologically to call them Conservatives.[28] Leroy-Beaulieu did not share their distaste for self-government, but he did agree that the modern state lacks intelligence because it is chosen by the suffrage of an unenlightened majority and is, as a result, "subject to all the successive prejudices which dominate human beings and carry them away." It puts into effect policies based on the enthusiasms that momentarily sweep a nation at election time.[29] Its actions are often incoherent, due to the frequent postelection turnovers of personnel and policies that cause government to lack continuity.[30] It expresses the will of a temporary and only apparent majority rather than that of the whole nation.[31] Since the officials of the modern state are chosen by popular vote, they cannot be impartial; instead they are the government of a party and serve special interests rather than the general interest.[32]

One can hear the voices of Metternich and Bismarck in these complaints, but the critique ends by positioning itself firmly in the tradition of Liberalism. Public officials in all states "have neither the stimulant nor the brake of self-interest," Leroy-Beaulieu lamented. They do not suffer from the "sanction of an immediate recoil on them of the practical results of their work" in the way that a businessman does when he makes a bad investment. Second, state agencies are not subject to the conditions of competition.[33] Finally, he stated—using the same term that Metternich applied to the individual in his famous "Confession of Faith"—that the modern state, rather than humbly recognizing its limitations, is "presumptuous."

This dual suspicion of democracy and bureaucracy, earlier propounded by right-wing Liberals like Guizot, justifies Thomas R. Osborne's characterization of Leroy-Beaulieu as a "conservative liberal."[34] The emphasis should surely be on his adherence to Liberalism, since he never expressed any admiration of the Old Regime or authoritarian governments.

*I*n 1891, just two years after the publication of *L'Etat Moderne*, the book appeared in translation in England, a testimony to the regard it gained in the land of the Manchester School and Herbert Spencer.[35] About then, however, Leroy-Beaulieu's output of new books ceased for several years. In 1891 he had a burst of publishing activity, but it was confined to new editions of old works.[36] Between 1891 and 1896 he published only articles. During that time he devoted himself to the project he probably hoped would give him immortality as an economist, the *Traité Théorique et Pratique d'Economie Politique*. Even his usual schedule of producing a new edition of the *Traité des Finances* every two to four years was set aside while he concentrated on his most exceptional intellectual achievement, his four-volume summa of economic science (published in 1896).

Leroy-Beaulieu must have felt an urgency about his labors, because the tide of unorthodox economic thought was still rising.

New editions of Charles Gide's popular economics textbooks appeared in these years, and a doctoral program in economics was instituted at the Paris school of law, where Paul Cauwès, a leading dissident, had been teaching since the early 1870s. In 1893 Cauwès issued a prime challenge to Established Liberalism and to Leroy-Beaulieu's own ambitions: a four-volume "textbook," the *Cours d'Economie Politique*, which represented a revision on a grand scale of his two-volume *Précis* of the late 1870s. Thus, before Leroy-Beaulieu finished his immense project, it had a prominent rival. Because the *Cours* was a compendium of views that exasperated Leroy-Beaulieu, a summary of its doctrine will throw into greater relief the key features of Leroy-Beaulieu's four-volume treatise.

As in the late 1870s, Cauwès presented an extensive, forceful critique of existing economic teachings. He traced the main errors of Established Liberalism to the rationalist method of the early nineteenth-century English economists and to their treatment of the past as similar to the present.[37] In place of an economic theory derived by deduction from a few abstract principles, Cauwès called for an inductive economic science based on systematic observation of past and present. Economics must start, he declared, with empirical, historical study of the economies of specific countries rather than from conceptions of universal laws of nature. Once the discipline discovered regularities in each society, it could begin to make generalizations to cover them all. Until that time its theories could claim to be only relatively rather than absolutely true and, therefore, subject to revision.[38]

Challenging directly one of the views dearest to Leroy-Beaulieu, Cauwès denied the existence of natural laws of economics that exert a compelling force over human and social behavior. Although observation and reason can discover universal standards, he stated, in practice a people can only approximate these standards. Each nation must adapt its economic life to circumstances and cultural heritage.[39] Cauwès's relativism bolstered his rejection of the doctrine of universal, unchangeable Economic Man; he agreed that self-interest is a powerful human motive, but not that it is the only motive that matters in economic affairs.[40] Furthermore, human beings are not "constants"; rather, human nature is changeable, varying over time and according to the stage of a society's development.[41] On these grounds and because few specific economies had been thoroughly studied, Cauwès denied the cherished Established Liberal view that economics was a fundamentally finished science.[42]

Cauwès also rejected the established doctrine's productivist standpoint. Calling this view *chrématistique* (the science of riches), he countered: "To produce a great deal is fine but on condition that we do not sacrifice man in order to make wealth, that we do not treat him as an instrument or simple agent of production in somewhat the same way as we do machines."[43] The emphasis on production, Cauwès said, leads to mistaken views about the distribution of income and thus to mistreatment of workers. If economists consider the needs of production as the sole criterion of institutions and policy, they logically would advocate that costs should be cut by reducing wages as far as possible.[44] Cauwès further criticized the productivists for believing in the concentration of wealth. Disliking their judgment that large fortunes are particularly useful in bringing about increases in production, he argued for a more equitable distribution of incomes.[45]

Cauwès urged making justice, not production, the measure of the effectiveness of an economic system. Economic science should not simply "say what is or simply . . . describe movements of quantities or riches." Instead, when economists see "the strong . . . using the pretext of liberty as a cloak for oppressing the feeble," they should demand "intervention of the sanctions of positive law" to prevent the abuse. For example, wage bargains that result from economic or other kinds of coercion rather than from voluntary agreements should be judged illegitimate.[46] Although he supported freedom for entrepreneurs and the principle of free labor and stated that the rights of property are vital and justifiable, Cauwès also declared that economic rights are far from absolute. The principle of justice must take precedence over economic efficiency and output.[47]

Cauwès went much further than Leroy-Beaulieu to correct what even the latter considered an overemphasis on the individual in Established Liberal doctrine. Cauwès rejected the conception of society as an aggregation of individuals who associate for reasons of personal benefit. Rather, he saw society as just as basic and natural as the family. Furthermore, everywhere, at all times, people work in a coordinated fashion to supply one another's needs.[48] This positive valuation of the importance of groups led, for one thing, to approval of labor unions. Unlike Leroy-Beaulieu, Cauwès never criticized unions for suppressing the freedom of their members, even though he also regarded personal liberty as a central value.

For Cauwès trade unions and the state were essential parts of the response to the Social Question. Cauwès believed wages were insufficient and working hours too long, because of "the more nomadic and precarious existence" modern workers lead in comparison to their medieval and Old Regime predecessors.[49] He scorned the idea that wages are determined by iron laws of supply and demand.[50] The source of excessive hours and low incomes is competition among insecure workers for a limited number of jobs and the weakness of the individual worker vis-à-vis employers. The state should regulate work hours and support the right of workers to associate in unions.[51]

In Cauwès's eyes the state is responsible for both guarding the interests of humanity and ensuring national vitality.[52] Quoting the German-Swiss theorist Johann Bluntschli, Cauwès proclaimed, "The first duty of the individual is the development of his faculties. Similarly the State is a moral being whose mission is to develop the latent forces of a nation, to bring about the blossoming of its faculties, all of which implies, in two words, conservation and progress."[53] He argued that public officials are indeed competent to achieve this desired end, especially where the government is freely chosen. Cauwès believed in the excellence of representative government, and he held that regular elections would keep authorities from intervening in economic affairs in ways that would threaten freedom. He took issue with Leroy-Beaulieu's charge that the contemporary French state showed that democratic states fall under the control of a particular political party.[54]

In his own treatise published in 1896 Leroy-Beaulieu responded to every challenge posed by reformers such as Cauwès. The massive "textbook" is outstanding for the clarity of its organization and the lucidity of its exposition of Leroy-Beaulieu's values. But its literary qualities are of minor importance for students of modern history. The *Traitè d'Economie Politique* is one of the last and in many ways the most monumental compendium of the ideas championed by Say, Bastiat, Chevalier, and other leading lights of the established school of French Liberal economics. Every one of Leroy-Beaulieu's fundamental beliefs about knowledge, method, economic institutions, and social arrangements find a place in this summa. An account of the treatise, therefore, is a synopsis of his outlook on practically every issue of importance that he ever addressed.

The treatise has a hybrid character. Although many chapters are mainly polemical, in other sections Leroy-Beaulieu dropped his confrontational tone in order to struggle with questions of economic theory. In these sections he tried to come to terms with the approximately thirty years of economic experience and debate that had elapsed since he began his first book. The contrast with the polemics of *Le Collectivisme* and *L'Etat Moderne* is often startling. He even accepted modest contributions from Lassalle and Marx.[55] Entire chapters deal with theoretical matters, even though their conclusions are often polemical.

Much of the *Traité d'Economie Politique* centers on the same concern that preoccupied the Physiocrats and Adam Smith: the sources of the wealth of nations and the means to bring about a continuous increase in the output of factories, mines, and fields. Following the standard organization of textbooks of political economy, Leroy-Beaulieu included a description of fundamentals, followed by analyses of production, distribution, and consumption. There is, in addition, almost another book within the treatise or, rather, almost another organization of ideas in it. This incomplete subtext is a historical or quasi-historical account of the rise and development of the capitalist economic system.[56] Both the historical and theoretical parts of the treatise have the same themes: the inevitability of the division of labor into investors, managers, and workers, the legitimacy of private capital and capitalists, and the essential and indispensable role of the entrepreneur. To bolster the capitalist system Leroy-Beaulieu relied on the same economic positions that he drew from Established Liberalism in the 1860s. That is, the four thick volumes of the *Traité d'Economie Politique* presented production as society's key need and justified the capitalist, the entrepreneur, private property, freedom of initiative, and free labor as vitally important to fostering a high level of production.

The first part of the treatise deals with fundamentals—the nature, usefulness, and method of economics. Underlying these early chapters is one of Leroy-Beaulieu's chief convictions and central strategies for defending Liberal society. He believed and taught that we know with certainty that the existing social structure and economic institutions are natural, useful, and good. Leroy-Beaulieu shared with most of his contemporaries the belief that the findings of the physical sciences are unchallengeable absolute truths. Building upon this assumption, he defended the idea that Established Liberal economics is a science in the same way as astronomy, geology, and biology are. These sciences, he pointed out, are based on objective observation rather than on mathematics and experiment, and in

France economics has the same character. Classifying the discipline as part of "natural history," Leroy-Beaulieu invoked the research of two biologists, Buffon and Darwin, as models for economic science. He claimed that the French school had always approached economic phenomena in the same way as these two great biologists approached the natural world. Undertaking "minutely detailed studies," the French economists employed the "positive" method—the procedure controlled by careful attention to "facts" that resulted in inductively established conclusions backed up by a myriad of indubitable bits of evidence.[57] Consequently, these conclusions were as certain, absolute, and universal as those of the kindred physical sciences.[58] Since established economics in France had followed scientific procedures in the strictest sense of the term, the laws it had discovered were beyond doubt.[59]

Yet Leroy-Beaulieu tried to avoid rigidity in his description of economics. His 114-page introduction took into account the critiques of Liberal doctrine by the "historical" schools, the socialists, and academic dissenters like Cauwès. He apparently was willing to grant that abstraction and analysis, essential as they are to science, distort reality.[60] He distanced himself from Malthus, Ricardo, and the Manchesterians, saying they erred by creating a deductive, rationalist science that imitated mathematics and ignored history. In contrast to Adam Smith, whom Leroy-Beaulieu praised for his systematic attention to the empirical world, these economists spun theories out of deductively produced abstractions and generalized too much from modern conditions. Their gravest fault was their reliance on the concept of Economic Man, which describes every human being as exclusively a self-interested, rational calculator concerned only with personal material gain. Leroy-Beaulieu recognized fully that Established Liberal economists exposed themselves to attack when they reduced all human urges to rational economic self-interest. He saw his own interpretation as departing from that of English Liberals because he took into account the findings of economic historians and ethnographers on the historical relativity of human behavior. Thus he wrote that human nature is "very variable and very disparate" (inégal) depending upon national, ethnic, and individual factors, and he accepted the contention that noneconomic motives influence economic behavior.[61]

Leroy-Beaulieu even moved haltingly toward modifying the concept of natural law, a keystone in the edifice of Established Liberalism. By the time he wrote the Traité d'Economie Politique he had to admit that economic laws do not explain all economic events. His answer to this difficulty was that economic phenomena are intertwined with other kinds of social and psychological forces. The operation of the laws is inhibited by the "friction" from these other forces, just as friction in the physical world modifies the impact of the laws of mechanics. To some extent, then, the rules governing economic activity are contingent upon the social and mental stage of a society. Some societies, during certain periods of their development, resist the operation of economic constants.[62] Economic laws, he concluded, do not act in isolation, and other laws could even annul their impact.[63]

This discussion seems to exhibit some alteration of Leroy-Beaulieu's convictions. But Leroy-Beaulieu also sought to attenuate the impact of his concessions to critics of natural law. In a fashion typical of the economists of his time, he contrasted *pure* science with *applied* science. Pure mechanics, he noted, must ignore a variety of complicating factors in describing the force of gravity or the velocity of objects. But the mechanical engineer who constructs railroads or builds bridges must rely upon applied mechanics, making allowances for the wind and other stresses that do not appear in the laws of the pure science. Similarly, Leroy-Beaulieu contended, the "inductive" French school of economics to which he belonged taught a pure economics whose truths were firmly established while making the proper allowances with regard to practical policies. Yet his key response parallels that of Alfred Marshall, whose great text had appeared five years before the *Traité*. Although he agreed with Marshall that in the short run the natural laws of economics operated in only approximate and incomplete fashion, he insisted that the laws have an overriding influence in the long run.[64]

Leroy-Beaulieu refused to budge from his claim that the Established Liberal economists knew how to find the truth and had done so. Despite the complications produced by "frictions," he stated that elite minds could make the careful distinctions and impartial observations that are necessary. Blessed with "a rare circumspection" and "a singularly penetrating understanding," such gifted thinkers could discover the basic truths about the world.[65] The natural laws he and other economic scientists had established did indeed govern all areas of economic activity, whether people like those laws or not.

The limits of Leroy-Beaulieu's modification of natural law doctrine are evident in his attack on the definition of economics propounded by Emile de Laveleye, the outstanding French-speaking representative of academic dissent. De Laveleye insisted in his *Eléments d'Economie Politique* (1882) that "the laws that concern political economy are not those of nature but, rather, the edicts of the legislator." To Leroy-Beaulieu such a statement was "full of confusion" and "in contradiction to all the principles of the science." Rejecting even the term "*political economy*," he proclaimed, "Economics, to use the *correct term*, does not have to do only with the lawmaker; it is involved with all freely made industrial and commercial arrangements and with a multitude of activities of individuals. Its laws do not emanate in the least from the will of individuals but dominate that will and impose upon it."[66] This last sentence not only reveals his basic allegiance to Established Liberal doctrine but also hints at his political agenda. Economics for Leroy-Beaulieu "had been for a long time and often is still a protest against the sins and errors of the legislator."[67] The pretensions of human will must be circumscribed by the authority of science, especially the science of economics. The movement of Leroy-Beaulieu's thought, therefore, was circular. Despite his apparent receptivity to a few new ideas, even in the introduction to the treatise he edged back to the starting points of Established Liberalism.

His fundamental ideological immobility is apparent from the rest of the text, in which he made no effort to recast economics as a whole into an applied doctrine and a pure doctrine. Although here and there he operated as an empiricist, examining data rather than imposing a preconceived conclusion upon them, he generally treated the laws as if they rule over social existence. When he considered actual features of contemporary society, he often invoked natural laws to defend free-enterprise capitalism and social inequalities against the claims made by the workers and claims made for the state.

Having demonstrated, with some ambiguities, the scientific certainty of established economics, Leroy-Beaulieu devoted the remaining three-and-a-half volumes to the other standard subjects of the discipline. When he took up the topic of distribution, the second main division of economic theory, he filled with distinction the role of economic reporter. The bulk of volume two of the treatise analyzes the situation of wage earners and deals with the determinants of wages, the nature and role of unions, state intervention in earnings, and the value of profit-sharing and cooperatives as alternatives to the wage system. A chapter on farm earnings and prices fully justifies Leroy-Beaulieu's claim that he based his ideas on observation rather than on deduction. After he surveyed the output of varying kinds of land, he identified a number of significant variables and voiced his conclusions in terms of tendencies rather than natural laws.[68] His discussions of wages display, to an extent not found in other parts of the treatise, an attempt to be fair to criticisms of Liberal doctrine. He also confronted the issue of justice, reiterating many of his long-held ideas, but sometimes stating them less positively than he had at the outset of his career. For example, he gave more credit to unions for helping workers and was somewhat more tentative about the future of cooperative businesses. In discussing the system of piecework he outlined more completely and with more understanding why workers object to the system, and he acknowledged that employers can and do take advantage of innovations in equipment to make subtle decreases in rates. Nevertheless, he still insisted that piecework is the best system of payment, since it most closely correlates wages with productivity and responsibility, but he laid down strict conditions for its use.[69]

When Leroy-Beaulieu considered the determinants of wages— one of the most controversial issues of economics—he made the most use of the revisionist ideas whose value he conceded in the introduction. First, he boldly sided with the Socialist critique that under the Capitalist System "labor is a commodity." That does not make the *worker* a commodity; the "thing furnished and the furnisher are not identical," he stated. However, he did not explore this position. Instead he discussed the relation of morality and equity to the wage system. He accepted the possibility that sentiments of sympathy and benevolence might legitimately play a role in setting rewards for working people. Other sentiments also affect compensation. Feelings and habits frequently lead a worker to remain in one place even though he would receive higher wages if he moved.[70] Family relationships, preference for a particular kind of work, custom, and even resignation can play roles.[71] All in all, Leroy-Beaulieu was less absolute on the question of wages than on other topics. Further, he again stated his conclusions in terms of tendencies, contradicting his assertion in the introduction that economics stated laws rather than tendencies.[72]

Nevertheless, Leroy-Beaulieu still held that the price of labor is fixed by "causes that are more general, more permanent, more precise, less individual, and not as continually variable as feelings."[73] Productivity, not bargaining strength or any other psychological factor, determines the basic rate of pay.[74] Leroy-Beaulieu took the stand that distribution, like production, is ruled by natural laws. On this point Leroy-Beaulieu opposed John Stuart Mill's important dissenting belief that patterns of distribution could be reformed through legislation. Repeatedly Leroy-Beaulieu turned from describing the actual distribution of wealth and income to combat criticisms of the current economic hierarchy.[75] Thus the polemical, ideological side of his thought did not disappear.

Despite his admission that the concept of Economic Man is inadequate, Leroy-Beaulieu based his final judgment about distribution heavily on it. Differences in earnings must persist in order to motivate people to work hard, whether as laborers or managers. As he put it: "In their impact on the general conditions of our existence, economic motives are so powerful that the majority of human beings cannot free themselves from their influence for very long or very completely." That is particularly true, he added, in a "very civilized society," which he characterized as one "where the milieu is very sensitive to motives from the economic sphere."[76] Despite his flexibility and caution, at least in comparison with his other writings, these statements illustrate the way he defended the same fundamental positions he had always held.

If Leroy-Beaulieu's section on distribution amounts to a defense against critiques of the Liberal conception of economics and social organization, his section on the factors of production was even more defensive. Taking up the topic of "the general conditions for the development of modern societies and the effect of these conditions on production,"[77] Leroy-Beaulieu offered a concise and elegant vision of the good society. This is perhaps one of the finest statements of the predominant Liberal ideal of the nineteenth century. The vision is expressed in four chapters—on liberty and individual responsibility, property, inheritance, and competition—that are, not surprisingly, the most highly ideological in the entire four volumes. The now-familiar argument is that capitalist institutions and bourgeois supremacy are good for society because they are natural and because they are essential to society's chief interest, increasing the output of material goods.

The institution of free labor is among the most important causes of growth. In speaking of *liberté de travail*, Leroy-Beaulieu praised the untrammeled ability of employees to take and leave jobs as they saw fit. All Established Liberals, including Leroy-Beaulieu, boasted that Capitalism was inimical to slavery, serfdom, and urban forms of labor bondage. They believed the modern European economy, grounded in private property and the pursuit of profit, had been a powerful emancipator of human beings. Leroy-Beaulieu scorned the medieval guilds since they prevented workers from bargaining over their conditions of employment. The modern worker, he asserted proudly, was in a far better legal position than the slaves and serfs who had been the property of others or of the land they worked on. "Through the efforts of many centuries," he declared, "humanity has gradually gone from the regime of constraint, servitude or serfdom, of diverse forms of subjection, to the regime of full individual liberty." Western society's great achievement was its provision of the freedom to choose a job or profession—or an area of investment—because this freedom more than any other force releases human energy and inventiveness.[78]

Leroy-Beaulieu considered the wage system an essential concomitant of free labor and defended it in his pseudohistorical subtext. As he had done in *Le Collectivisme*, Leroy-Beaulieu asserted that wage labor originated in primitive times because most people were incompetent and intellectually limited. To support themselves and their families they had to work for the elite few who had the self-control to build up their capital. The division between owners and laborers is thus legitimate because it parallels the division between the able and the unable. But Leroy-Beaulieu regretfully noted that for thousands of years, as a consequence of prejudice and greed, slavery, serfdom, and guild labor were the predominant forms of work. Although he did not explain the reasons why for millennia these factors were stronger than the forces of nature, he said experience eventually taught the vital lesson that bonded laborers are less productive than those who are their own masters. This account of society's development reinforced his opposition to the efforts of the new labor unions to control the supply of labor and thus stabilize or increase wages. Looking toward the future, he warned that the unions were reviving the old guilds and placing new chains on workers.[79]

Nineteenth-century critics of capitalism held that freedom of contract was a myth and that the wage system short-changed workers. To answer these charges Leroy-Beaulieu cited legislation that had improved the legal status of employees: the abolition of identity cards (the *livret*), the end of the law that accepted the employer's word in a court dispute with an employee, and the legalization of unions. Already in 1870 he had argued that unions made workers more powerful than employers; the latter could not withstand long strikes because they could not afford to leave their capital idle. In 1896 Leroy-Beaulieu's argument against profit sharing was that earnings would not be guaranteed, since they would go down when business is bad, whereas wages are a set and definite amount that has to be paid at an agreed upon level.[80] Leroy-Beaulieu was aware that slaves and serfs had a certain kind of security, but he pointed out that nineteenth-century workers generally considered themselves better off than their unfree predecessors because they were not legally tied to a job or a master. Leroy-Beaulieu seldom implied that economic liberties had unfortunate consequences.[81]

Leroy-Beaulieu presented capital as an even more crucial factor in promoting production than free labor and the wage system. He defined capital in conventional terms, as work embodied in accumulations of tools and provisions. The chapter on capital devotes a significant amount of space to such technical questions as how many types of capital there are, whether commercial paper and trade marks count as capital, and whether personal qualities can be counted as capital.[82] Whatever their character, however, in his estimation capital goods are worthy of the highest admiration. They enable people to fulfill their deep-seated desire to get a maximum of results out of production with a minimum of effort.

In his ideological defense of privately owned capital, Leroy-Beaulieu had to confront two important, hostile accounts of the origins of capital. One view, popularized by the German Socialist leader Ferdinand Lassalle, attributed the formation of privately owned capital to the conquest and enslavement of one people by another. Marx, in his powerful indictment of "primitive accumulation," claimed that European explorers, merchants, and English landlords obtained the funds for capitalist commerce and industry by using force, fraud, and ruthlessness to seize the possessions of others.[83] Leroy-Beaulieu answered Lassalle partly on the grounds of method, saying that his theory "did not rest upon any precise and universal *observation*."[84] In response to both Marx and Lassalle he offered an alternative historical account of primitive accumulation, designed to show that all the characteristic institutions of Capitalism were natural and, therefore, good.

Leroy-Beaulieu ascribed the first accumulations of capital to the insight, hard work, and self-denial of gifted individuals in primitive times. Private wealth, he asserted, is rooted in the conditions of the physical environment and evolves spontaneously because of permanent traits of human nature. As a consequence, it cannot be said to have originated in injustice.[85] Leroy-Beaulieu's "historical" explanation of the origins of capital and capitalists repeated the well-known "abstinence theory" of the creation of capital.[86] However, he skipped over the eras between primitive times and the present, giving no attention to the far different question of how people in contemporary society acquired the property that gave them a revenue. The implication was that they were simply modern versions of Leroy-Beaulieu's primitive heroes of foresight, self-control and abstinence from immediate pleasures.[87]

Society can maximize accumulation of capital only if its institutions encourage individual initiative and effort. Putting workers or the state in charge of capital formation is misguided, since neither can perform successfully the roles of capitalist and entrepreneur. Workers in general cannot resist satisfying their immediate needs; and "diverse vices, of which drunkenness is the principle one, reinforce this natural disposition and accentuate it."[88] As for public agencies, "most States, no matter what their governing institutions, have a stronger tendency to make imprudent expenditures than they have to make savings."[89] Capital is fully effective only when privately owned, and private capital does its job best only when aided by the division of labor, free labor and freedom of contract, the competitive free market, free exchanges between peoples, and the entrepreneur-managed firm. Over and over Leroy-Beaulieu referred to these institutions as the motors of progress while characterizing individual enterprise as the mainspring of the whole mechanism.

Commentators often regard eighteenth- and nineteenth-century Liberalism as fundamentally a defense of private property. Certainly Leroy-Beaulieu made such a defense and supported the corollary institution of inheritance. Leroy-Beaulieu defended private property as passionately as liberty, calling these the "two conditions that preside over society's operation and evolution."[90] He defined property as "the absolute right of a man over the product of his efforts, over the things which he is the first to improve and to which he gives a durable form."[91] Leroy-Beaulieu saw emancipation of the individual as dependent on protection of property rights, for freedom is impossible when "things continue to be submitted to the community" and "persons are in constant subjection to the group or to the collectivity."[92]

According to Leroy-Beaulieu, private property emerges spontaneously from individual effort and provides the security of tenure that promotes investment. "The regime of private property is the system that is best in accord with both the most effort and the most products," he wrote.[93] On the basis of his premise that production outweighed every other interest, Leroy-Beaulieu placed ownership rights beyond almost any legitimate interference by society, affirming that the right over what one possesses includes the power to abuse the possession as well as to use it. Morally it is wrong to damage what one owns or to leave it undeveloped, but arbitrary, prejudiced intervention by ignorant and meddlesome public authorities would make private ownership "conditional" and thus endanger more than enhance productivity.[94] "Permanent private property, together with liberty, low prices and unhindered conveyance of land, enables a nation to avoid serious social crises; it develops production greatly because there is no menace hanging over those who make improvements," he stated.[95] As ownership of goods and land became more secure, Leroy-Beaulieu asserted, individuals profited even more from their efforts and talents and suffered increasingly from their faults and vices. The result was "to render societies, through the stimulation of all the energies they contained, more prosperous and more progressive."[96] This system of private property remains both natural and ideal, and alterations to it would be contrary to the best interests of society. The growth of production throughout modern capitalist enterprises added to the persuasiveness of this argument.

Proceeding to a defense of the right of inheritance, Leroy-Beaulieu posed the problem in deliberately provocative terms by contending that heirs have the right to be indolent even though such behavior is morally reprehensible. Against those who proposed abolition of inheritance or the imposition of very high inheritance taxes, he used the same productivist arguments he employed in the other parts of his economic ideology. Love of family is the principal motivation for saving; therefore, abolishing or taxing inheritances would reduce the incentive to accumulate capital. Furthermore, inheritance ensures the preservation of the bourgeoisie, the driving force of progress. The virtues of this social group more than compensate for the fact that some who inherit large amounts of wealth become idlers. Besides, liberty and responsibility militate against idleness since inactive members of the bourgeoisie would expend their fortunes and decline into a lower class.[97] The reproach of conscience and loss of reputation and position must suffice as sanctions; legal intervention would be much too dangerous, since it would ultimately undermine liberty and property.[98]

Private ownership of capital, secure possession of property, the wage system, and free labor are all vital to a sound economy, but their fecundity depends upon two essential figures in economic life, the entrepreneur and the capitalist. Following J.-B. Say's analysis faithfully, Leroy-Beaulieu carefully distinguished between these two actors in the economy.[99] The capitalist accumulates capital, in the form of savings and equipment, while the entrepreneur organizes output, with his own or borrowed capital. The two have produced the modern innovations and inventions that have brought enjoyment and ease to others.[100] The contributions of these valuable social types require favorable conditions, however, including economic autonomy for businessmen, sufficient material rewards, and a disciplined labor force. Just as in *La Question Ouvrière* and *Le Collectivisme*, Leroy-Beaulieu declared that entrepreneurs should receive greater remuneration than their employees because good intellectual work is rarer and more valuable to society than manual labor.[101] Similarly, the capitalists acting through entrepreneurs should control the firms and the workers should always be subordinates.[102] Industry "would lose unity of action, élan, and the tendency toward progress" if the entrepreneur became merely a constitutional monarch or president instead of the real decision maker in a firm.[103] The entrepreneur is the hero of economic progress. Within the firm the entrepreneur is the "nerve center which provides the life, the intelligence, the direction."[104]

The entrepreneur and the capitalist can exist only in societies governed by the principles of liberty and personal responsibility. Liberty entails the right to choose one's career, to move freely, to emigrate, and to choose a place of residence. It also, of course, includes freedom for entrepreneurs from bureaucratic meddling. Freedom is beneficial because the prospect of gain is a more effective motivation than the threat of law. True liberty exists in the modern West because people are masters of themselves and, consequently, can be held morally responsible for their acts.[105]

Leroy-Beaulieu viewed accountability in economic life as the "great motive" behind the development of production. Everyone should profit or suffer from the results of his work and industry.[106] When entrepreneurs fail, it is because of personal faults such as imprudence and incapacity. The resulting hardship they experience is harsh but necessary. Personal responsibility is essential to efficient production, and therefore it is in the best interest of society not to weaken the force of personal responsibility in any way.[107]

Leroy-Beaulieu praised the "invisible hand" of the market for its role in disciplining economically wayward individuals. He characterized this impersonal regulating force as more efficient than social institutions in compelling people to contribute to economic progress. He drew a parallel between the way gravity and weight automatically produce a leveling of liquid in connected vessels and the way the market brings about an assignment of prices. Echoing faithfully the prevailing Liberal doctrine, he wrote that free competition launches society in a single direction "at full steam" but also provides built-in "counterweights" and "brakes."[108] Even though he admitted that noneconomic motives can disturb the productive and distributive machine, he maintained that the marketplace is substantially an automatic mechanism that operates without depending upon the error-prone faculty of human judgment and seldom needs outside correction. The market assigns profits and positions as they should be assigned, without conscious intervention by organized social authorities: "Whoever renders . . . service to society, by provisioning it more cheaply than others, receives his recompense, without any need to set into motion any examining boards, [which are] always hesitant or close-minded, full of prejudices."[109] Switching from mechanical terms to biological ones, Leroy-Beaulieu characterized competition as "an instinctive and spontaneous force." Such a force is the best means by which to bring order and coherence to the economy, because "instinct . . . is the result of the adaptation of a being to the milieu in which it lives."[110] While the market is not infallible, it acts "with precision, rapidity, and . . . an invariable (*habituelle*) sureness." Competition "constitutes the most energetic stimulant that could exist for humanity" because it "leads men by the two most powerful sentiments: hope and fear."[111]

Yet Leroy-Beaulieu moderated his claims for the market. Recalling his comparison of economics to pure and applied science, he conceded midway in his chapter on competition that these market forces have in theory "a more mechanical, more regular, and more ample action than one notices in practice."[112] Not only do individuals have other motives beside economic ones, but government has the right to supervise such matters as rights of way, water supply, and other services—though Leroy-Beaulieu almost immediately went on to list the disadvantages of public enterprises and the imperfections of government monopolies.[113] He limited the extent of free competition by clarifying that it must not compromise "the exercise of the rights of maintaining public order and security (*droits de police*), the protection of minors . . . and, obviously, the interests either of public health, morality, infants, or adolescents." Despite the qualifications, however, Leroy-Beaulieu continued to argue against governmental or social interference with the market and in favor of competition, not government, as the best protector of society's interests.[114] Production, he reiterated, depends on liberty. While he did not ignore the value of punishment for irresponsible uses of liberty, he wanted to leave this retribution largely in the hands of market forces. Thus he insisted that government must do nothing to shield individuals from the unfortunate consequences of their own economic failures. Freedom from excessive interference by the state is the most beneficial liberty for the creative businessman, and thereby for all of society.

There are no surprises, consequently, in volume four, where Leroy-Beaulieu discussed areas of possible collective action. In the interval between the publication of *L'Etat Moderne* and the completion of the *Traité* Leroy-Beaulieu had not undergone any fundamental change of heart on this score. He restated the dangers state action would pose to individual initiative and presented his standard objections to social-security programs in the same insistent manner, connecting government assistance programs with individual laziness as directly as if he had never doubted the concept of Economic Man. Leroy-Beaulieu delimited the state's role just as he had in his earlier writings, reluctantly but firmly assigning it a wide range of activities—such as preparation of colonies, promotion of population growth, and establishment of national systems of education—that strict adherents of laissez-faire rejected, but taking no significant additional steps. And he came no closer than he had in 1889—or in 1870—to suggesting a general principle that would determine when a proposed piece of economic legislation is wrong. Volume 4 shows how little the economist had changed, how little the new ideas he mentioned in the introduction had penetrated into his fundamental ideology. In the end the *Traité d'Economie Politique* is completely of a piece with *De la Répartition des Richesses*, *Le Collectivisme*, and *L'Etat Moderne*, even if lacking the stridency of those earlier works.

8
The Last Twenty Years

■ After the publication of the *Traité d'Economie Politique* Leroy-Beaulieu rested insofar as he was prone to rest, on his laurels. Even though he continued working long hours, he did not produce a significant doctrinal work for more than fifteen years. He did revise older books, but the revisions were often limited to the addition of new prefaces. Even in his lectures at the Collège de France he sometimes spent the year on a topic he had already covered, although he may well have added material in the process.[1] On the other hand, *De la Colonisation* grew in each new edition until it required two volumes. He also continued his unremitting labor for his own periodical, persistently fulminating against the income tax, the Radicals, and the protectionists just as he had been doing for decades. Finally, in 1913, Leroy-Beaulieu brought out a new book, *La Question de la Population*, based almost certainly on lectures he had given over the years at the Collège de France.

The public knew Leroy-Beaulieu mainly as a financial expert and as editor of *L'Economiste Français*. His journal continued to flourish, and in its pages Leroy-Beaulieu still gave advice to investors and scolded governments for their prodigality. *L'Economiste Français* also drew some notable advertising revenues from the Russian government, which through its agent Arthur Raffalovitch, placed a considerable number of financial notices. In the 1920s Raffalovitch wrote that he had used these advertisements and outright cash bribes to get a favorable press for Russian loans from a number of important newspapers and magazines. However, Leroy-Beaulieu's hands were always clean. From the beginning he had approved of investments in Russian government securities and willingly accepted promotional pieces from the Russian agent; there was no evidence that he had taken bribes. Indeed he appears to have been rigidly honest, and Leroy-Beaulieu prided himself on having warned the public against the Panama Canal scheme and other unwise and highly speculative investments.[2]

Even though he stopped running for the Chamber of Deputies after 1890, Leroy-Beaulieu never abandoned political activity.[3] He participated in the movement for colonial expansion, becoming a leading figure in such organizations as the Comité de l'Afrique Française and the Comité de l'Asie Française that promoted imperialism.[4] His main contributions to the cause were the four new editions of *De la Colonisation* that appeared between 1886 and 1908. On domestic issues Leroy-Beaulieu remained a persistent opponent of the republican governments. Generally the course of legislation drew his wrath, but above all he resented the government's refusal to reduce taxation of the well-to-do and its increasing regulation of private business.[5] In 1898 he recognized the existence of a "moderate party" and applauded its resistance to a progressive income tax. Nevertheless, the moderates also disappointed him because their support enabled the passage of a progressive tax on inheritances. More broadly, the constitution seemed to him to be fundamentally flawed. The country, he complained, had placed its faith in the Senate "as the means to ensure respect for our liberal traditions and the fundamental principles of our law," but this legislative body was totally failing to perform its function. From the turn of the century to the brink of World War I, he consistently protested that the Third Republic endangered the possessing classes because the regime was one of "pure universal suffrage without counterbalances."[6]

In the late 1890s the agonizing Dreyfus Affair became the dominating feature of French political life. As early as 1890 Leroy-Beaulieu had commented disdainfully on the rising current of anti-Semitism in his country.[7] Yet, although Aumercier declares that both brothers were Dreyfusards, Paul did not take any part that I can identify in the campaign to revise the sentence inflicted on Dreyfus.[8] Perhaps he shared the embarrassment and hesitations manifested in the *Revue des Deux Mondes*. At this time he was chair of the journal's Comité de Surveillance, and the editor-in-chief, Ferdinand Brunétière, was one of the leading Antidreyfusards among French intellectuals.[9] Rather late in the Dreyfus Affair, when the

Revue began to pay respectful attention to the demands for revision of the verdict, its political commentaries showed an uncomfortable effort to balance a concern for justice with a commitment to the Church and the army. At least the *Revue* did not take the stand that the individual did not matter, a position advanced by many Antidreyfusards. In any case, while Anatole Leroy-Beaulieu, by this time a prominent Catholic Liberal (and liberal Catholic), was one of the founders of a moderate organization that supported a retrial of Dreyfus, there is no sign that Paul lent his name and influence to that group or to any other.[10]

For about a decade and a half after the publication of the *Traité d'Economie Politique* probably the main development in the life of Leroy-Beaulieu was a personal or, rather, a familial one. His son, Pierre (b. 1871), began to make a mark for himself both in intellectual and in political life. Showing the same precocity as his father, Pierre published some notable works while still in his twenties. He even succeeded where his father had failed, achieving election to the Chamber of Deputies in 1906. In addition, he took on some of the editorial responsibilities for the *L'Economiste Français*.[11]

Yet in his own right the elder Leroy-Beaulieu remained a figure to reckon with. Strong in his opinions, capable of arduous hours of intellectual labor, imposing in his presence, he continued to command respect as a leader among French scholars. Weight of personality must have been a main source of the influence the grand bourgeois notable had in the Académie. After the death of Emile Levasseur in 1911 the economists of the old establishment signaled Leroy-Beaulieu's preeminence by electing him president of the Société d'Economie Politique, a post he held until his death.[12] Elsewhere his influence was not always as strong—at least in the aftermath of the Dreyfus Affair. In 1904, for instance, he backed the Antidreyfusard intellectual Ferdinand Brunétière for a chair at the Collège de France, but Brunétière lost the election. In a tone of angry contempt, Leroy-Beaulieu attributed this defeat to the efforts of the "false free thinkers" who, no doubt, opposed the editor of the *Revue* because of his Catholicism and because of his role during the Dreyfus Affair.[13] This defeat may indicate a decline in Leroy-Beaulieu's authority, but he remained one of the most visible publicists of the Liberal establishment until his death in 1916.

His last original work, *La Question de la Population*, permitted Leroy-Beaulieu to bask in the light of intellectual honor one more time. Before it was published, he read the proofs of the concluding sections at two meetings of the Académie and made a considerable impact. After a lively discussion, a committee of the august body recommended the award of a sizable prize to the author. At age seventy, Leroy-Beaulieu thus gained his sixth award from the Académie, this time without entering any competition.[14]

Although the work Leroy-Beaulieu did during the last twenty years of his life was seldom original, it is illustrative of the state of mind and opinions of the Liberal establishment. Still a major spokesman for Established Liberals and for dynamic business interests, he produced important propaganda in the campaigns against the growing forces of Socialism and interventionism, reiterating the time-worn Established Liberal theme that an enlarged state would endanger individual initiative and economic growth. Occasionally, he presented formerly heterodox solutions to new problems; in these cases his work informs us about changes in attitudes within the late nineteenth-century French elite.

The main new problems he confronted in the last two decades of his life revolved around fresh threats to France's security and prestige. Colonial conflicts with Britain culminated in the Fashoda incident of 1896–1898, while internally the Dreyfus Affair tore French society apart. After the Dreyfus incident was resolved around 1900, tensions between the European powers increased, and the threat of war with Germany intensified. Both domestic and international strife had a strong impact on Established Liberals. The battle over Dreyfus marked the passage of some former Liberals into the anti-Liberal camps on the political right. In the face of international conflict the nationalist feelings of men like Leroy-Beaulieu became stronger, and this nationalism warred with their Liberalism and with their often weak but still undeniable humanitarian impulses. For Leroy-Beaulieu this inner conflict can be traced in two areas of his late writings: on empire and on women.

There are three sides of the story of Leroy-Beaulieu and empire after he published the second edition of *De la Colonisation chez les Peuples Modernes*. One involves Leroy-Beaulieu's motivations for favoring overseas expansion, especially the relation he saw between colonial imperialism and peace. Another is his growing caution with regard to the future of the European empires. Finally there are his contradictory attitudes and actions with regard to the problem of the individual rights of the native inhabitants in French colonial territories. This last theme had the greatest bearing on the fate of his Liberalism.

Leroy-Beaulieu's colonial doctrine had a distinct humanitarian side,[15] but his nationalist motivations soon conflicted with his insistence that Europeans act on behalf of the native populations of the dependencies. The first signs of this conflict appeared in his inflammatory articles urging the conquest of Tunisia. Belligerent appeals to the masculine vanity of Frenchmen characterized his propaganda. On one occasion, with respect to a Moslem law the Bey of Tunis used to resist French economic penetration into his Regency, he declared: "We don't give a fig for the Hamefite rite or any other Moslem rite!" France must defend her dignity.[16] Similar insensitivity marked his response to the objections by English and Italian leaders to the annexation of Tunisia: "Let us do as Austria-Hungary did in Bosnia." The lukewarm supporter of self-determination had become a convert to the philosophy of "might makes right."[17] Significantly at this time he made one of his rare usages of the language of Social Darwinism, calling the conquest of Tunisia "a struggle for survival" for France.[18]

Nevertheless, soon after Leroy-Beaulieu wrote these almost brutal comments, he became president of a new organization, the Society for the Protection of the Natives in the Colonies, constituted in January 1882.[19] And in his many writings on French colonial territories he often stressed the need to protect native peoples from exploitation and oppression. In 1880 and 1882 he roundly criticized those among his countrymen who wanted Algeria incorporated immediately into France. Such a policy, he charged, ignores the existence of the natives and their mores.[20] From 1882 on he became more and more critical of French rule in Algeria. The generally optimistic preface to the first edition of his *L'Algérie et la Tunisie* (1887) showed some signs of apprehension. While he celebrated France's good fortune in having such huge territories so close to her southern ports, he warned that because of the native question the next quarter of a century would be decisive for France's rule over these lands. "Northwest Africa will belong to us definitively," he stated, "only if we conciliate the Arabs and, in a certain measure, Frenchify them."[21] Ten years later, in the preface to the 1897 edition of the same book, he wrote more pessimistically. Although the territories were an economic success, he felt that the "moral situation" of Algeria had deteriorated. "All elements of the population—colonists, indigenous peoples, Jews—are in a state of hostility and distrust toward the others," he lamented. The vice in the whole social structure, he implied, was the denial of voting rights to the natives, which "constitutes an artificial and illogical state such as no other society has ever known."[22] Leroy-Beaulieu clearly had not lost his Liberal humanitarianism.

Yet his inner struggle to reconcile the interests of the invaders and the natives persisted. In "The Philosophy of Colonization," a new chapter written for the 1891 edition of *De la Colonisation*, he expanded his justifications of the right of Europeans to intervene in the lives of Asians and Africans. Unless the active and progressive nations of Europe promoted change in the tropics, he claimed, the societies in that region would remain stagnant, failing to develop their resources. It would be a crime for productive Europeans to be crowded into their tiny homelands while "infantile" peoples had more land than they could use.[23] European and especially French interests always took priority over the welfare of the natives, even when Leroy-Beaulieu protested against the mistreatment of the native Algerians. While he wanted to increase the number of enfranchised Algerians, he also said the number of Algerian voters should never exceed the number of voters of European origin.[24] Moreover, he opposed those who wanted to treat the Arabs as an indigenous nation and leave their native customs untouched. Despite his sincere humanitarian sympathies he never reversed his statement of 1882:

> If one respected scrupulously and minutely all the usages, all the customs of the indigenous peoples, if one avoided bringing any disturbance into their property arrangements and their existence, one would not draw from the country the resources it contained nor assure to French Africa the future it could attain.[25]

Leroy-Beaulieu taught that imperialism must be accompanied by a civilizing mission, but he placed both world economic development and maintenance of France's greatness ahead of native rights.

Leroy-Beaulieu was deeply committed to protecting France's stature while preserving peace with other European nations. The relationship between imperialism, nationalism, and peace remained prominent in Leroy-Beaulieu's thought in the late 1890s and afterwards. Imperialist conflicts may well have strengthened his nationalism even beyond his fervor of 1880. When the French government in 1898 had to withdraw its exploratory mission from Fashoda in the Sudan in the face of a much larger British force, the humiliation evidently disturbed Leroy-Beaulieu for years. In 1904, in his book promoting the trans-Saharan railroad scheme, he emphasized that such a railroad network in 1898 would have allowed France to reinforce its troops in the Sudan, with the result that "Great Britain would then have lowered its tone; she would have discussed African issues peaceably and . . . on a footing of equality."[26] Leroy-Beaulieu did not want to be bellicose toward the British; on the contrary, he believed that one of the chief virtues of imperialism was that it could preserve peace among the Great Powers. In the 1891 edition of *De la Colonisation*, he optimistically suggested that the new field of activity for European nations meant the beginning of a long era without wars between them. He characterized colonization as the safety valve of Europe because the powers of the continent could satisfy their ambitions for expansion without battling each other.[27] Eventually, however, his hopes regarding the blessings of imperialism began to diminish, and before World War I his language about international affairs underwent a revolution. In 1908, expressing caution about whether France should take control of Morocco, he revealed a startling reversal of opinion: "A continental nation . . . should never lose sight of its need to defend its own frontiers."[28] By 1908 he was once again worried about France's security within Europe, and that year's edition of his treatise on colonization was the last. Instead he turned to a set of topics he had briefly examined earlier but which became an obsession in the prewar years: the relationship of the rate of French population growth to the emancipation of women, and to the military strength and world standing of his country.

To trace Leroy-Beaulieu's views on the connection between women, population, and national strength, we must begin with the monthly meeting of the Société d'Economie Politique in June 1884. There he participated in a discussion that enables us to see the stability of his views and the degree to which other Established Liberals agreed with him. The topic, placed on the agenda by Frédéric Passy, was: "Where, from the point of view of political economy, is a better place for woman: the family home or the workshop?" Among those taking part was Jules Simon, a senator and former prime minister whose pioneering 1860 book on working women, *L'Ouvrière*, had made him a recognized expert on the subject. Of the five speakers, only Simon argued strongly that the only proper role for a woman was as mother and homemaker. Above all, he disliked admitting the daughters of the bourgeoisie into secondary education, where they wasted their time studying algebra, geometry, chemistry, physics, and "historical curiosities good only for scholars." Instead he wanted them to learn how to cook, how to care for infants (by serving in nursery schools), and how to keep household linens in order. He breathed a sigh of relief that "he had not been put in peril of marrying a professoress" (agréegée).[29]

Everyone else who took the floor, including Leroy-Beaulieu, began by agreeing that it is preferable for women to stay at home raising children, but all made the point with far less enthusiasm. The first speaker, Passy, provided the strategy that the others followed. After he echoed Jules Michelet's formula that the wife's task is to direct the spending of what the husband earned, he quickly changed ground. Like Leroy-Beaulieu in *Travail des Femmes*, he insisted that circumstances made it impossible to eliminate women from the work force. Moreover, he felt women's economic role should expand in the area of medicine, because "the care of women and children seems by nature reserved to women themselves." Finally, he deplored the discrimination against women in the French code of civil law.[30]

E. Fournier de Flaix, an economic journalist, went even further. While he acknowledged that factory work was full of "grave inconveniences" for women, he added that they would inevitably have to work in factories, since large-scale industry would be in existence for a long time. Immediately he added, "In reality work is one of the forms as well as one of the conditions for the emancipation of women." He not only lauded women's contribution to "the task of production" but he also advocated improving their wages so that they could acquire "a necessary independence from their husbands, their fathers, and their brothers." His liberationist bent is explained at least in part by his final comment. He deplored the spectacle of the subjection of women revealed by the study of history and from travel in non-Western societies. As a Liberal he was repelled when he saw people deprived of the freedom to achieve autonomy.[31]

Emile Cheysson, a major figure in the effort to solve the Social Question by promoting paternalism among employers, also took the floor. To outflank Simon, he too relied on the practical arguments that women would have to continue working in factories because they had no other source of income and because society needed to keep goods flowing abundantly from the machines. A good example of the generosity of "reformers" like Cheysson was his support of legislation that would limit women to a workweek of six eleven-hour days so they would have some time left to maintain their homes.[32]

Leroy-Beaulieu similarly championed a limited but still real improvement in the working conditions of adult women in factories, and his remarks suggest that he shared Passy and Fournier de Flaix's approach to women's rights. Brushing off the comments of Simon, who had immediately preceded him, he repeated the judgment that in the modern world working-class women must have jobs outside the home. The only hope he held out for restoring the ideal of the woman maintaining the household and raising children was that technology would some day develop light, portable machines that would return production once again to the home (a possibility the optimistic Cheysson also mentioned). Yet the foreseeable tendency was for production to be carried out by big industries. Like Cheysson, Leroy-Beaulieu believed a shorter workweek was the practical means by which to combine employment and domestic duties. He recommended the British system, which limited work to half a day on Saturdays, as the way to permit married women to do housework. He also sounded the theme of emancipation, although more quietly than either Passy or Fournier de Flaix, when he reminded his audience that, in the past, women confined to the home had often held a status little better than that of a slave. The clear implication was that, since slavery was a terrible evil, a factory job marked a definite improvement for a woman of the humbler classes. However, Leroy-Beaulieu did not go so far as to admit that women had a right to their own lives, independent of their supposed biological function as mothers and homemakers. He focused on practical economic questions rather than on the concept of women as free and autonomous individuals. While his views tended (as they had in 1870) toward supporting the emergence of women from the home and even, under the right conditions, to their partial liberation from male authority, his deepest concern was for industrial efficiency and the protection of profits.[33]

With the exception of Simon, the contributors gave only lip service to the respectable position that women should be domestic creatures. They were, therefore, more favorable to women's right to work than were advanced republicans and radical reformers. Their position rested mainly on pragmatic foundations, as they argued that women needed paid employment to support themselves and their families and that society could not afford to lose them from the work force. But the Liberal principle of free labor also came into play, dictating that women had an unimpeachable right to be free economic agents. Even Simon carefully stated his opposition to government constraint as a means of keeping mothers from working outside the home. Self-interest as well as principles, however, may have played a role in leading the speakers to favor women being in the work force. Leroy-Beaulieu, Cheysson, and other economists, after all, were capitalists as well as intellectuals.

From a present-day feminist perspective, the views of these economists have serious limitations since none of them challenged head-on the dominant stereotype of women as biologically suited only for domestic activity. Still, Passy and Fournier de Flaix exhibited a strong element of idealism, while Leroy-Beaulieu and Cheysson agreed that mature individuals should be free from abitrary domination by others. Leroy-Beaulieu certainly understood that women had suffered terribly from their position of subjection. And all four believed that the opportunities offered by modern industry would put an end to that subjection. Despite their hesitations, these speakers illustrate the emancipatory side of nineteenth-century Established Liberalism. In this regard, Leroy-Beaulieu's support for women's right to work was in accord with an important Liberal current of opinion, and, judging from the speakers at this meeting, it was the prevailing view among Established Liberal economists. Although his position was partly a by-product of his desire to protect the interests of employers, this economic concern helped him become sensitive to postadolescent women's need for jobs and their right to work.

Leroy-Beaulieu never completely turned his back on women's claim to a degree of economic independence. Nevertheless, as the increased menace of war and his nationalist feelings eroded aspects of his Liberalism, he began to sense an incompatibility between women's right to work and the need of *la patrie* for more offspring. Toward the end of his life his concern over the rights of individuals declined as he felt more and more acutely the dangers faced by his homeland. Nationalism made even more acute the already existing tensions between his defense of women's economic rights, his proposals for maintaining their "purity" and encouraging them to become homemakers and mothers, and his desire to protect the economic system.

The problem of France's stagnating population gave rise to the conflict between Liberal views of the condition of women and nationalist fears and ambitions. During the last twenty or thirty years of the nineteenth century, theorists examining population trends still trembled under the shadow cast by Malthus's dire predictions of overpopulation and consequent misery for the masses. This timorous outlook hardly seemed justified as France experienced a number of years in the late 1800s when deaths actually outnumbered births and only immigration from abroad maintained the level of population. Around 1900 French social scientists and politicians came to recognize the irrelevance of Malthus's doctrines to their country. The prospect of war, on the other hand, became far more menacing. The defeat in 1905 of France's one ally, Russia, was followed by the 1906 and 1912 crises over Morocco, bringing France to the brink of war with its far more populous and prosperous antagonist, Germany. In this ominous context French nationalists saw the declining birth rate as a serious threat to the country's safety.

Leroy-Beaulieu turned regularly to the question of the causes of population decline in both *L'Economiste Français* and *Revue des Deux Mondes*, publishing an important study of the problem in the latter journal in 1897. Several times he also devoted his year-long course of lectures at the Collège de France to the topic. Although the yearly statistics on births and deaths troubled him throughout the 1880s and 1890s, he refused to use alarmist rhetoric and referred in quite calm terms to the military consequences of France's lack of population growth. In the first decade of the twentieth century, however, his attitude shifted. In 1911 he even told a session of the Académie of the shocking likelihood that the native French stock could die out within five generations, during which the country would become progressively weaker as a result of its small population and the large numbers of unassimilated immigrants within its borders. So serious was the situation that he accepted a remedy he had rejected earlier: family allowances provided by the state.[34] By 1913, in his five-hundred-page survey *La Question de la Population*, he was openly expressing "anguish" over the dangers posed by the decline in the birth rate.[35]

Leroy-Beaulieu always viewed demographic developments as the result of fundamental social changes. As early as 1877 he wrote that "the progress of civilization," combined with the increased desire for social mobility that had prevailed since the French Revolution, led fathers to limit the size of their families. And he characterized the wish for higher status as a democratic aspiration. He repeated this analysis—adding the erosion of religious belief as a key factor—in all his later writings on the topic.[36] The term *civilization* denoted changes he generally favored: the spread of modern industrial technology, the increase of production, the high degree of material comfort enjoyed by the "middle classes," the ability of the able to improve their status.[37] Regarding the impact of the yearning for social mobility he became much less sanguine in the 1890s. "A man," he said in 1897, "imagines that he might become more important in society" or that his family will achieve a higher rank if he has few children and passes on his property to only one or two offspring. He condemned these men of middling status for their egoism and unbridled social ambitions (which happened, of course, to threaten the position of Leroy-Beaulieu's own class). He also faulted workers in France and in Britain for their mistaken application of economic doctrine. Labor leaders were persuading workers that wages could be raised if the workers limited the number of their children and thus reduced the eventual supply of labor. Unions ignored the fact that the number of workers in all countries has an influence on wages in any particular country.[38]

After the late 1870s Leroy-Beaulieu wrote only a few brief remarks about the role of women in France's demographic crisis, but both his comments and his omissions are revealing. In discussing the use of birth control to limit the size of families, he implied that French *men* were the ones deciding to limit the number of their offspring. He apparently did not consider the possibility that wives may have joined in this decision, or that women were revolting against the miseries and dangers of multiple pregnancies. This area of the experience of women was utterly closed to him. Nevertheless, he did observe in 1897 that in every class of society "a number of young women resign themselves to being single or even choose this state because the more and more independent and varied life assured by modern civilization is sufficient for them."[39] Significantly, he did not condemn this attitude, but simply reported it. Thus he believed that the birth rate was suffering because some young women were making the (permissible) decision to avoid marriage and because the husbands of married women were making the (immoral) decision to avoid having children.

By 1890 he no longer confined his attention to women doing manual labor. Beginning in the 1880s, as France's secular-minded republican governments engaged in a massive expansion of educational opportunities for females as well as males, many teaching posts had become available to women. More women also were finding careers in medicine, as Passy had hoped. And, attracted in part by the cheapness and pliability of a female work force, government employers provided ever-greater numbers of clerical jobs for women in post offices and telegraph and telephone facilities. Looking at these transformations in 1890, Leroy-Beaulieu speculated that "young ladies who have adopted liberal or semiliberal careers" have fewer opportunities for marriage. He hastily added that "it is far from our intention to condemn either education in general or that of women in particular," but he did condemn the "craze of the age" for "unlimited and injudicious" education and philanthropy, although without proposing any answer to the problem.[40] In 1897 Leroy-Beaulieu pointed, presumably with disapproval, to another relationship between "the progress of civilization" and the resistance of women to having children. He wrote that "among the educated classes a great number of diverse and highly varied pleasures compete to a certain degree with the elementary pleasure of sexual relationships." He claimed that this factor was far from negligible and was particularly important for women.[41]

Leroy-Beaulieu's treatment of infant mortality, a problem intimately connected with any consideration of family life and population trends, provides further insight into his worldview. Others, including reformist Liberals connected with the Solidarist movement, were pointing to France's high infant mortality as a source of its population crisis.[42] Leroy-Beaulieu mentioned the problem in 1880 in the first of a proposed series of articles on population. The second article cited figures from Jacques Bertillon's *Statistique Humaine de la France* to support the view that commentators had "exaggerated" the rate of infant mortality in France. Leroy-Beaulieu granted that the Scandinavian countries had a better record, and he pointed out that France would gain 67,000 persons per year if it could match the Scandinavian mortality rate, but he emphasized that France's rate was average for Europe.[43] Since he never wrote the third article, in which he promised to draw conclusions from the data, we do not know how he might have proposed to decrease the mortality rate. From his writings of the 1890s and from *La Question de la Population* we discover that he practically ignored the subject afterward. In his 1897 article, for the *Revue des Deux Mondes*, he referred once briefly to the death rate in general and said that it should be reduced to that of England and Belgium.[44] But he gave no attention to the health of infants and children.

Similar indifference to the problem of infant mortality appeared in December 1911 when Leroy-Beaulieu took the floor at the Académie to respond to a report on the high correlation linking alcoholism and other adult health problems with stillbirths and infant deaths. Rejecting the report entirely, Leroy-Beaulieu asserted that the causes of population decline were almost exclusively "moral" rather than material; that is, the problem derived from conscious decisions to avoid having children, not from physical factors that damage the health of potential parents.[45] By this time Leroy-Beaulieu must have been working on *La Question de la Population*, yet the book completely ignored the subject of infant mortality. In effect Leroy-Beaulieu's silence implied that it was irrelevant to reform the conditions of factories where women were employed; those conditions had nothing to do with improving the physical health of potential and actual mothers.

The bafflement and ambiguity that characterized Leroy-Beaulieu's treatment of women's work and procreation in the 1890s are even more present in his last words on these topics. In *La Question de la Population* he repeated his analysis of 1890 and 1897, connecting the feminist movement of that day with the low birth rate in France. He described this movement as a "new feature of civilization," one seeking "the emancipation of women and their admission to every profession, whether industrial, scientific, administrative or political, many of which have been and are still either in practice or in law the exclusive province of men." He was not thinking primarily of France, where the feminist movement had not yet brought about major changes. Rather, he cited "the Anglo-Saxon countries" and remained uncertain as to what long-range developments would ensue in France. "Nevertheless," he reported, women were becoming "more and more numerous in public administration, education, postal, telegraphic, and telephone services, banks, and railroad offices, and they had infiltrated the medical profession." The ambiguity of his position is reflected in his half positive, half negative judgment of the principles underlying this process. In language reminiscent of Fournier de Flaix's 1884 speech, he declared that the desire of women for independence "is profoundly worthy of respect" and that women could justifiably claim equality with men. Then he shifted ground and declared that feminists demanded something else: "to become more and more like men and to live like them."[46]

The ambiguities continued as Leroy-Beaulieu advocated maintenance of "legally consecrated natural division of functions between the sexes." While "it is doubtless necessary," he went on, "to give more rights to women, to make them mistresses of their salaries and savings," feminist propaganda is "a serious peril to the civilization." It is "*déssechant et stérilisant*"; that is, it dries up the feelings and leads women to sterility.[47] Once more he refrained from suggesting repression through law, but his remarks on education and labor laws plainly reflected his sense that the national interest outweighed concern for individual well-being. He did not, however, go so far as to propose that women's duty to the nation should eradicate their interest in their careers, their personal independence, or their physical health. He had not become a complete antifeminist. Instead he had moved in two conflicting directions: toward a fuller recognition of women's claims for equality and toward frustration over the consequences of those claims.

Unwilling to quarrel with the egalitarian planks of the feminist program, Leroy-Beaulieu unleashed a barrage against the birth control movement. Designating it as Neomalthusianism, he protested the weakness of the government's response to propaganda for birth-control devices and abortion. He regretted that those who damaged the nation by disseminating birth-control leaflets and magazines could be prosecuted only under laws forbidding offenses to public decency, for which the punishments were light. He demanded that the legislature inflict heavy fines for this activity and heavy jail sentences (of up to three years) for repeat offenders.[48] There is no sign of misogyny in his polemic, as he did not single out women as the prime movers in the Neomalthusian cause; in fact, he refrained from any references to the gender of birth-control supporters. But he continued to demonstrate a complete ignorance of women's reasons for seeking greater control over the reproductive process.

La Question de la Population shows how little change had occurred in Leroy-Beaulieu's outlook on women and the population question since the early 1880s. Although he stated even more forcefully his support for the social and economic emancipation of women, his ambiguities and his criticisms of the women's movement reveal that he had moved very little not only from the position he held in 1884 but even from his paternalism-tinged views of 1870. The one major change was the degree to which nationalism had undermined his Established Liberal beliefs about legitimate state action. In 1870, in "La Question Ouvrière," he defended the traditional Liberal principle that all people have a right to propagate any point of view.[49]

But in 1913 he wanted strict repression of the ideas of family-planning organizations. In addition, despite his usual hostility to interference in the economic and social realms and his constant desire to reduce government expenditures, he reversed his previous stand by urging that the state subsidize families so as to promote population growth. Yet he suggested no other services, such as government-sponsored day care, that might have served as incentives for women. Instead he may have counted on a revival of religion and family-centered traditions to influence them to have more children.

La Question de la Population shows how much nationalism and the prospect of war with Germany had eaten away at Leroy-Beaulieu's Liberalism and his liberal attitudes toward women. He commented on the rise of professional women, especially primary-school teachers, and lamented their lack of children while grudgingly accepting their right to pursue careers. Although a secularist at heart, he called for a revival of religion as a means of turning families away from birth control. Finally, he abandoned his commitment to freedom of expression by demanding that the state prohibit birth-control propaganda. And he urged the state to favor large families even while he completely ignored the search for ways to improve France's infant mortality rate.

For several weeks after Leroy-Beaulieu had read from his manuscript in 1913, members of the Académie des Sciences Morales et Politiques came to the rostrum to respond. They enthusiastically accepted his values and much of his analysis. His interventionist stances did not outrage them, and most of these patriotic Established Liberals joined him in deploring the decline of French military strength and in attacking the birth-control movement. One speaker even went so far as to say that the propaganda for limiting family size amounted to the crime of "lèse patrie."[50] Most of the speakers supported punitive measures against the birth-control movement, although some said that legislation would be ineffective and that some other response must be found. Despite this disagreement on how to solve the problem, the areas of agreement were much greater. The unsolicited ten-thousand-franc prize the Academicians conferred on Leroy-Beaulieu demonstrated their admiration.

That achievement came at a time of sadness and on the brink of a period of tragedy for Paul Leroy-Beaulieu. In 1910 he lost his brother Anatole, and two years later his wife died. Then came the military test that Leroy-Beaulieu and his contemporaries had antici-pated with such dread. The economist devoted his immense energies and abilities as a publicist to the service of his country: from the outbreak of World War I, every one of his lead articles in *L'Econo-miste Français* surveyed the military developments of the previous week. In January 1915 he imposed on himself the awful task of writing the obituary of his son, an artillery officer killed in battle at the age of forty-three. Paul Leroy-Beaulieu's last major public role was as president of the Union des Pères et Mères dont les Fils sont Morts Pour la Patrie.[51] The widower and grief-stricken father survived his son by less than two years, succumbing suddenly in December 1916, after a one-week bout with influenza. Perhaps the story of his last words is apocryphal, but like many such stories it is appropriate. We are told that he asked for pen and paper because "I've work to do."[52]

9
Leroy-Beaulieu in the History of Liberalism

■ This account of Paul Leroy-Beaulieu's writings confirms that his friend and biographer René Stourm was right to stress the "unity and continuity" of his ideas and beliefs.[1] In an era when old faiths were shaken and reeling and when thinking people often searched for absolute verities to replace what the culture had lost, Leroy-Beaulieu was raised in a milieu saturated with the view of life expounded by postrevolutionary Liberalism. Neither family, teachers, nor members of his social stratum had encouraged him to think critically about his intellectual heritage. On the contrary, the self-evidence of these views must have constantly been brought to his attention. Furthermore, no experiences in his later life shattered any of his certainties. Consequently, from the mid-1860s onward Leroy-Beaulieu's views remained within a very narrow spectrum. Although the balance of forces within Leroy-Beaulieu changed as nationalist feelings came to play a more important role in his thought, almost every intellectual trait found in the young publicist still appeared in the mature and eminent economist. Throughout his life he was preoccupied with basically the same range of contemporary problems, and he approached them with the same set of values, intellectual tools, and presuppositions.

Leroy-Beaulieu's contemporaries saw him as a representative figure, one of the main exemplars of the leading school of social and economic thought of his time, what the French then and now have simply termed "Liberalism." In addition, the course of his career and his lifelong professional milieu and associations conformed to the grand bourgeois pattern. The movement of his thought, which was in a circular orbit rather than in a linear, evolutionary path, paralleled the intellectual development of his colleagues in the Liberal grand bourgeois intellectual establishment. As such a typical representative of this group, Leroy-Beaulieu also exhibits the impasses that Established Liberalism arrived at by the end of the nineteenth century. His identification with the Grande Bourgeoisie was not only the strongest influence on his outlook but also the source of the pessimism and growing antiliberalism that became a noticeable aspect of his thought as his life drew to a close.

These aspects of Leroy-Beaulieu's situation and life have been discussed in detail in the foregoing chapters. Now it is time for an overview of this French economist as a thinker, a Liberal, and a person. To see Leroy-Beaulieu as a whole we need to characterize his class position, his ideals, thought processes, and underlying assumptions. We will look at his basic convictions about the nature of truth, the universe, the individual, society, history, and change. Then we will be in a good position to understand why little of his thought ever developed but instead remained rooted in the place it had reached in 1870. To complete the portrait we began in the first chapter, we will place Leroy-Beaulieu in the history of Liberalism and especially the Liberalism of his time and ours. The result will be some cautionary observations about where we are today in the West.

Raised in a high stratum of the broad bourgeois sector, Leroy-Beaulieu succeeded in rising into the Grande Bourgeoisie while still in his thirties. Even before then, in the waning years of the Second Empire, his professional associations were exclusively in milieux dominated by the Grande Bourgeoisie. He quickly succeeded in gaining admission to the Liberal establishment. Shortly before his socially and financially advantageous marriage, he was writing articles for the *Revue des Deux Mondes* and in the early 1870s he began contributing pieces to the other outstanding mouthpiece of the Liberal Grande Bourgeoisie, the *Journal des Débats*. His participation in the Ecole Libre des Sciences Politiques is also a sign of his class allegiance, since that school was designed to prepare the offspring of elite families for political and administrative posts. By the early 1880s he was an active participant in the Société d'Economie Politique and the Académie des Sciences Morales et Politiques, elite groups that strengthened his inclinations to celebrate the superiority of his social class and to dedicate himself to preserving the existing social structure. Since he never sought or obtained a university post, he did not have to engage regularly in the discipline of considering opposing sides of a question, as was normal in French higher education. Instead, as a member of the Academy and the economic establishment, he was surrounded by others who were just as certain that they had possession of the truth and that it was their duty to propagate and defend it uncompromisingly. Furthermore, his elite status during an era of growing social segregation meant that Leroy-Beaulieu lived at a great emotional and physical distance from working people. He almost always relied on published statements and reports, not personal experience, when he described the attitudes and desires of laborers or even of the shopkeeping middle class.

Leroy-Beaulieu's politics further confirms this class analysis. He was truly an heir of the Orleanists of the July Monarchy, remaining faithful to the spirit of that heritage if not to all its details. Before the fall of the Second Empire he praised constitutional monarchy, and during the political struggles of the 1870s he was close to the Centre Gauche and the *Constitutionnels*, two political groupings composed largely of figures from the old bourgeois elite. His limited success and bitter frustrations in politics also matched that of the Grande Bourgeoisie. Like so many others of his class he achieved election to a departmental *Conseil Général*. During the 1880s, while others of his status were losing their seats in the French parliament, Leroy-Beaulieu too failed in his races for national office. Even though his ambition to become a deputy met with repeated disappointment, he refused to modify his positions. While the French public repudiated or ignored Established Liberal orthodoxies, he made only very modest, often superficial changes in his social and economic doctrines.

In ideology as in politics Leroy-Beaulieu remained faithful to the Liberal regime that the Grande Bourgeoisie had helped establish between 1789 and 1830. That means, above all, that he favored the modern institutions that issued from the French Revolution and capitalism. A few passing comments in Leroy-Beaulieu's works project a relatively positive view of the events of 1789. For example, he referred to "our great reform of the end of the eighteenth century," and he characterized the original reforms as the work solely of the bourgeoisie at a time when the uprising was "unstained" (*immaculée*).[2]

These statements, though fragmentary, have a specific and crucial role in the economist's account of history. They indicated unequivocally to his contemporaries that he approved the way of life brought about by the revolutionaries and other modernizers of the early nineteenth century and rejected the historical doctrine of the Conservatives and reactionaries that saw the taking of the Bastille and the abolition of the Old Regime as kindred to a second fall of humankind.

As is true of any well-developed ideology, Leroy-Beaulieu's Liberal doctrine contains a vision of the good society. Leroy-Beaulieu's ideal society is epitomized by the word "civilization," a word he used constantly with strong emotive undertones. To him the attainment of "civilization" was the goal of historical development; conversely, the most reprehensible behavior possible was that which threatened to undo civilization and to return humanity to a state of "barbarism." Although he never formally defined these two concepts, his generalized, abstract sketches of the "state of nature" suggest that by barbarism he meant the primitive deprivation in which early men and women had lived. The forces of history, according to Leroy-Beaulieu, had gradually, almost unconsciously, and therefore naturally moved human beings from a state of savagery to the state of civilization. Leroy-Beaulieu associated barbarism with a lack of personal freedom and believed that civilization exists when servile labor is abolished and free enterprise is established. He also equated advanced stages of social development with flexibility (*plasticité*), technological dynamism, and ever-increasing material prosperity. For example, in the second volume of his economics treatise he wrote that a civilized society is "supple and adaptable, wide awake and intellectually keen." In such a society education, scientific knowledge and technological notions spread rapidly, and "new arrangements are hatched at every moment," especially new business ventures founded by enterprising individuals.[3] In 1913, in *La Question de la Population*, he gave another revealing definition. "By civilization," he stated, "we understand—besides the development of towns and of the middle class—the almost universal spread of prosperity (*l'aisance*) and education, the extension of leisure, the rise of individual and familial ambitions, the opening up of prospects for ascent of the social ladder." In such a society there is "access for all inhabitants to all positions."[4] In these evocative words he summed up the heritage of 1789 as his Established Liberal forebears had delivered it to his generation.

Leroy-Beaulieu's contrast between primitive and developed societies reflects his age's view of history as a story of material progress. Although he vaguely mentioned moral and intellectual development as the goal of social evolution, his concept of progress predominantly emphasized the slow but successful struggle to create abundance. Improving the human condition depended primarily on providing *more*: more material goods and more leisure. To Leroy-Beaulieu this was the basic duty of human beings. As he put it, "the development of the entire globe is the preeminent human task" because "it is profitable for everyone, though most profitable to the least well-off classes of civilized countries as a result of the abundance and cheapness of natural resources."[5] He identified two main, interlocking processes that made this greatest achievement of humankind possible. First, knowledge and techniques steadily improved because, in the absence of "extraeconomic causes, . . . every invention, every old discovery would be preserved."[6] Second, over the ages capital is maintained, renewed, and replaced, and saving adds new "parcels of capital." Thus, "the action of economic causes, when external factors do not trouble their action, appears to engender a continuous growth, however irregular, of production."[7]

Leroy-Beaulieu's ideal society would not be egalitarian, but deferential and stratified. Although he spoke favorably of the increase of equality and democracy, he remained attached throughout his career to a stratified society with the *classe bourgeoise* at the top. The guiding rule of the social structure would be imposed by nature: the inequality of social conditions tempered by the possibility of social mobility for the able and self-disciplined. The upper classes must be responsible and compassionate, unmarred by "levity and thoughtlessness." The lower classes should be full of "habits of respect for law, of deference for the elevated positions of society."[8] Perhaps the clearest illustration he gave was his very first: the description in *L'Etat Moral* of the ideal factory in which zealous, inventive, honest workers would still be respectfully subordinate, though out of "respect and deference" rather than "fear and necessity."[9] The ideal society, therefore, would be harmonious because individuals would know their places and their duties and all people would have the freedom to make their own future. Above all, it would be productive because of unanimous dedication to society's greatest moral duty: work. This is the dream that underlies all of Leroy-Beaulieu's social thought, and it is a grand bourgeois utopia.

The aspect of Leroy-Beaulieu's ideal that most transcended class egoism was his individualism. He would permit no administrative or social group to inhibit the endeavors of gifted individuals. He prized the right of every person, with or without property, to absolute liberty from control by any group: guilds, the state, unions, fellow workers.[10] The most deeply liberal aspect of his thought was his commitment to the sanctity of the autonomous, self-directing individual.

Leroy-Beaulieu believed he was serving the needs of all humanity when he defended the dominant institutions of the West and the dominant social class of his nation. For him free enterprise, class society, and elected governments characterized the highest form of human existence. Indeed he equated them with civilization itself. There is not a hint that he ever imagined the possibility of a stage of social existence superior to that found in France, Britain, and the United States in the 1870s. All his beloved institutions, of course, were the ones Liberals had developed or worked diligently to maintain. Thus we can call Leroy-Beaulieu's ideal the Liberal Regime, a term that is more precise and more usable than "civilization" or any other label he used.

Confidence certainly pervaded not just Leroy-Beaulieu's proclamation that the Liberal Regime was the best of all possible worlds; it was deeply rooted in all his thought processes. Such terms as "irrefutable" and "incontestable" appeared regularly when he made assertions about other people's motivations and behavior, the proper forms of social organization, or economic life. A primary source of his certainty is that he shared the belief of his time in an infallible scientific method, capable of producing unquestionable conclusions. Repeated comments in his writings show that Leroy-Beaulieu generally regarded the discovery of truth as quite unproblematic. The scientific method was totally reliable because of the character of the world it investigated. True knowledge is composed of statements of natural laws, and "all the laws of nature . . . are simple," he wrote in the *Traité d'Economie Politique*.[11] Despite occasional gestures toward other points of view, he accepted fully the mid-nineteenth-century dictum that laws of nature were rigid, immutable commands imposed on both the physical world and society. Objective observation and the establishment of absolutely true and universally valid generalizations were possible because of the invariability of nature. Since these permanent unalterable regularities are "relations between things," the existence of the laws does not depend upon human thought or fantasy; they are in nature whether we like them or not. [12] Even though European and American thinkers had challenged this view in the last third of the nineteenth century, Leroy-Beaulieu never offered proof for his contentions. His works of the 1880s and 1890s still proclaimed the nineteenth-century commonplace that natural laws "are the necessary relations that derive from the nature of things," a definition he took from Montesquieu. [13]

All observers should see the same *things* "out there" in the external world as long as they were perceptive and honest. Leroy-Beaulieu thus presupposed that such objective observation could uncover absolute verities about society and the economy. Using the term in currency for generations, he occasionally declared that important truths were "self-evident" (*de toute evidence*) to anyone who followed the proper scientific method. [14] Although Leroy-Beaulieu recognized that there are some realities that are not on the surface of things, he took it for granted that partially hidden aspects of the world could also be found by employing objective, cold observation. [15] Truth, then, is a set of uncomplicated, universally valid statements about nature that we are forced to live by even when we might perversely refuse to recognize their reality. Leroy-Beaulieu confirmed what his audience wished to believe: that truth is not relative or ambiguous or paradoxical.

According to Leroy-Beaulieu, statistics and historical study held a privileged status among the positive methods for uncovering those truths about society that are not self-evident. First, he treated knowledge that was quantifiable as especially authoritative. Seemingly unaware that statistical tables require interpretation, he commented on them as if they provided clear, unambiguous information. Second, history represented a storehouse of facts uncovered through thorough, unprejudiced research. Facts were documentable, and all coldly impartial investigators would come up with the same information about the past. When research is grounded in such indubitable data rather than on questionable abstractions, enlightened thinkers easily perceive the truth about society.

Leroy-Beaulieu's delight in solid facts is symptomatic of his unimaginative style of thinking. Indeed he explicitly scorned imagination, insisting that this mental process produced unrealistic social utopias. At first, however, this just-the-facts attitude did not translate into indifference to humanitarian concerns. Occasional comments in his early writings display his painful knowledge of the terrible conditions in which many people were living and working. He apparently experienced a struggle between such feelings and the unsentimental imperatives of Established Liberalism. Later he sympathized with efforts by private charities to build inexpensive housing for working people, and he participated in the activities of the Société d'Economie Sociale, which encouraged business owners to adopt paternalist policies toward their employees. However, Leroy-Beaulieu's lack of imagination often prevented him even from attempting to enter empathetically into the world in which others lived. This gap of understanding led him, for instance, to contend that allowing working wives half a day off on Saturdays would enable them to do the housework that would keep their homes and families in order. He also scorned limiting the workday to eight hours, not only on productivist grounds but because this reform would encourage "idleness, indiscipline, and flabbiness at work."[16] Thus he was expecting women to have energy left for housework after not forty-four but fifty or sixty hours a week of physical labor. He never seemed to question whether this was reasonable; after all, he himself found such contentment in a long day of writing, editing, and estate management.

Although Leroy-Beaulieu correctly asserted that he "did not have the honor of being a Positivist" (by which he meant a follower of Auguste Comte), he shared with that prophet of scientism the same materialistic, realistic, and earthbound ways of feeling and seeing.[17] His comments on morality and religion show that he had no more sense of the divine than did his Materialist and Positivist contemporaries. As a nonmystical person typical of his time, he also "did not like paradoxes one bit," and he "did not like to dress up reality."[18] Throughout the nineteenth century Liberals and others, most notably Comte and his school, had condemned abstract speculation and argumentation as "metaphysics." Leroy-Beaulieu joined them in condemning this type of thinking; thus in 1874 he praised the members of Chambers of Commerce for being men "who by the habits of their spirit and the direction of their interests are little inclined to be impassioned for abstract and general questions."[19] In the *Traité d'Economie Politique* he stated similar sentiments, claiming that the goal of his study was "a book thoroughly impregnated with reality" and rudely scoffing at those "subtle professors" who for thirty years "have expended a prodigious dose of ingeniousness in transforming economics into a new scholasticism, something frightfully complicated and desperately empty, infinite spider webs, woven with a marvelous art, and which serve no function."[20] Leroy-Beaulieu complained about the widespread "sophistries" about society and the economy, errors promulgated by thinkers whose wishes, angers, and resentments corrupted their judgment and caused them to rely on imagination rather than on objective observation. Socialists in general and Karl Marx in particular were his chief examples of sophists engaged in convoluted, fantasy-ridden reasoning. Airy metaphysicians, they fell into the error that social institutions had begun with some kind of social compact and deduced the equally mistaken corollary that people could intentionally remake society by means of a rationally and abstractly conceived plan.

Leroy-Beaulieu almost always entered intellectual debates as a prosecutor, reading Marx or Henry George or Albert Schaeffle not for illumination but in order to refute them. He preferred to poke holes in opposing arguments rather than to see if even their apparently weak statements might contain worthwhile insights. He generally does not appear to have engaged in self-critical analysis of his own theories or of key concepts such as liberty, state, or society. Although on the surface Leroy-Beaulieu's books and articles seem extremely social-scientific, statistic-laden, and fact-oriented, they often take on a ritualistic nature. The catchwords of Liberalism and Established Liberal economics—"individual initiative," "responsibility," "freedom, the basis of civilization," "progress," "foresight and sagacity," "imprudence and inertia," and so many other phrases—are invoked regularly to slay the demons of error. The result, rather than any real intellectual engagement with alternative theories, is a series of formulaic statements and a litany of familiar truisms, occasionally combined with attacks on carefully camouflaged straw men. Leroy-Beaulieu used invective skillfully to discredit enemies of the nineteenth-century Liberal Regime. His writings drive home the message that these critics were simply fools for failing to recognize the superiority of capitalism and Liberal social institutions.

This contemptuous attitude toward his intellectual opponents indicates that Leroy-Beaulieu's conception of truth became an ideological weapon for beating down opposition to the nineteenth-century Liberal Regime. William James, a contemporary of the economist and one well acquainted with the intellectual scene in France, characterized this method as one of "coercive demonstration." This desire to compel others to accept supposedly obvious truths is related to

Leroy-Beaulieu's refusal to acknowledge the possibility of shades of meaning or degrees of validity. By holding fast to the conviction that truth is simple, evident, and readily available, he could treat dissent as unreasonable, perverse, and contemptible. Since Leroy-Beaulieu never doubted that Established Liberal views about the economy were scientific and that science provided absolute truths, he rejected entirely the claim that many schools of economic thought could legitimately coexist. Gaëtan Pirou's comment about kindred thinkers Guy de Molinari and Yves Guyot applies to Leroy-Beaulieu as well: they "were convinced that their doctrine was the only true one, the only scientific one, that a society absolutely could not function if it renounced the principles of competitive free enterprise and private initiative."[21] The method of debate, in short, was intellectual authoritarianism.

Leroy-Beaulieu rested his Established Liberal edifice not only on a positivistic philosophy of knowledge but also on assumptions about human nature. When he portrayed our drives and behavior, he accepted without demur that we are part of the animal kingdom.[22] He stressed the *nature* in human nature. Although Leroy-Beaulieu insisted on the ability of individual "will" and of such immaterial factors as ideas and moral habits to shape events, he never accepted the slightest supernatural component in the universe. Nor did he give any justification of his naturalistic approach; for him the questions of human origins and human nature had already been resolved. In addition, when he discussed the intrinsic character of the race, he emphasized uniformity, invariability, and certainty just as firmly as in his comments about physical nature. All human behavior obeyed laws, he insisted. "Modern science," he observed in his economics treatise, "has shown . . . that the spirit has its laws just as matter does . . . offering nothing that is fortuitous . . . manifesting itself with an admirable constancy and regularity."[23]

Yet Leroy-Beaulieu claimed that he had departed from the analysis of Classical Liberalism in some important ways. As we have seen (in Chapter 7), he tried to incorporate the historical relativity of human behavior into his theories, and he agreed that noneconomic motives influence economic behavior, especially as wealth increases. Nevertheless, he made only vague gestures toward relativism; his most reiterated teaching was quite different, and usually, more by reflex rather than by reflection, he depended on the concept of inflexible Economic Man in his thinking about society. "Without doubt," he wrote, "the core of man . . . [is] always the same and the rules which determine his activity . . . [have], despite differences of intensity, the same nature."[24] That core, for Leroy-Beaulieu as for all Established Liberals, was self-interest. Liberal economists had always held that material self-interest and rational economic calculation were the strongest motivating forces inside all human beings at all times in history. Despite his occasional statements that he had repudiated the doctrine, Leroy-Beaulieu actually retained it, for it was a vital support of the broader claim that the Liberal Regime was universal and natural. He stated as a universally valid axiom that men and women want to maximize their utilities while minimizing the energy expended in doing so. While stating that motives are "unequally powerful" depending on the state of a society's civilization, he cited his own experience with North Africans to justify the claim that in economic matters businessmen and workers of all places "act on the same maxims, which are hardly different from the usages of the civilized world."[25] The emphasis for him was always on the existence of natural laws. In agreement with Classical Liberals, Established Liberals, and even some reform-minded Liberals, he asserted that in the area of production, in contrast to the realm of distribution, the self-seeking economic motives of the individuals become *more* predominant as a society becomes more civilized.[26] A few times Leroy-Beaulieu argued, although very briefly, that distribution and consumption are influenced by such motives as devotion to family, love of country, a taste for honors, a desire for adornment and finery (*parure*), and ambition for power.[27] He attributed the charitable use of wealth to religious motivations, "the pleasure from ennobling oneself in the eyes of fellow citizens, or in [one's] own eyes, the taste for admiration, . . . a refined type of sporting activity." Another force that he mentioned that leads people to use their wealth to benefit others was "the quest for the ideal."[28] Once in his discussion of human nature in *L'Etat Moderne* he wrote, "It is false that the human being is uniquely guided by personal interest, at least in its grossest form, pecuniary interest." Yet he went on to attenuate the force of this statement by asserting, "having to fight against so many obstacles to his self-preservation and well-being, man obeys mainly a motive which is the principal, the most habitual, the most constant, the most intense," the desire for gain.[29]

Leroy-Beaulieu's vindication of the motive of self interest rested upon his assumption that human beings are animals. Since we are totally embedded in a naturalistic environment, he said, many of our requirements are instinctual. But as we evolve we acquire additional needs, and as a result our wants can never be surfeited. Each particular need is satiable, yet "man is never satisfied" because "human needs, although having a certain immutable and fixed basis . . . are indefinitely variable and expandable in their forms and objects." Our protean urges lead us to go on acquiring. Even after we get as much as we want of necessities, we aspire next to the comfortable and "decent," then beyond that to the elegant and refined, and, still unsatiated, to the opulent and magnificent.[30] At no point did Leroy-Beaulieu ever suggest that being human might entail transcending this innate drive to limitless consumption. In adhering to this view of humans as consumers Leroy-Beaulieu again spoke for many people of his time and for most members of his own school of Liberal thought.

Leroy-Beaulieu believed in social progress, but not because of any high opinion of human capacities. He was no humanist who gloried in the varied and extraordinary gifts of humankind. On the contrary, although he found some faults in the instinctual equipment of the human race, he argued forthrightly that our animal urges guided our behavior better than reason did. Often we read that Liberalism involves a high regard for reason, but it is vital to be very careful about what that idea means. Leroy-Beaulieu joined Herbert Spencer, William Graham Sumner, and many French Established Liberals in believing that human thinking powers are poor guides for behavior. Although he boasted that trained minds can discover truths about the universe and society, he denied that rational judgment would generally lead to wise courses of action. "Human discernment and will" are both so uncertain, he cautioned, that automatic natural processes (i.e., instincts) are preferable.[31] This denigration of reason as an aspect of human personality was an openly stated part of his ideology. In this respect, Leroy-Beaulieu's Established Liberalism was markedly different from the reformist Liberal doctrine being shaped around 1900 by such thinkers such as Lester Frank Ward and John Dewey in the United States and T. H. Green and J. L. Hobhouse in Great Britain.[32]

The word "nature" carried generally positive connotations for Leroy-Beaulieu, but he saw one important limitation in human nature: we are naturally perverse. In *L'Etat Moderne* he explicitly criticized those who counted on education to produce moral improvement: "At present there is no longer anyone among those whose views carry some authority who is thoughtless enough to believe that man is born good, that his fortunate instincts flower naturally, that the bad ones develop only because of outside intervention."[33] Here is a secularized version of Christian teaching about the fallen state of human beings. Most of his statements along these lines, however, are far less dramatic than the harsh Augustinian view that people have an inborn desire to do evil. Rather, again in accord with the Liberal tradition, he presupposed that individuals are born lazy, seeking to satisfy their needs with a minimum expenditure of energy. Because of this innate lethargy, only the proper upbringing and the right kind of family and social environment can give people the virtuous inclination to work hard. This line of argument, of course, established the superiority of the bourgeoisie.

As his contrasts of bourgeois with working-class character illustrate, Leroy-Beaulieu tended toward a rigidly moralistic view of people and events, but he drew his morality from Liberal economic principles rather than from philosophy or religion. Like many other Established Liberal economists he refused to judge the doctrines of political economy by standards drawn from conventional or religiously based moral teachings. Instead he found his morality within the precepts of his discipline. For an economist this meant defining moral behavior as that which contributed to the promotion of production. Leroy-Beaulieu accepted this belief from his youth and, as far as we can tell, never questioned it.

From the 1860s to the 1910s Leroy-Beaulieu invariably proclaimed that the duty to work was the chief moral commandment, an obligation so absolute that Europeans had the right to force hard labor upon the peoples of other continents. Since the increase of the world's wealth was essential to social peace and personal well-being, "backward" peoples had no right to leave their lands underdeveloped. If they did not have the skill, energy, and desire to tap the resources of their land, Europeans should step in to do so. And work should be intense and efficient, producing as many items per hour—or as many pages of writing—as strength permitted. Leroy-Beaulieu hardly ever spoke positively of leisure, and he rarely acknowledged that efficiency or production should sometimes be sacrificed for the sake of family life. He also practiced what he preached, devoting his sojourns at Montplaisir to managing the estate and to putting out his weekly journal. When he did mention the love of family, he invariably treated this impulse as another motivation to work. Religious ways of seeing life were so foreign to him that, to take a striking example, he rejected the dedication of Jesus to poverty and self-denial as beyond the capabilities of human nature. On the contrary, he defended moderate indulgence in luxury—not due to the inherent value of pleasure, however, but because "the development of ease and comfort is favorable" to "the industry of a country."[34]

Although Leroy-Beaulieu used Liberal conceptions of human nature as a basis for his arguments, he also appealed to certain assumptions about the basic groups to which human beings belong. Nineteenth-century thinkers argued over whether nations, classes, or races were the most significant social group. Certainly race and nation are important categories in Leroy-Beaulieu's thought, but both of these concepts are narrower and less fundamental than the all-embracing association he called "society." This word is surely the key term that recurs most in his writings. Unfortunately its precise meaning is opaque, since he wrote as if his audience knew what he had in mind. In only a few places did he venture anything like a definition of the term, let alone probe deeply the nature of the phenomena it designated.

For Leroy-Beaulieu "society" clearly denoted a group of human beings organized into some kind of ongoing unity. His references to the primitive "state of nature" help us understand his meaning. He portrayed prehistoric villages as self-sufficient, self-contained associations of people living in close proximity and exchanging economic goods. He seems to have transferred this concept to modern times as well, treating a nation as a self-contained entity that needs trade but no intimacy with other national societies. That is partly because, as he said explicitly a few times, a society includes traditions. Tossing off a skeletal definition in the *Traité d'Economie Politique*, he referred to "society, that is to say the totality of the human group, of traditions, of education, of a specific collection of materials and equipment—whether intellectual or material."[35] Therefore, Leroy-Beaulieu viewed a society as a group of human beings distinguished from others by an inheritance of immaterial and material links and property. If this analysis is correct, then there is nothing unusual in his conception, and he was rightly confident that his readers would understand him.

Leroy-Beaulieu saw society in a positive light, especially in contrast with the state. As detailed in *L'Etat Moderne*, he believed that society formed first and then brought the state into existence to perform certain limited tasks. The social group, unlike the state, includes intimate private exchanges and private, noncoercive organizations. The private agencies are flexible and full of spontaneous creativity, while the state is rigidly bound to routine and therefore uncreative. Since he associated the natural with the spontaneous, this contrast also implied that society is somehow more natural in its operation (another favorable trait for Leroy-Beaulieu) than is the state.

On another important, related question—whether an all embracing social group is a distinct reality in itself or simply the sum of the individuals who comprise it—Leroy-Beaulieu never took a consistent stand on the issue and evaded a close examination of his own positions. He belonged to a school of thought famous for its emphasis on individual rights, but some passages in his writings indicate that he was occasionally uncomfortable with individualism of Liberal tradition and leaned toward an organic view of society in which the individual is a subordinate part of a larger entity. In an early essay, he appeared to criticize the extreme individualist view: "It is an illusion to imagine that one can found a real liberty and an efficacious (*administrative*) control in a society where everything is dust, where the implacable level of a geometric equality leaves in existence only scattered molecules that have no cohesion or power of resistance."[36] Almost twenty years later, in a functionalist characterization of sorts, he argued that a state must consider society as a whole rather than looking at "isolated parts" when it proposes to take a function away from the private sphere. To keep the creative forces of a people from atrophying, he declared, society must exercise its muscles and nerves.[37] In 1896 he even wrote that "Society is a living being which, in its development and self-improvement (*perfectionnement*), always creates more numerous and more complicated organs."[38] In passing the economist once recognized that human beings are interconnected in such a way that individuals and groups undergo the impact of the acts of others. Nevertheless, he did not pursue this idea—current in his time under the rubric of "solidarity."[39] Once in his economics treatise Leroy-Beaulieu took pains to underline that normally work was done in coordinated fashion by large numbers of people rather than by isolated individuals; hence the need for a figure like the entrepreneur.[40] But this insight was also an isolated one.

Leroy-Beaulieu's organic images imply that society resembles a super person, an entity with its own independent existence. However, he never explored this conception either, and his prescriptions for social and economic organization seldom treated the group as having interests different from those of the individuals comprising it. In *Le Travail des Femmes* he insisted that the basic unit of society was the individual, not the family (see Chapter 3). And he had no patience whatsoever for Joseph Chamberlain's claim that people in a democracy had nothing to fear from the state because they were the state. Such a view, he contended, was "a political pantheism that loses sight of separate citizens and considers nothing more than the aggregate they form," forgetting "the real life of the former" and seeing only "the fictitious life of the latter."[41]

Leroy-Beaulieu was unable to develop a truly organic view of society because he was so deeply committed to individualism—in several senses of the term. Throughout his writings Leroy-Beaulieu constantly drove home the point that the individual, not the group, is the source of progress. "Ever since humanity has been on earth," he wrote, "success has been the product of individual effort."[42] Every major improvement and each new idea in civilization came from a gifted and hard-working person who possessed "spontaneity of mind and spirit."[43] Therefore, societies must restrain themselves from seeking to be the main actor (e.g., through state action) and instead promote individual initiative. A prime source of his economic individualism probably was his habit of conceiving things through an analytical search for the "element," the atom. Leroy-Beaulieu remained so fully tied to individualistic thought patterns that he never could draw meaningfully on contemporary insights into the social nature of work. He automatically viewed economic processes as the result of the behavior of independent individuals, and he explicitly and forcefully contended that an economy can function well only when each individual is exposed to economic insecurity. Since he denied being an individualist, he seems unaware of his commitment to this way of seeing things.[44] Here is another area in which his views were representative. The description of economic life in terms of the activity of individuals was so deeply rooted in economic theory and so convenient ideologically and theoretically that even reform-minded economists held to it.

Another set of key presuppositions in Leroy-Beaulieu's thinking had to do with the relation of natural processes to historical processes. Once more he reflected completely and unquestioningly the dominant views of his times and articulated them in a fashion typical of early nineteenth-century Liberals. The inherent, basic character of a thing, he assumed, appeared over time. The natural, he said repeatedly, grew slowly as a result of the continual pressure of natural forces including, for animals, the force of instinct. He believed that social institutions developed properly when they evolved in the same way as living organisms: by slow, spontaneous, and tiny increments. By "spontaneous" he appears to have meant (following the Lamarckian rather than the Darwinian conception of evolutionary causation) that there were internal, instinctual causes as well as external physical ones. Only after long development could that which was inherent in the original phenomenon ripen into what nature meant it to be. This genetic interpretation of "natural" social development reinforced Leroy-Beaulieu's strictures against sudden, sweeping change.[45] In endorsing the natural he opposed the artificial, which in this case meant the violent external interference that hindered the natural ripening process. That which is natural is not created by human fiat; moreover, the natural has the capacity to endure while the artificial will be unstable and will disappear sooner or later. These presuppositions explain Leroy-Beaulieu's frequent comments that nature would keep a non-Liberal society from functioning successfully.

Central to his doctrine of historical progress was the argument that societies have only a limited ability to shape their own history. From such mentors as Guizot he took the notion that over a long period of time a particular people develops patterns that become embodied in their institutions. According to this view, old institutions become too deeply rooted in the historically created habits and "spirit" of a people to be swept away in short order by radical reforms. Therefore a society's advance toward civilization must be slow and gradual.[46] This doctrine provided yet another rampart against crusades for substantial social reform, but Leroy-Beaulieu could and did champion reforms as long as they were not too rapid or extensive.

Although he never explicitly admitted it, Leroy-Beaulieu's whole ideology was a weapon of intellectual warfare against reformist social-contract theory. His main line of defense was that science proved the existing (Liberal) society and economy to be the only natural ones and, consequently, the only right ones. The dichotomy he constantly created between natural and artificial institutions was the pivotal aspect of his response to radicals and reformers. The common feature he saw among all these enemies of the Liberal Regime was their belief that society could be reshaped by the conscious exercise of human reason.[47] Leroy-Beaulieu scorned the notion that progress could be planned by thinkers relying upon reason.[48] He countered that the external world is not shaped by "plans fully contrived by human intelligence; nature has other ways of operating and makes mock of the a priori systems to which men's imagination gives birth."[49] In order to improve society people must act as nature does, doing the modest work of each day rather than overturning everything at once.[50] They certainly should not expect to improve anything if they waste their time concocting unnatural, pernicious interventionist economic theories.

Leroy-Beaulieu's ideological doctrine of history carried the implication that, just as Western societies had arrived at an ideal state, the horror of regression to barbarism loomed on the horizon. The discussions of progress are anything but hopeful; his historical defense of Liberal civilization comes across as defensive, bitter, and even lugubrious. Leroy-Beaulieu, like others of his social class and ideological convictions, had become increasingly pessimistic about his society. Yet the despair that mounted in his writings from the late 1880s onward did not alter his basic ideas. The immobility of his thought left him unable to find intellectual resolutions and convincing programmatic solutions for the key social and political problems Established Liberals confronted after the coming of the Republic of the Republicans. In thought and action Leroy-Beaulieu wound up in a series of contradictions and impasses.

The course of his convictions about government offers a prime example. Leroy-Beaulieu's positions changed most significantly in two areas, foreign policy and political structures. In foreign policy he undeniably turned away from his early internationalism and antiimperialism; however, his nationalism was a set of feelings rather than a new set of ideas, and his imperialism was founded on the same Liberal beliefs he had always held. As for the second area, the development of his thought about governmental institutions resembled a spinning around in growing confusion. At first he was typically Liberal in his unsparing condemnation of personal power and absolutist monarchies. He detested the highly centralized administration in France, was contemptuous of bureaucrats, and praised self-government and universal suffrage. In the face of the collapse of the Second Empire Leroy-Beaulieu accepted the Republic and the increased share of power it gave to nonelite groups. After the advanced republican forces took power in the late 1870s, his attitude changed into a baffled opposition. From then on his commentaries on constitutional questions became more right-wing and less moderate than before. His writings grew more and more critical of the government of the Third Republic, and he even repeated early nineteenth-century arguments against electing leaders by universal suffrage. But he never explicitly repudiated Liberal ideals of parliamentary, constitutional government, and he never succeeded in constructing an alternative that would be in harmony with his basic Liberal convictions. Despite his disillusionment with universal suffrage, he refused to embrace any of the antiparliamentary movements of his time. In that sense he stayed faithful to Liberalism.

The same combination of superficial change and fundamental continuity characterized Leroy-Beaulieu's judgment of the state. As a young man he looked on the state organization with suspicion and hostility. Nevertheless, around 1870 he embraced the moderate Established Liberal stance by conceding that the rule of laissez-faire could not be applied strictly. By the end of the 1870s, when he saw that peoples everywhere were still attached to warlike ways, he accepted the view that a national government must be able to mobilize the resources needed to build strong military forces. Not only did military necessities force him to call reluctantly for a more active state, but he also recognized that in a society full of huge factories, mines, and estates, the central government too had to be strong; otherwise it would not be able to enforce the rules needed to prevent a return to what he himself called the chaotic period of early nineteenth-century industrialization. While he kept asserting that the French should rely mainly on social pressure to bring about the moral reform of abusive employers, he never claimed that this alone would be sufficient. Thus he never joined the holdouts among Established Liberals, such as Yves Guyot and Guy de Molinari, in demanding that the state authorities refrain completely from any activities other than those connected with providing for law and order, the sanctity of contracts, and national defense.

On the contrary, Leroy-Beaulieu made a series of concessions to expanding state interference in society. Admitting that the old Liberal formulas for differentiating the spheres of state and society no longer made sense, he adopted from Michel Chevalier and like-minded Established Liberals a basic principle that could be used to justify a broadly interventionist state. Government, in his words, must provide more services as a society becomes more "refined" and "civilized," or, to use other terms, more developed and more complex. In addition, he accepted another common Liberal view that government is obligated to protect those persons who cannot protect themselves from exploitation. On these grounds he argued in favor of child-labor laws, government subsidies and programs to promote population growth, publicly financed and administered educational systems with compulsory attendance in elementary schools, and government activity to acquire colonies and prepare them for investment and settlement. In doing so he represented the views of most Established Liberal economists. Whereas de Molinari and Guyot became rather marginal figures, Leroy-Beaulieu remained in the mainstream of Established Liberal thinking.

Yet he frequently resented having to make these concessions. Even as Leroy-Beaulieu helped to extend Established Liberalism's tolerance for state intervention, he undertook a long and only partially successful effort to set strict limits on the scope of legislation and government regulation. In the late 1880s and the 1890s he labored to articulate an alternative to laissez-faire that would keep the state from becoming overly powerful. Unfortunately for his peace of mind, he never found a new principle that would do that job as effectively as the principle of laissez-faire had. He could only warn in bitter language about the dangers the state posed. His writings are full of sarcastic sneers at the state, which often appear to be desperate attempts to keep his own concessions from being carried too far. When he needed a refutation of interventionist programs, he turned back to the familiar old ideas that an active state damages individual initiative, thus inducing lethargy and hindering material progress. Shaking his verbal finger repeatedly, he warned about the slippery slope: once we permit the state to take over what should be private functions, it will not and cannot stop until it abolishes freedom.

Leroy-Beaulieu's ultimate solution was to demand that the state prevent itself from infringing on individual liberty. This formula is an indication of the intellectual problems he faced in developing a doctrine of the state's relations with the individual and society. In the opening pages of *L'Etat Moderne* he indignantly reminded the interventionists that the state was not a person; it was a group of individuals who lacked the virtues that reformers attributed to the state.[51] Yet Leroy-Beaulieu himself, in all his writings, had treated the state as an individual actor. And he continued to do so even after rejecting that very practice in *L'Etat Moderne*. The habit of personifying the state, of treating it as a monolithic antagonist, had too much of a hold over his thought processes. He demanded that the state control itself and refrain from dragging society downward into intrusive and all-encompassing regulation of individual activities, but his reification of the state stood in the way of his specifying who was to take action and how. So he failed to replace the laissez-faire rule or to develop a convincing alternative.

While he was baffled on one hand by the question of how to restrain the state, on the other hand equally deep-seated thought patterns about the individual and society stultified his efforts to correct the exaggeration of Liberal individualism. Like most modern Westerners he tended to think about society as a collection of independent entities, yet occasionally he felt a need to move beyond this conception. Nationalist concerns pushed him toward desiring a more cohesive French nation, and he sensed that the atomistic model of society inhibited the development of national unity. Thus he complained that France was made up of isolated social molecules without sufficient cohesion.[52] Nevertheless, just as he failed to carry through his idea that the reality of the state organization was in part the people who comprised it, so he failed to make use of his insight about the atomization of the French people. When he used the term "society," he usually did so without any analysis. At other times he reduced the concept to representing the individuals that society contained. He never arrived at a vision of a society as a network of relationships, solidarities, and cultural inheritances that persist over time.

Furthermore, Leroy-Beaulieu was devoid of recommendations about how to produce more unity, for his ideological commitments kept him wedded to the individualist outlook. He was, in effect, trying to maintain both his Liberal individualism and the incompatible notion, associated with Conservatives and Socialists, that social groups have or should have an organic character. Throughout his career he achieved a precarious but unstable balance between the two conceptions by darting back and forth between them as he felt the need to do so. Although he regularly used organic metaphors when he called for unity among the French, he defended the individualist approach on those occasions when he attacked proposals for state intervention in the management of business firms.

Even with regard to his idolizing of production as humanity's ultimate value, we find one passage in his 1896 treatise that indicates an abortive second thought. Attempting to temper his era's belief in progress, Leroy-Beaulieu cautioned that some people expected too much from society. They overestimated the amount of growth already attained and did not see how distant the goal of providing plenty for everyone remained. As he put it:

> Many of the triumphant hymns of economists and statisticians give badly exaggerated ideas about real economic progress. For a century the growth of production has been, without doubt, very great; but the net result is quite a bit less than a superficial examination might lead one to believe. It is important to reestablish the truth because the truth is always good to know and to tell, and because, in the present instance, it can enlighten statesmen and administrators. Besides, it can calm impatience, soothe sufferings, and diminish resentments.[53]

Once again, unfortunately, Leroy-Beaulieu failed to reflect on an insight; the thought remained as isolated in his work as the other ideas that could have led him to reevaluate Established Liberalism. Nearly always production was the hope he held out for humankind.

The shifts and continuities in Leroy-Beaulieu's worldview followed a definite trajectory. At the outset of his career he moved away from strict laissez-faire convictions, and for a short time in the 1870s it seemed possible that he might move toward a version of Liberalism that approved more state intervention on behalf of workers than Established Liberals would ever accept. Then, under the impact of the social and political developments of the late 1870s and early 1880s, he recoiled to most of the positions he had held originally, except with regard to nationalism and imperialism. Although he never changed any of his basic convictions, in the early 1880s he began to systematize them and amplify his earlier defenses of the social and economic system to which he was so passionately attached. This effort was a response to new challenges or, more precisely, new forms of older challenges: the Socialism of Lassalle and Marx and the interventionism of nonsocialist reformers. While he eventually took some steps to adapt his outlook to changed conditions and ideas, he did not sacrifice any of the fundamental principles he had advocated in his youth. Leroy-Beaulieu never allowed any inner conflict over these intellectual matters to produce an intolerable strain on his perceptions and beliefs. Instead he merely glanced at a new perspective, quickly turned back to the old view—often without acknowledging that he had done so—and then closed his mind.

Class feeling ultimately checked Leroy-Beaulieu when he sought to unravel the dilemmas of modern society. As we have observed throughout the book, his whole career was a defense of his class's status against a dual assault from the working class and from the newly assertive middle and lower bourgeoisie. As time went on the threat of the latter group preoccupied him as much as the rise of socialism and other radical working-class movements. Whatever his worries, his intellectual options were always confined by his intense devotion to the supremacy of the Grande Bourgeoisie. Some Liberals of his time saw the inadequacies of atomizing thought and of an individualist conception of society. They moved out of the Established Liberal part of the Liberal spectrum and created what scholars tend to call the New Liberalism.[54] Leroy-Beaulieu remained an Established Liberal, aware of the inadequacies of laissez-faire and willing to permit modest expansion of state activities in the economic realm but unable to offer a specific, constructive program that would preserve free government and appeal across class lines. His only concrete agenda was to persuade France to return the government to the social elite who had once guided the country.

For about the first twenty-five years of his professional life Leroy-Beaulieu was more troubled by the danger of socialist, reformist, and working-class assaults on Liberal society than by any other contemporary problem. Undeniably humanitarian feelings also motivated his concern for the masses. Yet these feelings, though present in his early writings, never became a strong force in shaping his outlook as they did for reformist thinkers. Perhaps he muzzled his original sympathy as a result of his lack of imagination, indeed his desire to exclude imagination from his approach to life. But his dedication to promoting Grande Bourgeoisie dominance of the social and political order was surely the prime factor in closing his mind to reformist proposals. So he mobilized every possible argument in the Liberal intellectual armory to overwhelm them. Instead of finding both strong and weak points in the reformers, he responded with polemics. Given his fear of the slippery slope of interventionism, it is fair to judge that he feared any real intellectual revision would help to erode the "civilization" he worshipped. So, both in "La Question Ouvrière" and in his mature works, his basic answer to the Social Question was to call on the well-to-do to rally together and present a solid front of social and intellectual resistance. Invariably he relied on only one source of appeasement: constant increases in production resulting from the powerful force of individual initiative and the universal desire for higher profits and incomes. In that manner everyone's standard of living would rise without any harmful social upheaval.

After the triumph of the advanced republicans, Leroy-Beaulieu's specific identification with Grande Bourgeoisie became evident. Indeed, he appears to have seen the threat to the Grande Bourgeoisie from the middle level of French society as more pressing than that of working-class discontent. Beginning in the 1880s he began to protest the flocking of young men of the inferior classes into the liberal professions. He regretted the diffusion of secondary and higher education among the "middle strata." One undesirable result was an oversupply of people trained for the professions since the newly educated individuals felt that they deserved careers commensurate with their educational opportunities. In addition, the French now imagined that everyone "ought to be at the highest levels of society," and "therefore they disdain the obscure posts where most of them are born, in order to take the chance that might shove them . . . up to the most noteworthy places." The problem, he commented, was exacerbated by the way in which the recently created democratic regime "stupidly smears the magic word equality over all the walls."[55]

These complaints recurred in several of Leroy-Beaulieu's works. In the *Traité d'Economie Politique*, writing about mistaken policies of modern governments, he declared that

> peoples act against their permanent interests when, by a bad system of education, by the bait of overly numerous scholarships or artificial encouragements, they attract a growing number of rural inhabitants or skilled workers into either commercial or liberal professions or the civil service. They resemble an army that has developed an exaggerated number of general staff and auxiliary corps at the expense of the mass of fighting men.[56]

In other words, society must be hierarchical, with the higher positions and higher incomes reserved to a small minority. Such a point of view is a prescription in the ideological sense rather than a description or recommendation in a theoretical vein. Gripped by such strong class identification, he could never give in on any front where intellectual concessions might endanger the cherished supremacy of the Grande Bourgeoisie.

The elitist passages in Leroy-Beaulieu's books and articles restate the themes of the early or "Doctrinaire" Liberals, such as Royer-Collard and Guizot, who originated Established Liberalism in the early 1800s. This observation, however, raises again the question of whether Leroy-Beaulieu and like-minded figures of his time should be called Liberals at all. For the Doctrinaires drew much of their ideology of history and their justification of elite rule from the Conservative thinkers who began attacking the French Revolution in the 1790s. And Leroy-Beaulieu's stance does not parallel that of the often radical Classical Liberals of the seventeenth and eighteenth centuries, since his ideology was a defense of the prevailing social, political, and economic regime, not a critique of it. Still, despite the differences between Leroy-Beaulieu and Classical Liberalism and despite the kinship between Established Liberals and Conservatives, one profound continuity places Leroy-Beaulieu and his colleagues predominantly in the Liberal stream of thought. While the Conservatives fought to preserve a premodern, stable, agrarian, and rather authoritarian system, Leroy-Beaulieu and his school gave their allegiance to the Modern Regime. The contrast between the economist's outlook and that of such contemporaries as Count Henri de Mun or (to mention an extreme example) the pretender, the Comte de Chambord, remind us that Leroy-Beaulieu endorsed a dynamic, industrial society dominated by giant corporations and permitting social mobility. He never considered returning to the Old Regime as an ideal.

Leroy-Beaulieu adhered to a well-established antistatist version of Liberalism. But in the late 1800s thinkers like Paul Cauwès appeared, who were consciously committed to creating an alternative Liberalism. This newer version was reformist in character, although its ideas for practical reform were generally not as far-reaching or bold as their revisionist views about the nature of economics. These French reformers were tame in comparison to the British and American Liberals of the same era whose proposals for social-security systems anticipated the shape of the contemporary welfare state. Certainly the Reformist Liberals in France never even imagined that government should share with private business in the overall management of the economy, as present-day champions of a Liberal welfare state advocate.

The development of reformist Liberalism in the 1870s and 1880s gave Leroy-Beaulieu a wider choice of belief systems within the Liberal spectrum. He was sometimes able to agree with Cauwès and others that a totally individualist conception of society was invalid. Despite his commitment to the view that most human beings are lazy, he also recognized at least once that people hate being inactive. On another occasion he observed that human ability is distributed in gradations rather than simply into two groups, the assiduous and the indolent. One brief but eloquent passage admitted that a life devoted to work was not the highest end to which human beings could aspire. Although he generally treated the results of the free-market system as essentially fair, in his discussions of the distribution of wealth he accepted that a standard of justice drawn from outside economic life might be applied to an economic phenomenon. And for specific social ends—above all, the preservation of *la patrie*—he demanded extensive state interventions. Yet he never permitted these momentary insights to lead him very far down the road Cauwès traveled—the road Western Liberalism began to take in his own lifetime.

That road was toward the Liberal Welfare State and toward a Liberalism much bolder than that of the Reformist Liberals. It is possible that this form of Liberalism has finally run its course. In France, as in the United States and Britain where the change has been most dramatic, an outlook resembling that of Leroy-Beaulieu is once again influential after decades of seemingly irreversible decline. It is surely no accident that a French historian of economic thought, Luc Bourcier de Carbon, tried to revive Leroy-Beaulieu's reputation as an economist in the early 1970s, just as advocates of the free market became more and more vocal. Echoes of Established Liberalism can also be heard in the press. In December 1982, soon after France's Socialist Party had won the presidency and a majority in the Chamber of Deputies, a front-page editorial in *Le Figaro* protested the new government's orientation as a threat to freedom. "Freedom," wrote Guy Baret, "is the *sine qua non* for healthy enterprises and for economic recovery based on a growth in investment." A desire for economic efficiency, "outside of which there is no durable social progress," may have motivated the government's desire to control investment, but more important to economic health is "a conception of society." The issue is whether "to have more confidence in the constraining force of structures than in the liberty of persons." Baret concluded, "The liberty of enterprise is a form of liberty pure and simple, and it is rare to find a society that remains free when its enterprises are not."[57] Leroy-Beaulieu would undoubtedly applaud such a stance, despite the fact that not even the Guy

Barets of contemporary France would be likely to propose dismantling the current social-security system, a program that would have horrified Leroy-Beaulieu. This short, pointed article proclaims a theme Leroy-Beaulieu sounded loudly and persistently in the late nineteenth century—albeit under other circumstances. Leroy-Beaulieu, though now too forgotten to be a direct influence, is one of the ancestors of the Liberalism found in *Le Figaro*'s intense hostility to government control of big business.

The choice of appropriate standards of evaluation of historical figures is always a delicate one. Fortunately, Paul Leroy-Beaulieu provides us with one standard that we can apply to him as a person. Over and over he vaunted the trait of *plasticité*, a term that can be translated through a trinity of words as flexible, adaptable, and malleable. According to Leroy-Beaulieu, civilization has such plasticity. In addition, he characterized creative individuals as those who exhibited flexibility or adaptability along with spontaneity. Yet Leroy-Beaulieu himself was hardly such a person. Unbending, unyielding, resistant to revising his views, he also led a highly structured and even rigid personal life, the antithesis of spontaneity.

There is a more positive way of describing Leroy-Beaulieu that is faithful to nineteenth-century values and presents him in a better light. We can say that he held fast to principle. It is impossible with the sources at hand to outline a psychobiography of Leroy-Beaulieu, and that may be fortunate since such approaches often tend to be reductive. Nor is it fair to reduce him merely to a caricature of the stiff, humorless bourgeois defender of capitalism. He won the respect of the members of a demanding intellectual-journalistic circle and despite his reserve was elected by them to two important honors: annual president of the Académie des Sciences Morales et Politiques and president of the Société d'Economie Politique. And over the years, he came closer and closer to winning election to the Chamber of Deputies. It is at least possible that the real, breathing, feeling Leroy-Beaulieu was someone who engaged in a struggle with his limitations and who won out often enough to attain considerable esteem if not actual popularity.

However, our central concern has been with Paul Leroy-Beaulieu the ideologist rather than with Paul Leroy-Beaulieu the friend, colleague, or candidate for office. And as an ideologist Leroy-Beaulieu was indeed inflexible, often insensitive to social realities and social needs. He dogmatically insisted that the great majority of human beings were unwilling *by nature* to work except under the lash of need or the magnet of material gain. Constantly he classified all people into two types: an elite few whose family and class heritages made them self-disciplined, hard-working, and knowledgeable, and the remainder who were ignorant, dissipated, and lazy. He was barely capable of recognizing degrees of virtue and vice between these two extremes, yet he never allowed this realization to inspire any revisions in his doctrine. He was blind to the insights of more reform-minded Liberals who recognized that their doctrines had to be reexamined in the light of a different conception of human nature. And in the name of the freedom of social groups to shape their collective lives, they were willing to consider flaws in the so-called natural laws of economics. Leroy-Beaulieu, the self-proclaimed champion of individual liberty, used the intellectually authoritarian doctrine of natural law as a means of tying the hands of his community.

After this investigation of Leroy-Beaulieu it seems fair to conclude in retrospect that Established Liberals like Leroy-Beaulieu were more often wrong than right in their ideas and analyses. Even further, they contributed to the maintenance and even the creation of ills that might have been ameliorated earlier. Their promotion of imperialism, their attacks on social-security legislation, their propaganda against redistributive measures, their opposition to regulation of work hours—all these directly harmed people.

Possibly both Leroy-Beaulieu and Established Liberalism had a split character that became more pronounced during Leroy-Beaulieu's lifetime and that undermined Liberal values. The Classical Liberal heritage of the seventeenth and eighteenth centuries was generous, hopeful, and humanitarian. It valued highly every individual life. This was one vital sense in which the ancestral version of Liberalism was individualistic. Another positive aspect of individualism was the insistence that all persons should have the freedom to judge the truth for themselves. Balancing this view was the conviction that the authority of reason was limited to the here and now. These views on individual judgment and the limitations of the mind led inevitably to embracing a doctrine of tolerance. Another consequence of the intuition that each human being has a basic core of worth is the conviction that each of us, a priori, is of equal innate worth. But what is inner exists only as potential, and there is a crucial condition that must prevail before any person can realize in actuality his or her full humanity and personal selfhood. That condition is liberty: the liberty to pursue one's own path to higher selfhood. Liberty involves stopping public authorities from inflicting arbitrary treatment and irremediable damage upon the citizen innocent of any wrongdoing. As for fraternity, the last of the familiar trinity of the French Revolution, that precept was less clear in Leroy-Beaulieu's time and is generally ignored today; but Leroy-Beaulieu did inherit from his Liberal predecessors a humanitarianism that called upon the fortunate members of a society to help in improving the lot of the materially unfortunate.

Along with this heritage of humanism, humanitarianism, toleration, equality, liberty, and fraternity, however, Liberalism had another side. From its origins Liberals equated happiness with the consumption of material and immaterial goods. In such a view the value of any person is conceived essentially in relation to that person's contribution to production. Since people make unequal contributions to production, this side of Liberalism leads to valuing people unequally. Liberty also receives a narrower definition, as freedom from the interference of collectivities, especially the state, in the work of productive persons. And the nineteenth century saw the rise of a somewhat warped version of fraternity: the emphasis on nationalism, not just nationality and nationhood. While both the humanitarian and the materialist sides of the Liberal heritage are evident in Leroy-Beaulieu and Established Liberalism, it is also evident that the second set, especially when augmented by nationalism, tended more and more to outweigh the first set.

In Leroy-Beaulieu's case the shift is illustrated by his association with a crucial kind of symbolism, the symbolism of national mottoes. Liberty, equality, and fraternity—fraternity understood as belonging to a nationality—was the slogan under which Liberals fought for reform in 1789. Leroy-Beaulieu endorsed these principles, celebrating the work of the moderate revolutionaries whose ideals were embodied in the Declaration of the Rights of Man and the Citizen and in the August Decrees of 1789. He reaffirmed his allegiance to the revolutionary motto during the election of 1885. In the 1890s, however, he participated in an organization (the Comité de Défense et de Progrès Social, organized by his Liberal Catholic brother, Anatole) whose slogan indicates the transformation taking place in the values of Grand Bourgeois Established Liberals. This slogan was "Patrie, Devoir, Liberté" (Nation, Duty, Liberty). The willingness to accept nation and duty in place of equality and fraternity, as well as the acceptance of third place for liberty, illustrates the direction in which Leroy-Beaulieu was moving. It was a direction in which the individual was subordinated to one form of collectivity, the nationality as organized in a nation-state, and in which duties rather than human rights were stressed.

Others have interpreted Leroy-Beaulieu more favorably as a champion of a creative capitalism, a farsighted thinker who correctly anticipated the economic miracles of the twentieth century.[58] According to this interpretation, Leroy-Beaulieu was motivated by a sense of the contribution modern capitalist entrepreneurs could make if Western society would permit them to do so. He recognized the enormous productive potential of the capitalist economic machine, and he foresaw that the unleashing of this potential would raise the standard of living of wage earners so high that the danger of violent social strife would vanish. He promoted heroic capitalism because he knew it would work, and he promoted privileges for the capitalist Grande Bourgeoisie because that class was capable of the entrepreneurial creativity neither the state nor any other class could supply. This view of Leroy-Beaulieu, consequently, suggests that he identified with the Grande Bourgeoisie because he saw it as the very center of capitalist development.[59]

But there are at least two reasons to be skeptical of this generous interpretation of Leroy-Beaulieu's contributions and motivations. First, the standard of living of the mass of people in the West might never have risen as far as it has without the intervention of the state and of unions—interventions against which Leroy-Beaulieu fought diligently. Leroy-Beaulieu himself never suggested any process by which increased gains for employers would ensure increased earnings for workers. Second, as far as his motivations were concerned, a variety of unmistakable clues—his denigration of middle-class politicians; his demands that opportunities for higher education be narrowed so that middle-class youngsters would not compete with upper bourgeois youngsters for society's highest posts; his life-long fight to keep the working class "in its place"—all reveal the sentiments that dominated his heart and mind. Leroy-Beaulieu wrote sincerely about the days when all would prosper, but his deepest commitment was to the social and economic supremacy of his own class, the Grande Bourgeoisie.

Notes

ABBREVIATIONS

Books by Paul Leroy-Beaulieu

AL	*L'administration locale en France et en Angleterre*
DLC	*De la colonisation chez les peuples modernes* (1874 edition unless noted otherwise)
EM	*L'Etat moderne et ses fonctions*
EMO	*De l'état moral et intellectuel des populations ouvrières et de son influence sur le taux des salaires*
GC	*Guerres contemporaines, 1853–1866*
QO	*La question ouvrière au XIXe siècle*
RR	*Essai sur la répartition des richesses et sur la tendance à une moindre inégalité des conditions*
TDF	*Le travail des femmes au XIXe siècle*
TEP	*Traité théorique et pratique d'économie politique*
TSF	*Traité de la science des finances*

Other Abbreviations

Aumercier   Giselle Aumercier, "Paul Leroy-Beaulieu, observateur de la réalité économique et sociale française: *L'Economiste français* 1873–1892," Thèse, doctorat du troisième cycle, 4 vols. (Paris, 1979)

Eichtal,   Eugène d'Eichtal, "Paul Leroy-Beaulieu," *Revue des Sci-*
"PLB"   *ences Politiques* 37 (January–June 1917), pp. 1–7

EF   *L'Economiste Français*

JDD   *Journal des Débats*

JDE   *Journal des Economistes*

RDM   *Revue des Deux Mondes*

Stourm,   René Stourm, "Notice historique sur la vie et les travaux
"Notice"   de M. Paul Leroy-Beaulieu," *Séances et Travaux de l'Académie des Sciences Morales et Politiques* 89 (January–June 1918), pp. 151–84

Stourm,   René Stourm, "Paul Leroy-Beaulieu," *RDM* 38 (1 April
"PLB"   1917), pp. 532–53

PREFACE

1. Leo A. Loubère, *Radicalism in Mediterranean France; Its Rise and Decline, 1848–1914* (Albany: State Univ. of New York Press, 1974), p. xv.

CHAPTER 1: THE STUDY OF AN IDEOLOGIST

1. Marcel Proust, *A la recherche du temps perdu* (Paris: Gallimard, 1954), vol. 2: *Le côté de Guermantes*, p. 262. We know that Norpois means Paul rather than his brother Anatole Leroy-Beaulieu because Proust calls him at another point in the book "l'éminent économiste" (p. 151).

2. Just after the turn of the century, Gabriel Hanotaux listed the writers in his country who engaged in the "vast enterprise of rehabilitation and reform" in the years that followed the defeat of France in 1870–1871. Along with Renan, Quinet, Taine, Dupanloup, George Sand, Laboulaye, Boutmy, and de Laveleye, he also included Paul Leroy-Beaulieu. The inclusion of this journalist and economist in such a list of luminaries shows how important a figure he was in the intellectual life of the early Third Republic in France. Gabriel Hanotaux, *Histoire de la France contemporaine* (Paris: Société d'édition contemporaine, 1903–1909), vol. 2, p. 190. The great French sociologist, Emile Durkheim, in an 1895 lecture, used Leroy-Beaulieu's work on collectivism as the chief example of current thought on the topic. See his *Le socialisme* (Paris: PUF, 1971), p. 35.

3. Lucette Le Van Lemesle, "La promotion de l'économie politique en France au XIXe siècle jusqu'à son introduction dans les Facultés (1815–1881)," *Revue d'Histoire Moderne et Contemporaine* 17 (1980), p. 289. See also René Stourm, "Paul Leroy-Beaulieu," *Revue des Deux Mondes*, per. 6, vol. 38 (1 April 1917), pp. 534–35. Henceforth cited as Stourm, "PLB."

4. Michael Stephen Smith, *Tariff Reform in France, 1860–1900* (Ithaca, N.Y.: Cornell Univ. Press, 1980), p. 41.

5. Luc Bourcier de Carbon, a historian of economic thought, has recently defended Leroy-Beaulieu as an economist who anticipated a number of current positions in economic theory. See his *Histoire de la pensée et des doctrines économiques*, vol. 2: *Aux sources du scientisme et de l'humanisme économiques modernes* (Paris: Montchrestien, 1972), pp. 126–42. Douglas E. Ashford makes a similar point in his *The Emergence of the Welfare States* (Oxford: Basil Blackwell, 1986), p. 17, when he writes, "In France, Leroy-Beaulieu was a leader among the outspoken exponents of a totally untouched labour market, but he hardly represented French political thinking over the 1920s."

6. The Liberal was Thomas Jefferson, and the statement is worth quoting. Trilling wrote: "A unique originating power of mind Jefferson did not in fact have. He was, for example, a devoted student of philosophy, and it is possible for scholars to write learned books on the philosophy

of Thomas Jefferson, yet none of them asserts that Jefferson was, in the modern sense of the word, a genius of speculative thought. He did not give new answers to old questions or propose questions never asked before. He possessed himself of the ideas of the philosophical originators of his own time and of the past; he chose among these ideas and made use of them." Lionel Trilling, "Mind in the Modern World," *Times Literary Supplement*, 17 November 1972, p. 2.

7. Martin Seliger, *Ideology and Politics* (London: Allen & Unwin, 1976), p. 14, defines ideology as that type of "belief system" that "covers sets of ideas by which men posit, explain, and justify ends or means of organized social action, irrespective of whether such action aims to preserve, amend, uproot or rebuild a given order." He gives a more elaborate definition on p. 120. Willard Mullins writes, "I would define ideology as a logically coherent system of symbols which, within, a more or less sophisticated conception of history, links the cognitive and evaluative perception of one's social condition . . . to a program of collective action for the maintenance, alteration or transformation of society." Mullins, "On the Concept of Ideology in the Political Sciences," *American Political Science Review* 66 (1972), p. 510. Although Seliger (p. 61) criticizes some aspects of Mullins's analysis, their basic definitions are quite close. Closest to the language I have chosen is the definition in Maurice Duverger, *Sociologie de la politique* (Paris: PUF-Themis, 1973), pp. 19–20: "By ideology we understand here a system of explication of a society that tends to justify or criticize it and serves as a base for an action to maintain, transform or destroy the society. . . . Ideology contains a system of values."

8. Seliger, *Ideology and Politics*, p. 139.

9. A further element of confusion is the indiscriminate use of the term "new liberalism" whenever commentators come across a shading of the outlook that they have not encountered before. American authors, of whom Arthur Schlesinger, Jr., and Harry Girvetz are outstanding examples, believe a new phase in the history of Liberalism began in the last years of the nineteenth century or the first years of the twentieth century with a shift from an insistence on laissez-faire to a doctrine that favored state intervention in economic affairs. In recent years other scholars have described this movement of ideas in Britain, France, and Austria. Almost all these studies have used the rubric "New Liberalism" for the early twentieth-century version of the ideology. However, there have been other shifts as well in the history of Liberal belief, and partisans or commentators have applied the label "new liberal" (or "neoliberal") to many of these varieties. Incompatible doctrines have been so labeled; for instance, both the early proponents of the Welfare State and vigorous recent champions of the free market—such as Ludwig von Mises and Friedrich Hayek—have been termed neoliberals. The term has thus become a hindrance to clear thinking,

clear writing, and intellectual penetration into a stream of thought that has been winding and branching through the historical landscape for three centuries. See Girvetz, *The Evolution of Liberalism*, rev. ed. of *From Wealth to Welfare* (London: Collier-MacMillan, 1963), which has two parts, "Classical Liberalism" and "Contemporary Liberalism"; Schlesinger, "Is Liberalism Dead?" *New York Times Magazine*, 30 March 1980, pp. 42–43ff.; Michael Freeden, *The New Liberalism* (New York: Oxford Univ. Press, 1978); Jacques Cros, *Le néo-libéralisme, étude positive et critique* (Paris, 1951), who uses the term for von Mises and Hayek.

10. This account is hardly exhaustive, and not all would agree on what is the central, essential belief that defines a Liberal. Nevertheless, advocacy of some or all of these ideas suggests that an individual adheres to Liberalism in one or another of its forms.

CHAPTER 2: BACKGROUND AND YOUTH

1. The ideas presented here come from a number of sources and from over twenty years of reading and reflection. Among the key sources are Georges Gurvitch, *Le concept des classes sociales*, stenotyped course (Paris: Centre du documentation universitaire, 1954); Jean Lhomme, *La Grande Bourgeoisie au pouvoir, 1830–1880* (Paris: PUF, 1960); Herbert Luethy, *France against Herself* (New York: Praeger, 1955); Elinor Barber, *The Bourgeoisie in Eighteenth-Century France* (Princeton, N.J.: Princeton Univ. Press, 1955); and Harold Perkin, *The Origins of Modern English Society, 1780–1880* (London: Routledge and Kegan Paul, 1969). Particularly insightful are the pages Pierre Sorlin devotes to social class in his *Waldeck-Rousseau* (Paris: PUF, 1966).

2. François Guizot, *De la démocratie* (Paris: Masson, 1849). The first ancestor of the family of any note was François-Pierre Leroy, who served in the revolutionary assembly at the time of the condemnation of Louis XVI. See "François-Pierre Leroy," *Dictionnaire des parlementaires français . . . depuis ler mai 1789 . . . jusqu'en ler mai 1889* (Paris: Bourloton, 1891), p. 122; and *Dictionnaire historique et biographique de la Revolution et de l'Empire, 1789–1815* (Paris: Libraire historique . . . , n.d.). Giselle Aumercier uncovered new information about F.-P. Leroy. See her dissertation, "Paul Leroy-Beaulieu, observateur de la réalité économique et sociale française: L'Economiste Français, 1873–1892," Thèse, doctorat du 3ème cycle (Paris, 1979), vol. 1, p. 5. Henceforth cited as Aumercier.

3. Our information about Pierre Leroy-Beaulieu comes from two sources, the biography in the *Dictionnaire des parlementaires français*, p. 122, and an obituary of his son: Stourm, "PLB," pp. 532–53. Guizot represented Calvados in the Chamber of Deputies at the end of the Restoration, and Pierre might well have been one of the "gentlemen of the district" who

invited Guizot in 1829 to run for the seat. François Guizot, *Mémoires pour servir à l'histoire de mon temps* (Paris: M. Levy, 1857–1867), vol. 1, pp. 342–43.

4. Stourm, "PLB," p. 533.

5. Pierre Leroy-Beaulieu, "Aux électeurs des arrondissements de Lisieux et de Pont l'Evêque" (Paris, 16 February 1852), Bibliothèque Nationale, Le 77.23 Fol.

6. The unpublished dissertation by Giselle Aumercier is now the best record of the life of Paul Leroy-Beaulieu because his descendants gave her access to family papers. Three of the four volumes of this dissertation describe positions Leroy-Beaulieu took in the articles he wrote beginning in 1873 for *L'Economiste Français*. Aumercier does not discuss his books, and her accounts of the articles are marred by her frequent realization that they do not confirm her thesis that Leroy-Beaulieu was above all an acute observer of contemporary realities. In addition to Aumercier's work, two obituaries are helpful: René Stourm, "Notice historique sur la vie et les travaux du M. Paul Leroy-Beaulieu," *Séances et Travaux de l'Académie des Sciences Morales et Politiques* 89 (January–June 1918), pp. 151–84, hereafter cited as Stourm, "Notice"; and Eugène d'Eichtal, "Paul Leroy-Beaulieu," *Revue des Sciences Politiques* 37 (January–June 1917), pp. 1–7, hereafter cited as Eichtal, "PLB." There is also a useful biographical essay based on an interview: Paul de Lacroix, "Pierre-Paul Leroy-Beaulieu, membre de l'Institut," *Autographes du XIXe siècle* (BN, n.a.f. 22862), vol. 11, pp. 193–96. The article, illustrated with photographs of Leroy-Beaulieu and his homes, is clipped from an unidentified magazine, and it can be dated from 1903 or 1904 since it mentions that a book by Leroy-Beaulieu on railway communications in Africa was in press at the time. The reference can only be to his *Le Sahara, le Soudan et les chemins de fers transsahariens* (Paris: Guillaumin, 1904).

7. Stourm, "Notice," p. 173. On Madame Leroy-Beaulieu, Anatole and his inheritance see René Stourm, "Notice historique sur la vie et les travaux de M. Anatole Leroy-Beaulieu," *Séances et Travaux de l'Académie des Sciences Morales et Politiques* 83 (January–June 1915), pp. 169–91, esp. pp. 170, 173.

8. Eichtal, "PLB," p. 1. Eugène d'Eichtal was a lifelong associate of the Leroy-Beaulieu brothers. All three had been schoolmates at the Lycée Bonaparte (now the Lycée Condorcet) in the 1850s, and Eichtal succeeded Anatole Leroy-Beaulieu in 1910 as director of the Ecole Libre des Sciences Politiques.

9. Paul Leroy-Beaulieu to Junilla de Callac, 4 June 1861, in Aumercier, vol. 1, p. 14.

10. On Paul Leroy-Beaulieu's higher education and study in Germany, see Stourm, "PLB," p. 533 and also "Leroy-Beaulieu, Paul" in G. Vapereau, ed., *Dictionnaire universel des contemporains*, 6th ed. (Paris: Ha-

chette, 1893). On his choice of a career, see Stourm, "PLB," pp. 533–34.

11. Eichtal, "PLB," p. 1.

12. These developments and the Liberals' reactions are described in André Jardin, *Histoire du libéralisme politique: de la crise de l'absolutisme à la constitution de 1875* (Paris: Hachette, 1985), pp. 375ff., and Louis Girard, *Les Libéraux français, 1814–1875* (Paris: Aubier, 1985), pp. 188ff. A study from the point of view of a descendant of Orleanist notables is Gabriel de Broglie, *Histoire politique de la "Revue des Deux Mondes" de 1829 à 1979* (Paris: Perrin, 1979); see esp. pp. 106–25. Also helpful is Stuart L. Campbell, *The Second Empire Revisited: a Study in French Historiography* (New Brunswick, N.J.: Rutgers Univ. Press, 1978), pp. 27–35.

13. For examples of changing attitudes among the Established Liberals see Campbell, *Second Empire*, pp. 10–11.

14. Jardin, *Histoire du libéralisme*, pp. 375–76; Girard, *Les Libéraux*, pp. 191–92, 218–19.

15. de Broglie, *Histoire politique*, p. 110.

16. de Broglie, *Histoire politique*, p. 125.

17. The standard work on Prévost-Paradol is Pierre Guiral's *Prévost-Paradol, 1829–1870: pensée et action d'un libéral sous le Second Empire* (Paris: PUF, 1955). See also Jardin, *Histoire du libéralisme*, pp. 376–78, and Girard, *Les Libéraux*, pp. 194–201. Prévost-Paradol, like de Broglie, granted that a republic could be an acceptable regime; see Guiral, p. 517, citing *La France nouvelle*, p. 134.

18. For the economic history of France in this period, see Pierre Léon, "L'affermissement du phenomène d'industrialisation," in Ferdinand Braudel and E. Labrousse, eds., *Histoire économique et sociale de la France*, book 3, vol. 3 (Paris: PUF, 1976), pp. 475–618.

19. The best study of the creation of the liberal trade regime remains Arthur Dunham, *The Anglo-French Treaty of Commerce of 1860 and the Progress of the Industrial Revolution in France* (Ann Arbor: Univ. of Michigan Press, 1930).

20. Alain Plessis, *The Rise and Fall of the Second Empire, 1852–1871*, trans. Jonathan Mandelbaum (Cambridge: Cambridge Univ. Press, 1985), pp. 113–18, 159–61. For a firsthand testimony about the workers' meetings that took place after the liberalization of 1867, see Paul Leroy-Beaulieu *La question ouvrière au XIXe siècle* (Paris: Charpentier, 1872), pp. 16, 143–45.

21. The regime's degree of success with the working class is much debated. Campbell, *Second Empire*, pp. 135–40, discusses the state of the debate as of 1978, noting the diverse findings of such scholars as Pierre Léon, Michelle Perrot, Charles Tilly, and David Kulstein. Campbell's conclusion seems to be that the artisan elite of the Parisian working class was not strongly republican in outlook and was impressed by the emperor's

social policies while the mass of workers, more republican in its politics, was hostile to the regime. Nevertheless, the strikes of 1869–1870, Campbell indicates, had a variety of causes, economic as well as political and local as well as national. Plessis, *Rise and Fall*, p. 161, disagrees with Kulstein's conclusions about the working-class elite.

22. This view of the character of Established Liberalism appears in John B. Christopher, "The Desiccation of the Bourgeois Spirit," in E. M. Earle, ed., *Modern France: Problems of the Third and Fourth Republics* (Princeton, N.J.: Princeton Univ. Press, 1951), p. 50. An example of the defensive attitude of Established Liberals can be found in François Guizot, *Mémoires pour servir à l'histoire de mon temps* (Paris: Michel Levy Frères, 1857–1867), vol. 1, pp. 165–67; for an assessment of Benjamin Constant along these lines see Roger Soltau, *French Political Thought in the Nineteenth Century* (New Haven, Conn.: Yale Univ. Press, 1931), pp. 40ff.

23. Pierre Rosanvallon, *Le moment Guizot* (Paris: Gallimard, 1985), pp. 225–27, describes the refounding of the Academy, quoting Guizot's *Memoirs*.

24. On the Liberal establishment in general see Campbell, *Second Empire*, pp. 29–31. Guiral, *Prévost-Paradol*, pp. 165–67, gives an excellent, brief account of one component of the establishment, the *Journal des Débats*. On the Académie and the economists in the establishment see also Lucette Le Van Lemesle, "La promotion de l'économie politique en France jusqu'à son introduction dans les facultés, 1815–1881," *Revue d'Histoire Moderne et Contemporaine* 17 (1980), p. 283; idem, "La Faculté de droit de Paris et l'introduction l'économie politique dans son enseignement, 1864–1878," in Donald N. Baker and Patrick J. Harrigan, eds., *The Making of Frenchmen: Current Directions in the History of Education in France, 1679–1979* (Waterloo, Ont.: Historical Reflections Press, 1980), pp. 327–36.

25. On the establishment economists see the two articles by Le Van Lemesle cited in the previous note and also: Madeleine Ventre-Denis, "Sciences sociales et Université au XIXe siècle," *Revue Historique*, no. 520 (October–December 1976), pp. 321–42. Michel Lutfalla, "Aux origines du libéralisme économique en France, le *Journal des Economistes*: analyse du contenu de la première série, 1841–1853," *Revue d'Histoire Economique et Sociale* 50 (1972), pp. 496–97, provides a concise yet complete description of the economic establishment, with its "four pillars": the Société d'Economie Politique, the Collège de France, the Conservatoire des Arts et Métiers, and the journal.

26. The established economists have long been depicted, by such notable figures as Joseph Schumpeter, as a narrowly dogmatic group who took an inflexible and uncompromising stand in favor of laissez-faire, free trade, and the deductive method in social-scientific thought. *History of Economic Analysis*, edited by Elizabeth Boody Schumpeter (Oxford: Oxford Univ. Press, 1954), pp. 840–43. Recently a French historian of economic thought

has come to their defense, insisting that they relied upon observation as well as upon deductive reasoning and that many of them understood that the natural laws of economics had to be tempered in application. Luc Bourcier de Carbon, *Essai sur l'histoire de la pensée économique et des doctrines économiques*, vol. 1: *De Montchretien à Karl Marx-trois thèmes centreaux: l'Etat, l'individu, la société* (Paris: Montchrestien, 1971), pp. 224–40; vol. 2: *Aux sources du Scientisme et de l'humanisme économiques modernes* (Paris: Montchrestien, 1972), p. 70. On Joseph Schumpeter, see Bourcier de Carbon, vol. 2, p. 125. Believing that the old picture of the establishment is roughly accurate but overdone, I have tried to present important nuances that are lacking in both older and newer accounts.

27. Two key works that helped form the ideology of peace were Benjamin Constant, *De l'esprit de conquête* (1813), and Henri de Saint-Simon, *Catéchisme des industriels* (1823). A discussion of this ideology and of its prevalence among intellectuals in the 1860s in France is found in Claude Digeon, *La crise allemand de la pensée française (1870–1914)* (Paris: PUF, 1959), pp. 12–14. Guy Palmade, "Le *Journal des Economistes* et la pensée libérale sous le Second Empire," *Bulletin de la Société d'Histoire Moderne* (May 1962), pp. 13–14, comments on the depth of the pacifism of the contributors to the *Journal des Economistes*.

28. Palmade, "Le *Journal des Economistes*," gives the best account of the outlook of the Established Liberal economists during the 1860s. See also Lutfalla, "Aux origines du libéralisme économique" and Charles Gide and Charles Rist, *A History of Economic Doctrines, from the Time of the Physiocrats to the Present Day*, trans. R. Richards and Ernest F. Row (2nd English ed., New York: D.C. Heath, 1948), pp. 329–54.

29. Palmade, "Le *Journal des Economistes*," p. 10.

30. See Lutfalla, "Aux origines du libéralisme économique," p. 516, and Gide and Rist, *History of Economic Doctrines*, pp. 329–34.

31. Frédéric Bastiat, *Harmonies économiques* (Paris, 1851). Robert Heilbroner has a few fine pages on Bastiat in his *Worldly Philosophers*, a text which has gone through numerous editions since its first appearance in 1953. The discussion appears in the early part of the chapter called "The Victorian World and the Underworld of Economics." See also Gide and Rist, *History of Economic Doctrines*, pp. 334–52. A recent dissertation has added considerably to our knowledge of Bastiat and his thought: Robert M. Hendrick, *Frédéric Bastiat, Forgotten Liberal: Spokesman for an Ideology in Crisis* (Ph.D. diss., New York University, 1987).

32. Charles Dunoyer and Michel Chevalier are two major figures who illustrate the extremes of the Liberal spectrum regarding government's role. Dunoyer, known for his adherence to the strictest conception of laissez-faire, excluded government from the realm of education on the basis that schooling was the business of parents and of private associations. Bourcier de Carbon argues that Dunoyer was not dogmatic, but the two pages of

quotations he presents do not in the slightest support his argument. Dunoyer also declared that the true aim of economic policy must be to promote conditions that would bring a flood of goods from machines and fields. This attitude represents a shift from Adam Smith's emphasis on the needs of the consumer to the assertion that the producer's needs are primary. On Dunoyer, see Gide and Rist, *History of Economic Doctrines*, pp. 352–54, and Bourcier de Carbon, *Essai sur l'histoire*, vol. 1, pp. 240–42. On Chevalier, see Bourcier de Carbon, vol. 1, pp. 238–40, and Jean Walch, *Michel Chevalier, économiste saint-simonien, 1806–1879* (Paris: Vrin, 1975).

A posthumous article by Jules Duval and Joseph Garnier's reply in an 1870 issue of the *Journal des Economistes* illustrate the differences within the establishment. Duval argued that the role of the state had to expand with the improvement of civilization. Garnier, while admitting that the role of the state at that time had to be greater than that desired by supporters of laissez-faire, expressed the hope it would diminish over time. Jules Duval, "Les fonctions économiques de l'Etat," and Joseph Garnier, "Observations sur l'article précédent," *Journal des Economistes* (hereafter JDE) 17 (March 1870), pp. 382–98. A similar interchange occurred between Louis Wolowski and Notelle at the 5 October 1874 meeting of the Société d'Economie Politique; see report, *JDE*, 3rd. ser., 36 (October 1874), pp. 134–38, 143.

33. Palmade, "Le *Journal des Economistes*," pp. 12–13.

34. A survey of the tables of contents of the *Séances et Travaux de l'Académie des Sciences Morales et Politiques* in the late 1860s reveals frequent reviews of books on the problems and discontent of the "popular classes," as well as lengthy reports, read to and discussed by the membership, on the conditions of workers.

35. Guiral, *Prévost-Paradol*, pp. 518–19. See also p. 303 for Prévost-Paradol's skepticism about the deterministic rule of supply and demand over the level of wages. In the early 1870s, when the faculty of the school of law in Paris was debating curriculum reform, a number of instructors expressed considerable skepticism regarding the ideas of the economists, whom they found dogmatic and out of touch with the complex realities of social life; see *Registre de la Faculté de Droit*, 17 and 29 April 1872, Archives Nationales, AJ[16]1791.

36. One should not overemphasize the resistance of the leading Bonapartists to Established Liberal economic principles. Jules Baroche, one of the three leading ministers of Louis Napoleon, opposed government intervention in the economy and favored free trade. See Campbell, *Second Empire*, pp. 123–24, which draws on Jean Maurrain, *Un bourgeois français au XIXe siècle: Baroche* (Paris: Alcan, 1936). Similarly, the Imperial Senate invoked the law of supply and demand in rejecting a petition in which workers requested the right to form unions. See Guiral, *Prévost-Paradol*, p. 303.

37. A letter by an official of the University of Paris, Octave Gréard,

reports on disturbances at the opening lecture by Anselme Batbie, the first professor of political economy at Paris. The students shouted, "Down with the police. Open the doors," a reference to the presence of police agents in the lecture hall and to the exclusion of students who wanted to get into the room. See Octave Gréard to the Rector of the University, 2 October 1864, Batbie dossier, Archives Nationales, AJ[16]6947. Students were not required to take an examination in the subject and therefore were not under any compulsion to attend the lectures.

38. In 1867, when Leroy-Beaulieu won his first prize, the president of the Academy was Esquirou de Parieu (b. 1815), who held a high post in the financial section of the Conseil d'Etat and who evidently regarded himself as a "political economist." See his "Discours d'ouverture prononcée à la séance annuelle du samedi 28 décembre 1867," *Séances et Travaux*, 5th ser., 13 (January–April 1868), pp. 208–28, esp. p. 221. G. Vapereau, ed., *Dictionnaire des contemporaines*, 5th ed. (Paris: Hachette, 1880), pp. 1405–6, describes de Parieu as a politician and scholar whose interests included political economy, natural history, and philology. Palmade, "Le *Journal des Economistes*," p. 9, lists twelve key members of the Société d'Economie Politique who were members of the Academy in the 1860s or who became members after the establishment of the Third Republic.

39. Palmade, "Le *Journal des Economistes*," p. 9. Lutfalla, "Aux origines du libéralisme économique," pp. 497–98, cites similar remarks by Louis Reybaud in 1842, Th. Fix in 1843, and Joseph Garnier in 1846.

40. de Lacroix, "Pierre-Paul Leroy-Beaulieu." For Laboulaye consult Girard, *Les Libéraux*, pp. 188–90; Jardin, *Histoire du libéralisme*, pp. 386–87, 408; and Jacques Flach, "La vie et les oeuvres de M. Edouard Laboulaye" (Inaugural lesson, Histoire des Législations comparées, Collège de France), *Revue politique et littéraire (Revue Bleue)* 21 (17 May 1884), pp. 610–18.

41. Stourm, "PLB," p. 535.

42. *Recherches économiques, historiques, et statistiques sur les guerres contemporaines (1853–1866)* (Paris: Verboeckhoven-Lacroix, 1869).

43. The list of the officers of the organization is on the inside cover of the pamphlet version of the book. Some of the publication history is found in the preface of the complete version, pp. vii–ix. Frédéric Passy recounted other aspects of its publication history in a review published—belatedly—in 1873: *JDE*, 3rd ser., 19 (September 1873), pp. 457–58.

44. Stourm, "PLB," p. 537.

45. de Broglie, *Histoire politique*, pp. 106–7.

46. Stourm, "PLB," p. 541. Leroy-Beaulieu faced few competitors for his prizes. Only two manuscripts were submitted in the contest for the study "of the education and wages of women employed in industry and of the means to reconcile their work and family life," and the prize committee considered the other submission completely irrelevant and

dismissed it out of hand. Leroy-Beaulieu's first work, on the influence of morality and education on wages faced two rival submissions. Among the other three 1870 contests, three monographs were submitted on local administration, four on land taxes, and four on modern colonial systems. Judging from the reports of the prize committees, however, Leroy-Beaulieu's manuscripts must have been considered major works. Few authors would have undertaken the challenge of producing the extensive and probing discussions demanded by the Académie. The information about the number of contestants can be found in the reports on the competitions (for specific references see the notes to Chapter 3).

47. Stourm, "PLB," p. 541.

48. Aumercier, pp. 108–13, gives a detailed account of Leroy-Beaulieu's fortune.

CHAPTER 3: THE JOURNEYMAN PUBLICIST

1. Hippolyte Passy, "Prix Bordin: rapport sur le concours," *Séances et Travaux*, 5th ser., 12 (July–September 1867), p. 22.

2. *Guerres contemporaines, 1853–1866* (Paris: Librairie Internationale, 1869), pp. 8–9, 325. Hereafter cited as *GC*.

3. *De la colonisation chez les peuples modernes*, 1st ed. (Paris: Guillaumin, 1874), pp. vi–vii. Henceforth cited as *DLC*.

4. *L'administration locale en France et en Angleterre* (Paris: Guillaumin, 1872), pp. 13, 15. Hereafter cited as *AL*.

5. *Le travail des femmes au XIXe siècle* (Paris: Guillaumin, 1873). Hereafter *TDF*. The first half of the book presents the history of women's work, summarizes research on women in contemporary industry, and points out the weaknesses in the various schemes to protect women and the family. The second half describes and evaluates private efforts, mainly by employers, to enable women to work while raising children.

6. *TDF*, p. 189.

7. *De l'état moral et intellectuel des populations ouvrières et de son influence sur le taux des salaires* (Paris: Guillaumin, 1868), pp. 9, 70–71, 208. Hereafter *EMO*.

8. *La question ouvrière au XIXe siècle* (Paris: Charpentier, 1872), pp. 2, 66, 123. Hereafter cited as *QO*.

9. *QO*, p. 61; see also *EMO*, pp. 47, 61, 69.

10. *QO*, p. 63.

11. *GC*, pp. 291, 5–7.

12. *AL*, pp. 41–50.

13. *AL*, p. 61.

14. *AL*, pp. 58–61.

15. *EMO*, p. 3; emphasis added. We will see that Leroy-Beaulieu repeatedly described the views of "political economy" as beyond dispute.

16. *EMO*, pp. 3, 36; see also pp. 109–11, 112, 164. Leroy-Beaulieu blamed unions for attacking individual freedom by coercing workers.

17. *AL*, pp. 22–23. On the basis of this gradualist perspective Leroy-Beaulieu could reject too great a break with the elite control of the state; he could conscientiously seek to restrict the role of the majority of French people to the relatively small privilege, for example, of electing their "betters" as Conseillers Généraux.

18. *QO*, pp. 243–46, 248; quotation is from p. 165.

19. *QO*, pp. 166, 232; on the natural hierarchy and inborn inequality, pp. 251–52; on social mobility, pp. 35–36.

20. *EMO*, pp. 192–93, 208, 214, 215.

21. *TDF*, p. 192. "Société soit un être complet, spontané, indépendant, produit et résultante de l'action des forces individuelles, ayant en soi son propre moteur et sa loi de développement."

22. *TDF*, p. 195; emphasis added.

23. "Tout empiètement de l'Etat au delà de ces limites amène necessairement des empiètements ultérieurs; il devient impossible de fixer un point d'arrêt." *TDF*, pp. 196–97.

24. *AL*, pp. 178ff., 189, 190, 208. These viewpoints appeared in sections that must have been part of the original prize treatise.

25. *EMO*, p. 146.

26. *TDF*, p. 196.

27. *TDF*, pp. 200–202.

28. *EMO*, p. 18.

29. "Il ne faut pas croire à une solution unique, exclusive," he wrote (*QO*, p. 65). On his experience with public meetings of radicals, see *QO*, pp. 144–45.

30. The expressions of an ideal society are found above all in *EMO*, but his comments about the deferential lower classes of Britain in *AL* also indicate his concept of an ideal political system.

31. *EMO*, p. 70.

32. *EMO*, p. 208.

33. *EMO*, p. 10.

34. In *EMO*, pp. 99–100, for example, Leroy-Beaulieu repeated typical Established Liberal arguments to refute the Malthusian theories that implied conflict between classes for scarce resources.

35. Passy, "Prix Bordin," pp. 8–9.

36. Passy, "Prix Bordin," pp. 11–12.

37. Passy, "Prix Bordin," pp. 16–17.

38. Esquirou de Parieu, the lawyer and Imperial official who served as president of the Académie that year, summed up the results of the competition by remarking that "Political economy, through such useful information, comes powerfully to the aid of morality and even of politics." "Discours d'ouverture prononcée à la séance publique annuelle du samedi 28

décembre 1867," *Séances et Travaux*, 5th ser., 13 (January–April 1868), p. 221.

39. E. Cauchy, "Rapport sur le concours relatif à l'administration locale en France et en Angleterre," *Séances et Travaux*, 5th ser., 23 (July–September 1870), pp. 119, 144–45, 1,55.

40. Conservatives (i.e., those suspicious of modern civilization), other Established Liberals such as Guizot and Prévost-Paradol, and republican Radicals including Jules Ferry and Léon Gambetta all demanded an end to the administrative centralization that characterized the Second Empire as it had the Jacobin Republic, the First Empire, and the Conservative and Liberal regimes from 1815 to 1848. For a description of the state of opinion in the 1860s on decentralization, see Pierre Guiral, *Prévost-Paradol*, pp. 535–36.

41. The commentator, Louis Reybaud, also declared that the other submission was not on the topic assigned and that it was badly composed. Therefore, the prize committee, while "paying justice to the benevolent intentions of the author," ruled against his work because of its "illusions, its deviations and its lack of method." Reybaud, "Rapport sur le concours ouvert dans la Section de Morale relativement à l'instruction et au salaire des femmes dans les travaux d'industrie," *Séances et travaux*, 24 (October–December 1870), pp. 170–71, 172.

42. Reybaud, "Rapport," p. 169.

43. Reybaud, "Rapport," p. 193.

44. Reybaud, "Rapport," p. 193.

45. *EMO*, p. 77.

CHAPTER 4: LEROY-BEAULIEU DURING THE WAR AND THE CONSERVATIVE REPUBLIC

1. Charles de Mazade, "Chronique de la quinzaine," *Revue des Deux Mondes* (hereafter *RDM*), 2nd per., 85 (1 January 1870), pp. 241–43. Only a year later de Mazade wailed: "During the first days of 1870 who could have foreseen such a future. In those days the great affair was the ministry of January 2, the alliance of the *centre droit* and the *centre gauche*." De Mazade, "Chronique de la quinzaine," *RDM*, 2nd per., 91 (1 January 1871), p. 167.

2. For example, on July 1, 1871, de Mazade contrasted the situation before June, when the peace treaty was signed after the defeat of the Communards, with the present and future: "Above all we needed to pull the country free from the odious and bloody fatality that seemed even to menace its very existence. Today this fatality is vanquished, and there is no longer even a pretext for that painful uncertainty that kept everything in suspense." *RDM*, 2nd per., 94 (1 July 1871), p. 221.

3. The politicians of the center and the right and such publicists as de Mazade never failed thereafter to use an imprecation whenever they mentioned the Commune. See, for example, *RDM* (1 July 1871), p. 223.

4. "Les ressources de la France et de la Prusse," *RDM*, 2nd per., 89 (1 September 1870), pp. 151, 153.

5. "Les ressources," p. 136.

6. Blaming French levity for the military failures, Leroy-Beaulieu also flayed the "masses" for their "cynicism" and the Republican prefects for their "delirium." "La province pendant la siège de Paris: II. Sa situation politique et sociale," *RDM*, 2nd per., 92 (15 March 1871), pp. 301–2.

7. *Journal des Débats* (hereafter *JDD*), 15 August 1871.

8. Considering the subject at a time when the Communards were burning and fighting in Paris, Leroy-Beaulieu asserted once more: "Our excessive and clumsy centralization, that is the bad regime that is devouring us and that we must cure ourselves of before it becomes irremediable." "La reforme municipal en France: la Commune et le self government," *RDM*, 2nd per., 93 (15 May 1871), pp. 250, 265. In August 1871, when he had begun writing for the *Journal des Débats*, the conservative side of decentralization emerged plainly in his discussion of municipal reform. At that time he asserted that decentralization would be a weapon against radicals since it would remove much of the influence of the democratic cities over the conservative rural areas. *JDD*, 15 August 1871.

9. "La province pendant la siège de Paris: Sa situation politique," pp. 303–4.

10. Elme Caro, "La république et les républicains," *RDM*, 2nd per., 93 (1 June 1871), p. 529. Leroy-Beaulieu characterized Léon Gambetta, head of the Government of National Defense as a "capricious dictator." "La province pendant la siège de Paris: Sa situation politique et sociale," pp. 301–2. Yet nothing Leroy-Beaulieu wrote then or during the next few years about Gambetta or the Radicals matched the irony and anger expressed by de Mazade, on whom see *RDM*, 15 July 1871, p. 448, 1 November 1871, p. 229, 15 November 1871, p. 475.

At least one contributor to the *Revue* defended the republicans against the charge that they "had engaged in politics rather than truly engaging in defense." George Sand, "Journal d'un voyageur pendant la guerre (pt. 2)," *RDM*, 2nd per., 92 (15 March 1871), p. 229. "I believe," she wrote, that the republicans "were simply surprised by events."

11. Leroy-Beaulieu reported on these developments in such articles as "La navigation à voiles et la navigation à vapeur," *L'Economiste Français* (hereafter *EF* 2 (21 November 1874), p. 629, and "Les grands magasins universels et les petits détaillants" *EF* 3 (25 December 1874), pp. 801–3.

12. For a description of the situation, reactions to the Commune, and the treatment of the Communards see Jean Joughin, *The Commune*

in French Politics, 1871–1880, the History of the Amnesty of 1880, 2 vols. (Baltimore: Johns Hopkins Univ. Press, 1955). The repression lasted as long as the Conservative Republic.

13. Henri Germain, founder and president of the Credit Lyonnais, said in the National Assembly on December 21, 1871: "Since 1848 you have shown the masses that, when there was a sacrifice to make, you have undertaken the largest part of it. . . . It is for you to show the country that, if you have spent your blood prodigiously during the war, you will not be sparing of your fortune during the peace." Casimir-Perier told the same body on July 6, 1872: "As I examine England, I admire more and more its enlightened classes, its possessing classes, who always know to take the initiative when concessions become necessary." Quoted in Robert Schnerb, "La politique fiscale de Thiers: I. Un demi-siècle de luttes autour de l'impôt," *Revue Historique* 201 (1949), pp. 186–212. For the efforts to reform labor laws, see two articles by Leroy-Beaulieu in the *Journal des Débats*, 25 January and 3 February 1873.

14. Numa Fustel de Coulanges, "La politique d'envahissement: Louvois et M. de Bismarck," *RDM*, 2nd per., 91 (1 January 1871), p. 1.

15. de Mazade, "Chronique," *RDM*, 2nd per., 93 (31 May 1871), pp. 556–57.

16. See Elme Caro, "L'idée de la patrie: ses défaillances et son reveil," *RDM*, 2nd per., 91 (15 January 1871), pp. 243–62.

17. The first chapters of Claude Digeon's masterful *La crise allemand de la pensée française (1870–1914)* (Paris: PUF, 1959) are the best source on the reactions to the war, but see also an older work: Michel Mohrt, *Les intellectuels devant la défaite, 1870* (Paris: Correa, 1942), pp. 80–85, 141. On Ferry see Thomas Francis Power, *Jules Ferry and the Renaissance of French Imperialism* (New York: King's Crown Press, 1944), p. 4.

18. My description of the political factions relies on Odile Rudelle, *La république absolue, 1870–1889* (Paris: Publ. de la Sorbonne, 1982), pp. 59–60; for the Centrists see Jean Bouvier, "Aux origines de la Troisième République: les réflexes sociaux des milieux d'affaires," *Revue Historique* 210 (1953), pp. 271–301.

19. Bouvier, "Aux origines de la Troisième République," pp. 277–78.

20. Bouvier, "Aux origines de la Troisième République," pp. 292, 297, 300. Buloz, in common with the other ex-Orleanists who accepted the coming of the republic, remained as indifferent to the form of government as he had been during the 1860s. He demanded two things from a constitution: parliamentary government and a set of checks on those legislators elected through universal suffrage. See Gabriel de Broglie, *Histoire politique de la "Revue des Deux Mondes" de 1829 à 1979* (Paris: Perrin, 1979), p. 106 on Buloz's relative indifference with regard to the form of the regime; p. 195 on the Senate as a check on universal suffrage.

21. de Mazade, *RDM* (15 May 1871), p. 359; see also his chronicle for 28 February 1871.

22. Garnier sat with the republican left in the Senate while Batbie was an outstanding orator for the Centre Droite. On Batbie consult Roger Vidal, *Batbie: homme politique, économiste, juriste* (Paris: Pichon, Durand-Auzias, 1950); on Garnier, L.-A. Morel, *Clément-Joseph Garnier, 1813–1881: l'homme et l'oeuvre* (St. Germain-en-Laye: Penot, 1906), pp. 13, 17–19.

23. On the Ecole Libre see Thomas R. Osborne, *A Grande Ecole for the Grands Corps: The Recruitment and Training of the French Administrative Elite in the Nineteenth Century* (New York and Boulder, Colo.: Social Science Monographs, 1983), and Guy Thuillier, *L'ENA avant L'ENA* (Paris: PUF, 1983).

24. Quoted in Lucette Le Van Lemesle, "La promotion de l'économie politique en France au XIXe siècle jusqu'à son introduction dans les Facultés (1815–1881)," *Revue d'Histoire Moderne et Contemporaine*, (1980), p. 290n.105.

25. Paul Leroy-Beaulieu, letter of candidature, 12 June 1878, Paul Leroy-Beaulieu dossier, Archives de l'Institut de France.

26. See the letters in the dossier for *L'économiste français* in the Archives Nationales. The police report to the Minister of the Interior characterized Fontpertuis as "constantly involved with religious writing," publishing in *Le Monde Catholique* and *L'Avenir Catholique* as well as contributing to the *Journal des Economistes*. "As for his political views, his sympathies are attached to the monarchist party." Prefect of Police to the Minister, 29 April 1873, Dossiers de Presse, *L'Economiste Français*, Archives Nationales, F18 343. Aumercier, pp. 172–281 (esp. p. 183), has a very detailed account of the founding and character of *L'Économiste Français*. However, she could not determine with certainty the role Leroy-Beaulieu played in the formation of the journal.

27. Leroy-Beaulieu, "Programme," *EF* 1 (19 April 1873), p. 2. See also his "De la representation des intérêts industriels et commerciaux en France," *EF* 2 (7 November 1874), 353. One earlier sign of his identification with the industrialists was his attack on a proposed tax on corporate revenues. He argued that corporate profits should be regarded as the reward for the intelligent directors who developed the country's natural resources. *JDD*, 3 January 1872.

28. Aumercier, vol. 4, p. 1264.

29. Stourm, "Notice," pp. 154, 157. Leroy-Beaulieu expressed these convictions in a November 1872 letter he wrote to Jules Simon, then Minister of Public Instruction in the Thiers cabinet: "I am one of those . . . who have strongly applauded the reform you have had the courage to propose. This renovation of the classical curriculum was indispensable. The education given in the *collèges* had degenerated into an empty and verbose

rhetoric, which did not improve the mind, but swelled it without nourishing it. . . . I know that you undoubtedly will face battles against the partisans of the old routine: you can count on the assistance of the greatest part of the press and in particular of the *Journal des Débats*." Leroy-Beaulieu to Jules Simon, 8 November 1872, Jules Simon papers, Archives Nationales, 87 AP4.

30. The article was "Les aspirations des ouvrières et de leurs projets de réforme sociale: rapports de la délégation ouvrière à l'exposition de Vienne," *RDM* (1 July 1875), which was later published as a pamphlet and which discussed the moderate demands made at an international gathering of workers at the exposition at Vienne.

31. Prefect of police to the minister, 21 January 1873, Dossiers de Presse, *L'Economiste Français*, Archives Nationales, F18 343.

32. Leroy-Beaulieu, "Programme," p. 2.

33. "Le mouvement politique et économique aux Etats Unis," *EF* 2 (14 November 1874), p. 598. See also "Le mouvement politique et économique aux Etats Unis," *EF* 2 (12 September 1874), pp. 308–11; "Le budget de 1874," *EF* 1 (29 November 1873), p. 901.

34. "Le Programme ministeriel," *EF* 4 (18 March 1876), p. 353.

35. An English scholar who was acquainted with Leroy-Beaulieu also placed him in this political camp. John Courtenay Bodley, *France* (London: MacMillan, 1898), vol. 1, pp. 98–100, 128–29.

36. "Les grands magasins et les petits détaillants," *EF* 3 (25 December 1875), pp. 801–3.

37. Michael Stephen Smith, *Tariff Reform in France, 1860–1900* (Ithaca, N.Y.: Cornell Univ. Press, 1980), p. 74, discussing the late 1870s, also sees Leroy-Beaulieu as an ally of internationally oriented enterprises.

38. On Thiers's fiscal policy, see Schnerb, "La politique fiscale."

39. *Traité de la science des finances* (Paris: Guillaumin, 1877), vol. 1, pp. 546, 547, 552. Hereafter cited as *TSF*.

40. *JDD*, 19 June 1871 and 25 January 1872; "Le transit et les droits sur le transport," *EF* 1 (1 November 1873), pp. 789–91.

41. *JDD*, 19 February 1871; "Le transit et les droits," pp. 789–91.

42. If the progression were modest, he argued, the effect on the distribution of income would be too insignificant to be worth pursuing. If the wealthy had to pay a much heavier percentage than the lower-income groups, the impact on the economy and society would be deplorable. The principle that taxation should be based on "equality of sacrifice," (that is, on progressivity) would produce an "invincible tendency" to use the government to correct social inequalities, and that "fatal impulsion" would ruin society. *TSF*, vol. 1, pp. 139–40.

43. He also wanted surplus revenues from indirect taxes to be used to lower, and eventually to eliminate, taxes on essential items such as salt. *TSF*, vol. 1, pp. 136, 725.

44. On his boredom on the Council, see Aumercier, vol. 1, pp. 70–74. Aumercier also reproduces the electoral leaflet, dated 27 October 1877, which consists of a long appeal by Michel Chevalier on behalf of his son-in-law and a shorter statement by Leroy-Beaulieu himself. Two important Established Liberal economists, Joseph Garnier and Anselme Batbie, had already achieved election to the National Assembly. See note 22 above.

45. Léonce de Lavergne, economist and leader in the pivotal group of Constitutionnels in the National Assembly, and Hippolyte Passy heaped praise upon the book. Although the former qualified his compliments by pointing out that the science of public finance was a young one, Passy's remarks were entirely flattering. See "Bibliographie," *JDE*, 3rd per., 48 (October 1877), pp. 142–44, in which their comments to the Académie were published.

46. For the quotation, see *JDD*, 27 February 1873. See also *JDD* for the entire period from January to April 1872; "Programme," p. 2; Eichtal, "PLB," 2.

47. He wrote: "We have in faraway countries only a few trading posts and traders. . . . This inertia, which nothing justifies, does singular harm to France. . . . Our industry would have infinitely more activity and make greater profits if we knew how to seek out clients at the extremities of the globe." *JDD*, 1 May 1873.

48. *TSF*, vol. 1, p. 725.

49. As we see from the statement cited in note 47 above, one of his chief preoccupations in the years just following the war was to encourage France's foreign trade. This trade, he felt, was being harmed by Thiers's policies.

50. These proposals appeared in one of three articles in *L'Economiste Français* on Algeria, articles which perhaps coincided with the publication of *De la Colonisation chez les peuples modernes*: "La colonisation de l'Algerie" (pt. 1), *EF* 2 (22 August 1874), pp. 213–14.

51. "La question de la population en France," pt. 1: *EF* 4 (14 July 1877), p. 419; pt. 2: *EF* 4 (21 July 1877), pp. 450–51.

52. Roger Soltau pointed out this aspect of French Liberalism long ago in *French Political Thought in the Nineteenth Century* (New Haven, Conn.: Yale Univ. Press, 1931), p. 296.

53. *TSF*, vol. 1, p. 88; see also pp. 5, 8.

54. *TSF*, vol. 1, p. 88.

55. *TSF*, vol. 1, pp. 87, 88, 90; the discussion continues to page 95.

56. *QO*, pp. 301–3, 400.

57. *QO*, pp. 12–15, 88.

58. *QO*, pp. 310ff.

59. He conceded, "The other side of the coin of the magnificence of contemporary industry is excessive instability." *QO*, p. 331. His review,

in December 1871, of a British consular survey of workers' conditions around the world noted the unemployment problems of unskilled American workers, but he did not explore the meaning of the situation. "Une enquête anglaise sur la condition des travailleurs," *RDM*, 2nd per., 97 (1 December 1871), pp. 658–59.

60. "Les aspirations des ouvrières et de leurs projets de réforme sociale (pt. 1)."

61. *TSF*, vol. 1, pp. 115.

62. *QO*, p. 335.

63. *QO*, p. 327.

64. *QO*, p. 317. Early in 1873 Leroy-Beaulieu made one slight departure from his position that discontent should be cured by morality rather than law: he supported legislation regulating child labor. Shortly after the publication of *La question ouvrière* Leroy-Beaulieu wrote two columns in the *Journal des Débats* in which he stated that public disapproval was an insufficient sanction to prevent employers from mistreating the women and children who worked for them. He urged the passage of a law that would provide inspectors to protect working women and children. *JDD*, 3 February 1873 and 10 February 1873.

65. *QO*, pp. 305–9, 317–18.

66. *QO*, p. 339. The book concluded, "So there is one phrase that ought to sum up this entire book: the only dike that we can raise successfully to the constantly rising tide of the populace's demands is the honesty and the union of the upper classes."

67. *QO*, pp. 136–37, 154–56, 159.

68. *JDD*, 11 March 1872; see also *JDD*, 8 March 1872.

69. In one new passage in *La question ouvrière* he attributed the insurrection to "the breakdown of all public authority, frightful national catastrophes, the passions over-excited by suffering." *QO*, p. 136.

CHAPTER 5: THE TURNING POINT

1. Michael Stephen Smith, *Tariff Reform in France, 1860–1900* (Ithaca, New York: Cornell Univ. Press, 1980), p. 41. Smith emphasizes the role played by *L'Economiste Français* in the free trade campaign, but the reports in the *Journal des Economistes* indicate that Leroy-Beaulieu did not figure among the leading speakers of the organization. See "Bulletin: Association pour la défense de la liberté commerciale et industrielle," *JDE*, 4th ser., 3 (July 1878), pp. 120–23. On the organization's speaking tours see, e.g., "Chronique économique," *JDE* 4th ser., 7 (July 1879), p. 164.

2. Paul de Lacroix, "Pierre-Paul Leroy-Beaulieu, Membre de l'Institut," Bibliothèque Nationale, n.a.f. 22862. Apparently Leroy-Beaulieu presented himself as a candidate in 1877 in competition with Frédéric Passy. Passy was elected and Leroy-Beaulieu had to wait another year to gain

his seat. The two men were also rivals for the Chair of Political Economy at the Collège de France in 1880. F. Passy to Jules Simon, 24 January 1877, Jules Simon Papers, Archives Nationales, 87 AP 6.

3. On the election see the dossier on Leroy-Beaulieu in the archives of the Institut de France and the dossier, "Candidates for the Chair of Political Economy, Collège de France," Archives Nationales, F17 13556. He was chosen over Passy and Emile Alglave, one of the founders and editors of the *Revue Bleue* and professor of financial theory at the Faculté de Droit in Paris. One contemporary observer, Léon Walras, attributed Leroy-Beaulieu's rapid advancement to nepotism. See Walras, *Correspondence and Related Papers*, ed. William Jaffé (The Hague, North Holland Publishing Co., 1965), vol. 1, p. 627.

4. Aumercier, pp. 108–13. See p. 118 and note 52.

5. Paul Leroy-Beaulieu, *Traité théorique et pratique de l'économie politique* (Paris: Guillaumin, 1896), vol. 1, p. ii.

6. de Lacroix, "Pierre-Paul Leroy-Beaulieu"; Edwin R. A. Seligman, "Paul Leroy-Beaulieu," *Encyclopedia of the Social Sciences*, 1st ed. (New York: Macmillan, 1933), p. 415; Stourm, "PLB," p. 549. For his role in the Caves du Rocquefort, see Chapter 8 below, and also "Caves et producteurs réunis de Rocquefort," *Moniteur de Banque et Bourse*, 19 July 1907, in the dossier of the Société des Caves et des Producteurs Réunis de Rocquefort, Archives Nationales, 65 AQ R. 429.

7. Stourm, "PLB," p. 547. A full-length photograph of Leroy-Beaulieu in his uniform as an academician is included in Paul de Lacroix's article on him. He appears to be in his late thirties or early forties. In contrast to the well-stuffed figures one so often associates with the epoch, we see a fairly slim and very erect form. De Lacroix, "Pierre-Paul Leroy-Beaulieu."

8. G. Schelle, "L'oeuvre de Paul Leroy-Beaulieu," *JDE*, 6th ser., 54 (April–June 1917), p. 20. Schelle described him as "a man of distinguished manner, perfectly courteous, although outwardly a bit cold." Schelle also commented on "the regularity of his features, his wavy hair, his imposing beard, the slightly guttural timbre of his voice."

9. Marcel Proust, *A la recherche du temps perdu* (Paris: Gallimard, 1954), vol. 2: *Le côté de Guermantes*, p. 151.

10. Aumercier, vol. 1, p. 10, states that she did not find any evidence that he had any close friends. The accounts of his reserved and cold nature also point to this conclusion.

11. On Leroy-Beaulieu's political life consult Aumercier, vol. 1, pp. 65–83; de Lacroix, "Pierre-Paul Leroy-Beaulieu," who reported that at the time of that article that Leroy-Beaulieu had held the seat on the Conseil Général for eighteen years; Stourm, "PLB," p. 550, René Stourm, "Paul Leroy-Beaulieu," in G. Vapereau, ed., *Dictionnaire universel des contemporaines*, 6th ed. (Paris: Hachette, 1891). Leroy-Beaulieu's own brochure on

the 1889 election is also informative: *Un chapitre des moeurs electorales en France en 1889–1890* (Paris: Guillaumin, Librairie Chaix, 1890).

In 1961 M. Paul Leroy-Beaulieu, the grandson of the economist, told me that his grandfather's political failure was the result of differences in temperament between the candidate and the voters. Aumercier, p. 65, agrees: "In April 1964," she wrote, "we heard an old friend of the family at Lodève say to Monsieur Paul Leroy-Beaulieu: 'Your grandfather spoke to the peasants around here as if he were giving a course at the Institut.'" Nevertheless his electoral record was a respectable one. In the special election of 1883 he at first drew more votes than Auguste Galtier, who won the runoff. In 1885 in the Hérault the republican winners received between 49,143 and 52,411 votes, and Leroy-Beaulieu topped the opposition list with 42,694 votes. In the Department of the Rhone, where he was also on the slate, he again topped the opposition list with 45,454 votes while the five republicans got between 49,898 and 63,686 votes. His own argument that the election of 1889 was stolen from him is quite persuasive. For the election figures see the dossiers in the Archives Nationales for the races in the Hérault during these years (file C 3507) and *Le Temps*, 5 October 1885, pp. 1E, 2C.

12. On the role of Cordelia Leroy-Beaulieu, see Aumercier, pp. 78–79. On his boredom as councillor, see his letters of 1879 to his wife, cited by Aumercier pp. 72–74. On April 8, 1883, he wrote to Cordelia: "le spectacle de tant d'imbéciles et méchants gens et tous ces petits intérêts si mesquinnement traités fatiguent singulièrement le cerveau. . . . Aucun temps pour la reflexion, ni pour le travail. Je t'assure que j'ai bien peu de gout pour me lancer dans une lutte electoral à Paris. . . . C'est un suicide de l'intelligence de se consacrer à cette vie agitée et bruyante. Ici je n'ai le coeur à rien. Je ne puis ni corriger une épreuve, ni faire un article" (Aumercier, p. 82).

13. "Chronique du Midi," *Messager du Midi* (Montpellier and Nimes), 51st year, no. 175 (18 June 1878), p. 2. See also p. 85 and note 53.

14. Clipping in Leroy-Beaulieu dossier, "Candidates for the Chair of Political Economy, Collège de France," Archives Nationales, F17 13556.

15. Joseph Garnier, "Chronique économique," *JDE*, 3rd ser., 44 (May 1877), pp. 321–24. The possibility that the conflict would involve the other European powers also preoccupied Charles de Mazade: "Chronique," *RDM*, 3rd ser., 21 (1 May 1877), pp. 227–36 and 3rd ser., 22 (1 July 1877), pp. 236–38.

16. Joseph Garnier, "L'année 1877," *JDE*, 4th ser., 1 (January 1878), p. 10. See also Charles de Mazade, "Chronique," *RDM*, 3rd ser., 21 (1 May 1877), pp. 227, 232, 236, and 3rd ser., 25 (1 January 1878), p. 231.

17. Garnier, "Chronique," *JDE*, 3rd ser., 45 (March 1877), p. 475.

18. One speaker claimed that the country had "pretty much escaped" the worldwide depression until the middle of the year, but that was the

only comfort the assembled economists had. "Discussion: Les causes de la crise actuelle" (report on the meeting of the Société d'Economie Politique, 5 December 1877), *JDE*, 3rd ser., 48 (December 1877), pp. 446– 56; see esp. the remarks by Henri Fould, p. 449, by Clapier ("ancien député de Marseille"), p. 448, and by Clamageran, pp. 446–48. In March 1879 Maurice Block, a leading economic journalist, again expressed alarm over the failure of natural forces to do their work; see Block, "La crise économique," *RDM*, 3rd ser., 32 (15 March 1879), p. 432.

The economists wanted to explain the crisis (and exonerate their natural laws) by identifying some culprit whose misbehavior could be blamed for the troubles. So Clamageran and Ernest Brelay, at the December 1877 meeting, chastised the right-wing government installed in May 1877 because it provoked insecurity and fear among business circles. At the same meeting Frédéric Passy launched into a polemic against the aristocratic leaders of the government who treated businessmen and their concerns with disdain ("Discussion," pp. 450–53). He characterized the former as "hommes de joie" and the latter as "hommes de peine." Others pointed to the speculation, overexpansion, and protectionism unleashed in the United States after the Civil War and in Germany after the war of 1870–1871. Garnier, in "L'année 1877," p. 11, focused on wars and speculation, while Guy de Molinari blamed American tariffs in "L'année 1880," *JDE*, 4th ser., 13 (January 1881), p. 8. For Block these explanations were insufficient because "the distress is more profound and more general" than previous commentators had seen. He attributed the crisis to long-term changes in the distribution of population between cities and countryside and to the exhaustion of the productive potentialities of steam and electric power ("La crise économique," pp. 453–59).

19. Paul Degoix (Ingénieur), "Les grèves et la question ouvrière," *JDE*, 4th ser., 3 (August 1878), pp. 177–87; "Le Congrès ouvrier de Marseille" (report of the meeting of the Société d'Economie Politique, 5 November 1879), *JDE*, 4th ser., 7 (November 1879), pp. 307–8.

20. See Jean Joughin, *The Commune in French Politics, 1871–1880, the History of the Amnesty of 1880* (Baltimore: Johns Hopkins Univ. Press, 1955), on the fate of the repressive policies, and Michelle Perrot, *Les ouvriers en grève, France 1871–1900*, 2 vols. (Paris: Monton, 1974).

21. On Renouvier see his *Science de la morale*, 2 vols. (Paris: Ladrange, 1869), and William Logue, *From Philosophy to Sociology: The Evolution of French Liberalism, 1870–1914* (DeKalb: Northern Illinois Univ. Press, 1983). Walras's studies and lectures from the 1860s are reprinted in his *Etudes d'économie sociale: théorie de la répartition de la richesse sociale* (Lausanne and Paris: F. Rouge, Pichon, Durand-Auzias, 1896, rpt. 1936).

22. Among the Socialists of the Chair were Adolph Wagner, Gustav Schmoller, Lujo Brentano, Adolph Held, and (according to Donald O. Wagner), Albert Schaeffle, whom Leroy-Beaulieu regarded as a Socialist.

Wagner's short but excellent introduction to the group appears in the book of readings he edited, *Social Reformers: Adam Smith to John Dewey* (New York: Macmillan, 1934), pp. 486–88. Especially valuable is James J. Sheehan, *The Career of Lujo Brentano: A Study of Liberalism and Social Reform in Imperial Germany* (Chicago: Chicago Univ. Press, 1966). For a thorough and recent analysis of the German economists of the late nineteenth century, see Luc Bourcier de Carbon, *Histoire des pensées et des doctrines économiques* (Paris: Montchrestien, 1971–1979), vol. 2.

23. On Emile de Laveleye, see his "Les tendances nouvelles de l'économie politique et du socialisme," *RDM*, 3rd ser., 45 (15 July 1875), pp. 445–68. A German scholar, S. Feilbogen, in "L'évolution des idées économiques et sociales en France depuis 1870," *Revue d'Histoire des Doctrines Economiques et Sociales* 3 (1910), pp. 1–10, 347–72, summarized the developments, focusing on Paul Cauwès and Charles Gide.

24. Paul Cauwès, *Précis d'un cours d'économie politique: professé à la Faculté de Droit de Paris; contenant avec l'exposé des principes l'analyse des questions économiques* (Paris: Larose et Forcel, 1879), vol. 1, p. viii. The second edition appeared quickly for two reasons. The first edition was full of faults that Gustave Courcelle-Seneuil scornfully pointed out in *JDE*, 4th ser., 2 (May–June 1878), pp. 315–17, and *JDE*, 4th ser., 5 (November 1878), pp. 328–29. But also, it was so popular that it sold out in less than two years, according to an advertisement from the publisher. This advertisement is included in the Cauwès family papers, which were graciously put at my disposal by the granddaughter and great-grandson of Paul Cauwès, Mme. Collette Goy and Professor Raymond Goy of Versailles, France.

25. Cauwès, *Précis*, vol. 1, p. vi.

26. Cauwès, *Précis*, vol. 1, pp. 25–26, 70ff. These stances are stated even more forcefully and unequivocally in the second edition.

27. Cauwès, *Précis* (2nd ed.), vol. 1, pp. 84–87, 649–51.

28. Cauwès, *Précis* (2nd ed.), vol. 1, pp. 5, 65, 171.

29. In January 1878, when Garnier reviewed the events of 1877, he wrote happily that France, "a country formerly so prompt to have recourse to the dangerous and costly weapon of revolution," showed in the October election that "the peaceable right of suffrage and the mere menace of a refusal to pay taxes sufficed to rout the politicians of the seize mai." See Garnier's articles, "L'année 1877," pp. 11–12; "Chronique," *JDE*, 3rd ser., 46 (June 1877), pp. 472–73, and esp. 3rd ser., 48 (November 1877), pp. 468–69. For de Mazade's reactions see his chronicles in *RDM*, 3rd ser., 21 (1 July 1877), pp. 230, 233; 3rd ser., 21 (15 July 1877), p. 473; 3rd ser., 22 (15 August 1877), p. 939; 3rd ser., 23 (1 October 1877), pp. 709ff.; 3rd ser., 24 (1 November 1877), pp. 224–31; 3rd ser., 24 (1 December 1877), p. 704; and 3rd ser., 24 (15 December 1877), pp. 945–46. De Mazade reacted at first with astonishment rather than indignation, but he grew increasingly upset over the electoral tactics of the Seize Mai government and

its lack of an understandable policy. Finally he bitterly criticized the de Broglie ministry for dividing France and making compromise between the parties even more difficult than before.

30. For de Mazade the year 1878 deserved "a good reputation in the history of our much tried country" because "it gave France only a profound internal peace." "Chronique," *RDM*, 3rd ser., 31 (1 January 1879), p. 224.

31. Smith, *Tariff Reforms*, on the tariff controversy; earlier historians, such as Gabriel Hanotaux, *Histoire de la France contemporaine* (Paris: Société d'édition contemporaine, 1903–1909), recount the disputes over the purges. The columns of the *Journal des Economistes* trace the Liberals' indignation over the protectionist tide, while those from the *Revue des Deux Mondes* illustrate the distress over the purges. Another issue dividing the two republican camps was amnesty for those jailed and exiled for participation in the Commune, as the Centre Gauche refused uncompromisingly to consider the total amnesty other republican parties urged. See Joughin, *The Commune in French Politics*.

A strong motive for a break between the new and the old republicans may have been that the latter did not trust the former. Some no doubt remembered how those who converted to republicanism just after the revolution of February 1848 later turned against the regime at a time when they had attained positions of power and influence. George Weill, *Histoire du parti républicain en France, 1814–1870* (Paris: Slatkine Reprints, 1980), p. 367, found similar distrust before the 1863 election, at which time the Orleanists pressed the Republicans for an alliance while "certains républicains se méfiaient; l'ancien pair de France d'Alton-Shée . . . supplia ses amis de ne pas oublier la perfidie des républicains du lendemain en 1848."

With regard to terminology, the French phrases for the new and old republicans were "républicains du lendemain" and "républicains de la veille," which Janet Lloyd has ably translated as "latter-day republicans" and "republicans of long standing." See Maurice Agulhon, *The Republican Experiment, 1848–1852*, trans. Janet Lloyd (Cambridge: Cambridge Univ. Press, 1983), p. 1. However, since long-term republicans like Jules Simon were part of the opposition to the anticlerical measures, I have tried to capture the distinction by referring to "right-wing republicans" and "advanced republicans."

32. The strongly anticlerical educational law Jules Ferry proposed in 1879 put the Centre Gauche in a difficult position. If it supported the law, it would alienate Liberal Catholics and drive a permanent wedge between itself and the Liberal monarchists whom it hoped to convert to a prudential republicanism and thus draw into an alliance. If it opposed the anticlerical policy, it would be in danger of losing votes from moderate but secular-minded republicans. The Centre Gauche and its allies chose to join the right in opposing Ferry's project. When elections took place

in 1881, the Centre Gauche lost a considerable number of seats, permanently ending its power in the Chamber of Deputies. Jean-Marie Mayeur, *Les débuts de la Troisième République, 1871–1898* (Paris: Seuil, 1973), pp. 99–100. On the struggle over the anticlerical legislation and its impact on right-wing republicans, see Philip Bertocci, *Jules Simon: Republican Anticlericalism and Cultural Politics in France, 1848–1886* (Kansas City: Univ. of Missouri Press, 1978). Also, Gabriel de Broglie, *Histoire politique de la "Revue des Deux Mondes" de 1829 à 1979* (Paris: Perrin, 1979), pp. 195–212; on the election of 1881, see p. 211. A striking example of the success of the advanced republicans' strategy is the "Protestation de Bienfait et Garnier au sujet de l'attitude de Jules Simon sur l'Article 7," a letter from two of Simon's constituents protesting that as republicans they would not be able to support him unless he accepted Article 7 (the anticlerical measure) of Ferry's educational law. Jules Simon papers, Dossier 10 (1878– 1890), "Lois sur l'enseignement. Protestation," Archives Nationales, 87 AP 10.

33. Dismissals in the early 1880s replaced numerous officials of elite social status with middle-class men. Odille Rudelle, *La République Absolue, 1870–1889* (Paris: Publ. de la Sorbonne, 1982), accurately describes the conflict as between "two personnels of which one, the new, symbolized the political society resulting from universal suffrage . . . and the other, the old, was simply the oddly assorted residue of the different regimes France had known since 1815" (p. 60). For a summary of the changes see Mayeur, *Les débuts*.

34. At the beginning of 1880 the editors of the *Journal des Economistes* warned that ostensibly philanthropic legislators were more of a threat to the "economic constitution of society" than the belligerent Socialists of the workers' congress at Marseilles. "L'Année 1879" (unsigned), *JDE*, 4th ser., 9 (January 1880), p. 11.

35. For Etienne Vacherot, at the same time a leading intellectual and a senator of unimpeachable antiauthoritarian credentials, the triumphant republican forces were "New Jacobins" engaging in reprisals instead of providing good government. Vacherot, "Les nouveaux Jacobins," *RDM*, 3rd ser., 40 (1 July 1880), pp. 40–74, esp. pp. 49–51. A highly visible opponent of the imperial government in 1860, Vacherot became so distressed by the country's political evolution during the 1880s that he reversed his ground and became a convert to the monarchist camp. See Henri Michel, *L'idée de l'Etat*, 2nd ed. (Paris: Hachette, 1899), pp. 336–38.

36. De Mazade, "Chronique," *RDM*, 3rd per., 31 (1 February 1879), pp. 713–14. In the January 15 issue, reflecting on the large majority the republicans had just won in the Senate, he declared there should be no further purges of the civil service (p. 471). About a year later he was deploring the displacement of the moderate republican faction by the republican left with its anticlerical policies, its desire to purge the administration, and its willingness to grant amnesty to the Communards. *RDM*, 3rd ser., 36

(15 December 1879), pp. 948–51; *RDM*, 3rd ser., 37 (15 February 1880), pp. 948–49.

37. De Mazade, "Chronique," *RDM*, 3rd ser., 39 (1 May 1880), pp. 230–32.

38. *RDM*, 3rd ser., 44 (1 April 1881), pp. 709–12. De Mazade complained for ten pages that the republican leader ignored other classes whose needs and aspirations "have their place in the state, with all the traditions and interests they represent."

39. "Du caractère de la crise économique actuelle," *EF* 5 (5 May 1877), p. 546. In *De la colonisation* (1874), p. 498, he had written that "the decline of profits, when it is exaggerated, despite the opinion of Ricardo and . . . others . . . , is in our eyes a real evil, a redoubtable symptom; it is, in effect, the death of the spirit of enterprise, it is the languishing of industry, it is a step towards that stationary state which, it is true, Stuart Mill praises, but which frightens us."

40. "Le régime économique et les intérêts généraux et permanents de la France," *EF* 8 (17 January 1880), p. 63; "Des causes de la crise industrielle et de la fin de cette crise" (pt. 1), *EF* 8 (31 July 1880), p. 125. Also see "De la continuité de la progrès économique," *EF* 8 (4 September 1880), p. 311.

41. "Des causes de la crise" (pt. 1), p. 127; "La crise financière et commerciale en Angleterre," *EF* 6 (21 December 1878), p. 769; "Les moeurs financières et la legislation," *EF* 6 (10 November 1878), pp. 610–11.

42. See, for example, his *L'Etat moderne et ses fonctions* (Paris: Guillaumin, 1889), pp. 246–49.

43. "De la portée de l'agitation socialiste et révolutionnaire en France et des responsabilités diverses (pt. 1)," *EF* 10 (28 October 1882), p. 543.

44. "Les intérêts coloniaux et exterieurs de la France et la situation gouvernementale," *EF* 11 (10 February 1883), p. 157. He also complained that the "professions of faith" of the Radical deputies and senators were, therefore, a "collection of follies" that poured oil on the fire the Socialists had ignited. "Une nouvelle invasion de la politique: la réprésentation de l'agriculture," *EF* 12 (23 February 1884), p. 217. Over the years his contempt did not abate; in 1896 he described contemporary politicians as "one of the most vile classes and the most limited to sycophants and courtesans that humanity has ever known." *Traité théorique et pratique d'économie politique* (Paris: Guillaumin, 1896), vol. 4, p. 618n.

45. "De la portée de l'agitation socialiste (pt. 1)," "De la portée de l'agitation socialiste, pt. 2: le program de M. Clemenceau," *EF* 10 (4 November 1882), pp. 573–77.

46. For expressions of this view see "La province pendant le siège de Paris," *RDM*, per. 2, 92 (15 March 1871), pp. 144–77; "L'association internationale des travailleurs," *EF* 1 (27 September 1873), p. 646.

47. "Un nouveau mode d'empiètement de l'Etat sur les droits de l'individu: les discussions de l'Académie de Médecine sur la thérapeutique officiel et la médecine de l'Etat," *EF* 9 (23 April 1881), p. 501.

48. *Le collectivisme: examen critique du nouveau socialisme*, 2nd ed. (Paris: Guillaumin, 1885), p. xiv.

49. G. de Molinari, "Chronique économique," *JDE*, 4th ser., 16 (October 1881), pp. 324–25.

50. *TSF*, vol. 1, p. 470.

51. *Essai sur la répartition des richesses et sur la tendance à une moindre inégalité*, 1st ed. (Paris: Guillaumin, 1881), p. 547. Hereafter *RR*.

52. Stourm, "PLB," p. 550.

53. The article declared that this "race of politicians" was found only in the Senate, but that they were seeking election to the Chamber of Deputies as well. "Elections générals du 14 Octobre 1877," *L'Indépendant de Lodève*, 12th year, no. 32 (21 April 1878), p. 1.

54. "Elections legislatives du 7 juillet 1878. A messieurs les électeurs de l'arrondissement de Lodève," reproduced, in Aumercier, pp. 61ff. According to a letter to his wife's aunt, he campaigned for only fifteen days. Paul Leroy-Beaulieu to Mme. Auguste Chevalier, 16 July 1878, Archives Nationales, AB 19 3357, Dossier 1, Correspondance addressée à Auguste et Michel Chevalier.

55. Paul Leroy-Beaulieu to Cordelia Leroy-Beaulieu, 16 November 1879, quoted in Aumercier, p. 76. Aumercier sees the silence as designed to retain royalist and conservative votes. However, Leroy-Beaulieu was careful in all his elections to identify himself as a republican. What he concealed was his reservations about universal suffrage.

56. Paul Leroy-Beaulieu to Cordelia Leroy-Beaulieu, 7 April 1880, quoted in Aumercier, p. 81.

57. Henri de Rochefort's newspaper treated him as a "candidate of the Centre Gauche." See *L'Echo de Lodève*, 43rd year, no. 52 (28 November 1883), p. 3.

58. *Le Petit Meridional*, 9 August 1881, p. 2. Leo A. Loubère, in his lengthy, extremely detailed study of the political life of the entire lower Midi, characterizes all of Leroy-Beaulieu's electoral opponents, including Arrazat, as moderate Radicals. Furthermore, in his careful accounts of voting patterns in the Hérault from 1849 on, he demonstrates that the department became a center of Radical Party strength at an early date, although the uplands, where Leroy-Beaulieu lived, were more right-wing in orientation than the other areas of the department. Leo A. Loubère, *Radicalism in Mediterranean France: Its Rise and Decline, 1848–1914* (Albany: State Univ. of New York Press, 1974), p. 133. For his analyses of the voting patterns in the Hérault see pp. 53–55, 125–27, 130–31, 147. Sanford Elwitt, *The Making of the Third Republic* (Baton Rouge: Univ. of Louisiana Press, 1976),

pp. 64–66, reviews the political evolution in the Hérault from 1869 to the time of Arrazat's election.

59. Elections générales, 1881–1884, Hérault, 1883, Archives Nationales, C 3507.

60. "Le comité républicain au électeurs de l'arrondissement de Lodève," *L'Indépendant de Lodève*, 24 November 1883, p. 1; "Leroy-Beaulieu jugé par de Cassagnac," *L'Indépendant de Lodève*, 24 November 1883, p. 2.

61. The paper quoted a diatribe from *L'Anti Sémitique* of December 1 that called him "the Jew Leroy-Beaulieu," a monopolist, the hired pen of the Rothschilds and of the Haute Banque. "M. Leroy-Beaulieu, économiste et candidat," *L'Indépendant de Lodève*, 8 December 1883, p. 2.

62. *Grandeur et décadence de Colladent: histoire d'un jacquette changée en casaquin et d'un économiste changé en chauve souris*. Elections, Chambre des Deputés, 1881–1884, Hérault, arrondissement de Lodève, élection partielle de 29 novembre 1883 et 9 décembre 1883, "Protestation générale de Mr. Paul Leroy-Beaulieu et pièces à l'appui," Archives Nationales, C 3507.

63. "Lodève" (lead article), *L'Echo de Lodève*, 41st year, no. 1 (7 January 1877), p. 1.

64. "Lodève," *L'Echo de Lodève*, 41st year, no. 19 (13 May 1877), p. 1.

65. "Lodéve," 41st year, nos. 19 (13 May 1877), p. 1, and 20 (20 May 1877), p. 1.

66. "Petit catéchisme conservateur (suite), IV: après les elections," *L'Echo de Lodève*, 41st year, no. 38 (23 September 1877), p. 3; "Lodève," (lead article), *L'Echo de Lodève*, 41st year, no. 39 (30 September 1877), p. 1.

67. Ch. Delpon de Vissec to "Messieurs les membres des comités conservateurs de l'arrondissement de Lodève," *L'Echo de Lodève*, 42nd year, no. 26 (7 July 1878), p. 1; "Chronique. L'élection de Lodève," *L'Echo de Lodève*, 42nd year, no. 27 (14 July 1878), p. 2.

68. "Aux électeurs de l'arrondissement de Lodève," 1881, quoted in Aumercier, pp. 67ff. See also *L'Echo de Lodève*, 45th year, no. 34 (17 August 1881), p. 1. An election flyer for 1883 signed by the conservative notables of the election committee repeated these points in its criticism of Galtier. Elections, Chambre des Deputés, 1881–1884, Hérault, arrondissement de Lodève, élection partielle de 29 novembre 1883 et 9 décembre 1883, Archives Nationales, C 3507.

69. "Aux électeurs," 1881, and "Elections legislatives du 25 novembre" (report of Leroy-Beaulieu's speech at the nomination meeting), *L'Echo de Lodève*, 47th year, no. 46 (11 November 1883), p. 1.

70. Rudelle, *La république absolue*, p. 120 n. 53. See pp. 119–21 for her account of the conservative campaign. For a superb contemporary

description of the campaign see André Daniel, *L'année politique 1885* (Paris: Charpentier, 1886), pp. 199ff. Rudelle also cites an account by a royalist leader: Louis Teste, *Les monarchistes sous le Troisième République* (Paris: Rousseau, 1891), pp. 84–90.

71. Leo A. Loubère, *Radicalism in Mediterranean France*, pp. 130–31.

72. "Tribune electorale. Bedarieux: Réunion publique conservatrice du 6 September," *L'Echo de Lodève*, 49th year, no. 37 (13 September 1885), p. 2.

73. Among the members of this fledgling group were close associates of Leroy-Beaulieu, such as Jules Roch. In fact, his brother, Anatole, became a member of the group's executive committee in the late 1890s. On the Union Libérale see André Daniel, *L'année politique 1889* (Paris: Charpentier, 1890). Anatole Leroy-Beaulieu is listed as a member of the executive committee in a notice in *Le Temps*, January 4, 1898, p. 2.

74. He declared: "Il faut . . . introduire en France le mesure démocratique connue sous le nom de Referendum. Elle consiste à consulter, quand une part déterminée des citoyens le demande, tous les citoyens de la nation ou tous les citoyens d'une commune, toutes les fois qu'il s'agit d'une mesure importante et sur laquelle chacun peut aisément se prononcer. C'est le frein, dont use la sage et prospère république Suisse, contre l'infatuation naturelle aux assemblées electives." "Elections Legislatives du 22 Septembre 1889, Aux Electeurs de l'Arrondissement de Lodève." See photocopies in Aumercier, pp. 66ff.

75. Aumercier, p. 69.

CHAPTER 6: THE PATH TO IMPERIALISM

1. For example, Robert R. Boutrouche, "Quelques aperçus sur l'opinion anti-coloniale en France depuis le XVIIIe siècle," *Revue Africaine* 74 (1933), pp. 377, 390, and Stephen H. Roberts, *History of French Colonial Policy (1870–1925)* (London: P. S. King, 1929), vol. 1, p. 35.

2. A significant trend in recent historical interpretation has challenged the once-dominant view that economic motives inspired the rise of modern imperialism. See, e.g., Raoul Girardet, *L'idée coloniale en France de 1871 à 1962* (Paris: Livre de Poche, 1978), and C. M. Andrews and A. S. Kanya-Forstner, *The Climax of French Imperial Expansion, 1914–1924* (Stanford, Calif.: Stanford Univ. Press, 1981), pp. 25–26.

3. Hubert Deschamps, *Méthodes et doctrines coloniales de la France* (Paris: Colin, 1953), p. 96.

4. For the period before the Second Empire, I have found two older works by Christian Schéfer valuable on these topics: *La France moderne et le problème coloniale* (Paris: Alcan, 1907), esp. pp. 85, 127–30, and *L'Algérie et l'évolution de la colonisation française: la politique coloniale de la Monarchie de Juillet* (Paris: Champion, 1928), pp. 26–27. See also Deschamps, *Methodes*

et doctrines, pp. 97–98, 103, 111–13. For a brief textbook account, see Gordon Wright, *France in Modern Times,* 3rd ed. (New York: Norton, 1981), pp. 202–5, which goes on to cover the colonial policy of Napoleon III.

5. For a survey of Liberal opinion as expressed by major journalists in the 1860s see André Masson, "L'opinion française et les problèmes coloniaux à la fin du Second Empire," *Revue Française d'Histoire d'Outre Mer* 49 (1962), pp. 366–435. Girardet's *L'idée coloniale en France de 1871 à 1962* remains the standard interpretation.

6. Despite the revulsion in France against *refoulement,* the government instructed a parliamentary commission in 1833 to consider this alternative. On the report of the parliamentary commission see Henri Blet, *Histoire de la colonisation française,* vol. 2: *Les étapes d'une renaissance coloniale, 1789–1870* (Paris: Arthaud, 1946), pp. 119–22.

7. Adam Smith, *The Wealth of Nations,* ed. Edwin Cannon (New York: Modern Library, 1937), pp. 531–32, 556, 557, 581, 592.

8. Jean-Baptiste Say, *Cours complet d'économie politique,* 2nd ed. (Paris: Guillaumin, 1840), vol., 1, pp. 248–49, 252, 297, 632–34, 636–37; vol. 2, pp. 191–93. See also, Archibald Thornton, *The Imperial Idea and Its Enemies: A Study in British Power* (London: Macmillan, 1959), pp. 11–12.

9. Say, *Cours Complet,* vol. 2, pp. 195–96.

10. Charles-Robert Ageron, *France coloniale ou parti coloniale* (Paris: PUF, 1978), p. 19; S. Herbert Frankel, *The Concept of Colonization* (Oxford: Clarendon, 1949), p. 9. Jacques Vallette only partly affirms the notion that the term "colony" was automatically equated with "settlements." On one hand, he quotes Jules Duval's definition from Maurice Block's *Dictionnaire de Politique:* "On nomme ainsi l'occupation, le peuplement, et la culture des parties du globe qui sont inoccupées, non peuplées, incultes." And he cites other similar views including the definition in Larousse's *Grand Dictionnaire Universel* of 1869. But he also argues that aspects of some of the definitions that implied economic development and domination of one people by another. Jacques Vallette, "Note sur l'idée coloniale vers 1871," *Revue d'histoire moderne et contemporaine* 14 (196), pp. 158–72, esp. pp. 160–66, 171.

11. J.-B. Say, for example, made a distinction between colonies ("establishments formed in faraway countries by an older nation") and trading posts founded by one nation in the midst of a populous country like China and Japan. Say, *Traité d'économie politique,* 6th ed. (Paris: Gallimard, 1841), p. 223. A leading opponent of overseas expansion during the July Monarchy, Amédée Desjobert, commented that England, "far from having adopted the colonial regime in [India], has proscribed its foundation, the possession of land by English citizens." Desjobert, *La question d'Alger: politique, colonisation, commerce* (Paris: Duffart, 1837), p. 48. I have found similar definitions and attitudes in John Stuart Mill, *Principles of Political Economy* (London: J. W. Parker, 1848) vol. 1, pp. 449–52, and vol. 2, pp.

296–306; John R. Seeley, *The Expansion of England* (Boston: Roberts, 1883), p. 168; and in speeches and pamphlets by French economists and politicians, most notably Hippolyte Passy (both an economist and a deputy), "Discours . . . dans la partie du budget de la guerre relative à la colonisation d'Alger (séance du 1er mai 1834), p. 11, in Chambre des Deputés, *Impressions diverses et feuilletons*, session of 1834.

12. Passy, "Discours," p. 28.

13. Desjobert, *La question d'Alger*, p. 223.

14. See Girardet, *L'idée coloniale*, pp. 43–45.

15. Girardet, *L'idée coloniale*, pp. 45–47, citing Prévost-Paradol, *La France Nouvelle*, pp. 418–19, 423.

16. Quoted in Masson, "L'opinion française," p. 415.

17. Emile Levasseur, "Rapport sur le concours pour le prix fondé par Mme. Léon Faucher (lu dans la séance du 19 mars 1870)," *Mémoires de l'Académie des sciences Morales et Politiques de l'Institut de France* 13 (1872), pp. 471–510.

18. Levasseur, "Rapport," p. 508.

19. *Guerres contemporaines*, pp. 84, 89–90, 310. He also addressed the expedition to Mexico (which collapsed a year before he started writing the book) commenting on the folly of those who expected a military promenade amidst a "rain of flowers" when instead the French were received by a "storm of musket balls."

20. *GC*, p. 84.

21. "Les ressources de la France et de la Prusse," *RDM* 89 (1 September 1870), p. 144.

22. Levasseur, "Rapport," p. 508.

23. Levasseur, "Rapport," p. 492. According to the archives of the Institut, Leroy-Beaulieu himself removed the manuscript, apparently in 1873 in order to prepare it for publication. Aside from Levasseur's report, J. J. Lefort, reviewing the published edition in *JDE*, 3rd ser., 34 (June 1874), pp. 460–62, called it fundamentally the same as the manuscript.

24. "Les ressources de la France et de la Prusse," p. 144.

25. *GC*, pp. 8–9, 94, 325.

26. "De la fondation d'une union douanière occidentale," *EF* 7 (11 October 1879), p. 435.

27. *JDD*, 27 February 1873.

28. *JDD*, 1 May 1873.

29. Agnes Murphy, *The Ideology of French Imperialism, 1871–1881* (Washington: Catholic Univ. of America Press, 1948), p. 139.

30. *JDD*, 5 November 1872. In the rest of the article he rebutted the charges that Algeria was an unpromising land that could not be turned into a bountiful home for Europeans.

31. *JDD*, 22 November 1872.

32. *JDD*, 27 February 1873. In *De la colonisation*, p. 237, he criticizes

Napoleon I for destroying the overseas empire in his vain attempt to conquer Europe.

33. *JDD*, 27 February 1873. "In order to have prosperous colonies," he wrote, "it is necessary to have a big commerce, and in order to have a big commerce, we must not place exorbitant duties upon all exotic products and all the ships that do not fly our flag."

34. Ageron, *France coloniale*, p. 34. Agnes Murphy, *Ideology of French Imperialism*, p. 108, believed that the appearance of the book represented the transformation of a theoretical into a practical interest. She stated that "as early as 1874 he had already emerged as a full-fledged propagandist, and . . . this work though alluded to by the author himself (p. 466) as a scientific study, was put forth in an effort to arouse France to her need." She was evidently responding to Parker Thomas Moon, *Imperialism and World Politics* (New York: Macmillan, 1939), p. 45, who believed that the original edition of the treatise "was put forth as a scientific study rather than as a propagandist appeal," just as the author claimed. Somewhat ambiguously Girardet, *L'idée coloniale*, p. 53, proclaimed that the book "appears to mark a decisive turning point," perhaps meaning only that the book provided the nascent imperialist movement with "a coherent doctrine of French imperialism." Apparently Girardet did not even see that there was a problem of dating the beginning of Leroy-Beaulieu's commitment to an active policy of overseas expansion.

35. As a positive argument, the book can be seen as a combination of those opinions of Adam Smith that were friendly to colonization with the more substantially favorable arguments of two mid-nineteenth-century defenders of overseas settlement, Herman Merivale and John Stuart Mill. Murphy concludes that Leroy-Beaulieu drew heavily on Merivale's *Lectures on Colonies and Colonization*, 2nd ed. (1861; rpt. London: Oxford Univ. Press, 1928). On the relation of the ideas of these three British thinkers with Leroy-Beaulieu, see Dan Warshaw, "Paul Leroy-Beaulieu, Bourgeois Ideologist: A Study of the Social, Intellectual, and Economic Sources of Late Nineteenth-Century Imperialism" (Ph.D. diss., Univ. of Rochester, 1966), chap. 2, esp. pp. 44, 55–59.

36. *DLC*, pp. iv, 431, 465–66. Out of 606 pages, 460 are devoted to the history of empire.

37. *DLC*, pp. i–ii.

38. *DLC*, pp. 195–200, 309–12, 341–42, 383, 594.

39. *DLC*, specifically citing Smith on p. 140; see also pp. 501, 506, 572–73. Most of the section on economic benefits described the general stimulation of European industry by increased production in the colonies.

40. *DLC*, pp. 466–67. The departure of capital from France was a main source of the ire of such antiimperialists of the July Monarchy as Desjobert and Passy.

41. *DLC*, pp. 473–76, 483. This view must have been one held by

Leroy-Beaulieu in 1870, and its presence in the first edition of *De la Coloni-sation* is further evidence that the book as we know it is essentially the same as the prize treatise. By 1874 he was expressing a somewhat different view. In his articles in that year he hoped that a slight emigration to Algeria would encourage the birth rate in the south of France.

42. Leroy-Beaulieu applied his classifications to Senegal, "an impor-tant colony that can become more important if we understand properly the role it is called to play and the perspectives before it. There is no question of settling on the banks of the [Senegal] river a numerous European popula-tion; the attempt would be folly. Our task . . . is . . . one of initiation; our principal means is moral influence." *DLC*, p. 364.

43. Although he rejected the idea that there could be a "general glut of commodities," he agreed with Merivale that a surplus of capital could cause a depression. *DLC*, pp. 491–97.

44. See, for example, *DLC*, pp. 534–37.

45. François Guizot, *Mémoires pour servir à l'histoire de mon temps* (Paris: Michel Levy, 1858–1867), vol. 6, pp. 270–71, 274–75.

46. *DLC*, pp. 341–42; see also pp. 356, 394.

47. *DLC*, pp. 13, 122–23, 164, 351ff., 463.

48. *DLC*, p. 356.

49. *DLC*, p. 383.

50. *DLC*, p. 606.

51. "La colonisation française et la colonisation anglaise," *EF* 2 (15 August 1874), pp. 181–83; "La colonisation de l'Algérie," pts. 1 and 2, *EF* 2 (22 and 29 August 1874), pp. 212–14 and 245–47. This series contains his most important pronouncements on the subject up to that time, for they were longer than his previous articles and more up to date than his book.

52. "Colonisation française et . . . anglaise," p. 181. On page 183 he wrote: "We consider . . . Algeria as the greatest chance that the French race has henceforth to exercise a great influence in the world." In the second article he again defended Algeria against its detractors, arguing that the colony's development was highly respectable even when compared to the miraculous ascension of Australia.

53. "De l'influence de la dernière guerre sur le mouvement de la population," *EF* 2 (25 November 1874), p. 663.

54. *JDD*, 17 November 1875.

55. "La question de la population: dialogue des morts entre Malthus et Cobden," *EF* 4 (9 September 1876), pp. 333–35. Shortly afterward one of his newspaper columns, *JDD*, 9 March 1877, connected emigration with the stimulation of the fertility of French families, placing him within a short logical step of advocating colonies as a possible solution to the popula-tion problem. But he still did not take that step yet.

56. Anatole Leroy-Beaulieu defended European settlement in Algeria

in *EF* 5 (6 January 1877), p. 17, and Paul mentioned the already existing colonies as areas for profitable investment in "Du caractère de la crise économique actuelle," *EF* 5 (5 May 1877), p. 547. As noted above, in 1874 he referred to "the expansion of the influence of the country abroad" as one of the nation's permanent interests. But two years later, in another list of these interests, "expansion of influence abroad" had given way to the simpler category of "foreign trade," a phrase he italicized. Both the context of his earlier remarks and his concerns at that time indicate that the French influence he wanted to expand abroad was economic in nature. Compare "De la réprésentation des intérêts industriels . . . ," *EF* 2 (7 November 1874), p. 565, with "Le programme ministériel," *EF* 4 (18 March 1876), p. 354.

57. Girardet presents Jules Ferry's arguments for imperialism following this format, *L'idée coloniale*, pp. 81–86. But, of course, Ferry framed his arguments in this fashion. See the preface he contributed to *Tonkin et la mère patrie*, Léon Sentupéry, ed. (6th ed.; Paris: V. Harvard, 1890). I used the phrase "three-part argument" in 1966 in my dissertation: pp. 178–79, 195.

58. "L'Egypte et les intérêts français," *EF* 6 (9 February 1878), p. 163.

59. He wrote: "England and France have diverse interests in Egypt: financial interests (those of their citizens who are creditors of the Khedive); political interests, traditional and new ones (those of preserving a tolerable organization of administration and of excluding from that country enemy influences); finally, a humanitarian interest, that of the fate of the fellahs." "La situation en Egypte et les intérêts français," *EF* 6 (28 September 1878), p. 385.

60. "Les causes et les remèdes de la crise économique," *EF* 6 (9 November 1878), pp. 577–79. "Frankly," he wrote, "this is not a remedy which would be immediately efficacious; our industrialists would have to wait a long time for profits if they could draw them only from eastern and central Africa."

61. "De la colonisation et de l'exploitation du continent africain," *EF* 7 (1 February 1879), pp. 129–31.

62. "De la colonisation et de l'exploitation du continent africain."

63. In October 1879 he did repeat the theme briefly in an article in which he considered France's relations with its neighbors. "Since the war of 1870–1871," he wrote, "we have often asked ourselves what ought to be the foreign policy of France." He concluded that the country should play a double role. Within Europe, France should "group around herself the secondary peoples who have preserved their independence, who have affinities with us either of race, language, mores, and institutions or of industry and commerce." He proposed a tariff union as the means of accomplishing this rapprochement. France's second role would be in North Africa, where it should "penetrate into the Sudan, with prudence and perseverance,

and attempt to constitute in that vast country a civilization that is inspired by our own and depends upon our own." He did not elaborate further on that point. "De la fondation d'une union douanière occidentale," *EF* 7 (11 October 1879), pp. 433–35.

64. "Des causes de la crise industrielle et de la fin de cette crise (pt. 2)," *EF* 8 (7 August 1880), p. 155.

65. "Les intérêts de la France et de l'Italie en Afrique," *EF* 8 (28 August 1880), p. 250.

66. "Des causes de la crise industrielle (pt. 2)," p. 155.

67. "Les intérêts de la France et de l'Italie en Afrique," pp. 249–51; "L'Algérie et la Tunisie: de la nécessité de proteger efficacement les intérêts français à Tunis," *EF* 9 (19 March 1881), pp. 345–47.

68. "L'Algérie et la Tunisie," p. 345. Almost every article Leroy-Beaulieu wrote on Tunis in 1881 stressed the Bey's "treachery."

69. "De la nécessité de l'annexion totale de la Tunisie," *EF* 9 (9 April 1881), p. 438.

70. "L'Algérie et la Tunisie," p. 347.

71. "De la fondation d'une union douanière occidentale," pp. 433–35.

72. "Le développement de la puissance coloniale de la France (pt. 1)," *EF* 8 (1 May 1880), p. 529.

73. "La politique continentale et la politique coloniale," *EF* 9 (7 May 1881), pp. 565–67.

74. "La politique continentale," p. 565.

75. Although in 1880 and 1881 Leroy-Beaulieu stressed the strategic value of colonization and the dangers of the continental policy, he did not neglect to point out economic and humanitarian aspects of the conquest of Tunisia. In fact, he tied all these arguments together. Once Tunisia was "pacified," he asserted, its commerce would increase, thus aiding both its own well-being and that of its European trading partners. Thus the conquest was one of the "superior interests of civilization" as well as one of the permanent interests of France. "L'Algérie et la Tunisie," p. 347. To sum up his attitude at this time, we could do no better than to quote a remark he made in 1879 when he proclaimed the promise of Africa for Europe and France. He declared that an imperialist role for France would be "an essentially pacific and civilizing role, full however of grandeur, future, and material profits." "De la fondation d'une union douanière occidentale," p. 434.

76. Hubert Deschamps, *Méthodes et doctrines coloniales de la France* (Paris: Colin, 1953), p. 125. Leroy-Beaulieu himself later recalled that in 1874 colonization was the concern of only a small minority in Europe while the majority disdained it as an anachronism. *De la colonisation chez les peuples modernes*, 4th ed. (Paris: Guillaumin, 1891), p. xi. Hereafter referred to as *DLC* (1891).

77. *De la colonisation chez les peuples modernes*, 2nd ed. (Paris: Guillaumin, 1882), p. 254. Hereafter referred to as *DLC* (1882).

78. *DLC* (1882), p. 249. This passage and the former one were parts of a new conclusion of one chapter. The preface refers to Cochin China as the "kernel of a new empire" (p. vi).

79. His remarks on Madagascar, however, show that he did set limits on his dreams of domination of large territories; he spoke of the occupation of that large island as "impracticable—or at least premature." *DLC* (1882), pp. 409, 410, 417.

80. Murphy, *Ideology of French Imperialism*, p. 109.

81. *DLC* (1882), pp. vi–viii.

82. *DLC* (1882), p. vii.

83. In 1874 Leroy-Beaulieu praised colonies because agricultural communities were less liable to economic crises and thus were better trading partners; in 1882 he replaced that sentence with a comment that commerce was more secure with colonies because there was less danger of war between parent and child than between foreign nations. For the same reason he deemed exportation of capital to colonies safer than investments in foreign countries. *DLC* (1874), p. 525; *DLC* (1882), pp. 541, 565.

84. *DLC* (1882), p. 572.

85. *DLC* (1882), p. 572.

86. *DLC* (1882), p. 541.

87. *DLC* (1882), pp. viii–ix.

88. *DLC* (1882), n. 1, pp. 192–93; see also pp. 60, 223, 289.

89. Girardet recognizes that the three-part argument for imperialism is one of the distinctive creations of French thinkers in the early history of the Third Republic, but he gives Jules Ferry credit for this innovation. Ferry's version may have been the most succinct and eloquent, but he did not invoke a three-pronged defense of imperialism until 1885, in justifying the conquests of Tunisia and Tonkin.

As for the extent of Leroy-Beaulieu's influence on other thinkers and on public opinion, I must leave that question to the specialists on imperialism and foreign policy. Although the similarities suggest that Ferry could have drawn heavily from Leroy-Beaulieu, only an examination of Ferry's private papers could prove that he read and digested the economist's works before formulating his own justifications. Girardet concluded that Ferry drew his arguments generally from the "body of doctrine elaborated during the preceding years by the diverse propagandists for the colonial ideal" and derived his economic position from Leroy-Beaulieu. Girardet, *L'idée coloniale*, pp. 82, 92.

There is no question that *De la Colonisation* received some favorable attention in high places. Murphy (*Ideology of French Imperialism*, p. 136 n. 87) notes that in February 1878 "François de Mahy, the colonial-enthusiast deputy from Réunion, eulogized the treatise in the Chamber" and that "In the discussion of colonization by the fifth group of the international congress of geography (1875) Levasseur referred to this work as among the most important and the most appreciated works on colonization. . . . It was one of the books used by the subcommission of this group in drawing up . . . [its] report." The book went through six editions during its author's lifetime. However, there is little evidence that the political leadership shaped their policies to conform to its ideas. Deschamps, *Méthodes et doctrines*, pp. 141–42, states that the French cabinets and parliaments almost completely ignored Leroy-Beaulieu's recommendations about establishing a free-trade regime for the empire and a policy of assimilation for Algeria. The colonies were ruled bureaucratically, and in black Africa respect for the indigenous institutions of the natives replaced the policy of assimilation. At least this is the interpretation of Deschamps, and I am in no position to quarrel with it.

90. In the 1891 edition of *De la Colonisation* Leroy-Beaulieu made these ideas explicit in a chapter on the "philosophy of imperialism." There he argued that Europeans had the right to conquer "backward" peoples who were shirking their duty to humankind by not pursuing perpetual and rapid increases of production. The obligation was not imposed only on the natives: the French and other "advanced" nations had both the right and the duty to rule and develop economically those lands whose inhabitants were too sunk in inertia and ignorance to make their farms, natural resources, and trade reach their full potential.

91. See E. de Laveleye, "L'exploration de l'Afrique centrale et la conférence géographique de Bruxelles," *RDM* 20 (1 April 1877), pp. 584–606; Vesin, "La colonisation d'Algérie (suite et fin)," *JDE* 6 (June 1879), pp. 406–39; Adalbert Frout de Fontpertuis, "L'Afrique centrale: son exploration et sa colonisation," *JDE* 7 (October 1879), p. 10–35. Fontpertuis, associated with Leroy-Beaulieu in the founding of *L'Economiste Français*, noted the quickening of activity in the region. But, like Leroy-Beaulieu at this point, he apparently had visions of a peaceful penetration of the region, establishing French hegemony by economic activity (e.g., building railroads) rather than by force (see pp. 28, 34–35).

92. See C. W. Newbury and A. S. Kanya-Forstner, "French Policy and the Origins of the Scramble for West Africa," *Journal of African History* 10 (1969), pp. 253–76, and Henri Brunschwig, "Scramble et 'course au clocher'" in his *Le partage de l'Afrique noire, questions d'histoire* (Paris: Flammarion, 1971), pp. 153–56.

93. "La guerre en Orient," *EF* 5 (21 April 1877), p. 481.

94. "La question de la population en France (pt. 1)," *EF* 5 (14 July 1877), p. 418. Steven Englund correctly has pointed out to me that Leroy-Beaulieu's nationalism was mild compared to that of some contemporary fanatics.

95. "De la fondation d'une union douanière occidentale," p. 434.

96. For an excellent, up-to-date account of the imperialist attitudes and activities of Gambetta, Ferry, and Leroy-Beaulieu, see Pierre Guillen, *L'expansion (1881–1898)* (Paris: Imprimerie Nationale, 1985), pp. 95–105. Guillen's interpretation of Gambetta follows Robert Ageron, who has revised the view expressed by Pierre Renouvin in his Sorbonne lectures, *La politique extérieure de la IIIe République de 1871 à 1904* (Paris: Centre de Documentation Universitaire, 1948), pp. 138.

97. "La situation de la France en Europe et hors d'Europe," *EF* 11 (1 September 1883), p. 254.

98. "La politique continentale et la politique coloniale," pp. 565–67.

99. Ageron, *France coloniale ou parti coloniale*, pp. 44–53, finds this safety-valve argument in the writings of a number of mid-nineteenth-century and early Third Republic figures. Sanford Elwitt attempts an elaborate but ultimately confusing linkage between fears of social unrest and the Tunisian expedition in his "French Imperialism and Social Policy: The Case of Tunisia," *Science and Society* 31 (1967), pp. 129–47; see also his *The Making of the Third Republic*, p. 300. He asserts that the expedition was not economically motivated but was designed to satisfy the yearning for social stability. However, he fails to show that Third Republic leaders made or implied such a connection as Leroy-Beaulieu did.

CHAPTER 7: THE MATURE WRITINGS OF LEROY-BEAULIEU

1. "Leroy-Beaulieu (Pierre-Paul)," *La Grande Encyclopédie* (Paris: Lamirault, n.d.), vol. 22, p. 79.

2. Osborne, "Social sciences at the Science Po," p. 71. On the Société d'Economie Sociale see the lengthy and illuminating discussion in Sanford Elwitt, *The Republic Defended: Bourgeois Reform in France, 1880–1914* (Baton Rouge: Univ. of Louisiana Press, 1986), pp. 19–38.

3. A. Béchaux, *Les écoles économiques aux XXe siècle*, vol. 1: *L'ecole économique française* (Paris: Rousseau, Guillaumin, 1902), pp. 9, 12, 20–23; Auguste Oncken in *Deutsche Literaturzeitung*, 22 August 1903, p. 2096, quoted in A. Béchaux, *Les écoles économiques aux XXe siècle*, vol. 2: *L'ecole individualiste, le Socialisme de la chair* (Paris: Rousseau, Guillaumin, 1907), p. 329.

4. Stourm, "PLB," p. 548.

5. John Courtenay Bodley, *France* (London: Macmillan, 1898), vol. 1, pp. 18–19.

6. Stourm, "PLB," p. 551.

7. Two notable exceptions are Guy de Molinari and Yves Guyot, who succeeded Joseph Garnier as the next two editors of the *Journal des*

Economistes. On these two economists see Gaëtan Pirou, *Les doctrines écono-miques en France depuis 1870* (Paris: Colin, 1925), pp. 104–15. Pirou entitled his chapter on these two thinkers "L'individualisme extrême."

8. *RR*, pp. vii, 551.

9. *RR*, pp. vii, 551.

10. *RR*, pp. 544–45.

11. *RR*, p. 547.

12. Adalbert Frout de Fontpertuis, review of *RR*, *JDE*, 4th ser., 13 (March 1881), pp. 500–505. The review is considerably longer than the usual and is full of praise.

The prediction about declining interest was criticized by René Stourm, "Notice historique sur la vie et les travaux de M. Paul Leroy-Beaulieu," *Séances et Travaux de l'Académie des Sciences Morales et Politiques* 86 (January–June 1918), p. 167, and Charles Brouilhet, *Le conflict des doctrines dans l'économie politique contemporaine* (Paris: Alcan, 1910), pp. 61–67. In his economics treatise Leroy-Beaulieu replied at length to earlier criticisms by Charles Gide. See the *Traité théorique et pratique d'économie politique* (Paris: Guillaumin, 1896), vol. 2, pp. 111–12n.

13. Albert Schaeffle (1831–1903) was an Austrian official whose description of the socialist regime of the future was receiving a great deal of attention in the 1880s.

14. *Le collectivisme: examen critique du nouveau socialisme*, 2nd ed. (Paris: Guillaumin, 1885), pp. 116–17.

15. *Le collectivisme*, pp. 245–46; see also pp. 106, 115, 217.

16. *Le collectivisme*, pp.106, 233–234, 245–246, 268.

17. *Le collectivisme*, p. ix.

18. *L'Etat moderne et ses fonctions*, 1st ed. (Paris: Guillaumin, 1889), p. 18–24, esp. p. 18. Hereafter cited as *EM*.

19. *EM*, p. 39.

20. *EM*, pp. 16–17, 24–29, esp. 24–25.

21. *EM*, p. 39.

22. *EM*, p. 41.

23. *EM*, p. 40.

24. *EM*, p. 42. On railroads, see pp. 205–21; on aid to the incapacitated, pp. 211–13; on social security, pp. 377–79. He also reversed his previous judgment that public agencies were best for promoting transportation; see pp. 148, 202.

25. *EM*, pp. 89, 96, 240.

26. Leroy-Beaulieu illustrated this point by referring to the economic life of the Middle Ages. After the dynamic merchants of medieval times shaped a commercial code to regulate their dealings at the great international fairs of the time, governments took these codes under their protection and made them the law for an entire kingdom. The initiative, however, came from private individuals. *EM*, pp. 41–46, 56.

27. *Le collectivisme*, p. 195.

28. *EM*, pp. 55–75. Edward Tannenbaum once stated to me that I was talking about "reactionaries" rather than Conservatives, but I believe applying the term Conservative, with a capital c, to the opponents of the modern regime is both more accurate historically and ideologically.

29. *EM*, p. 63.

30. *EM*, pp. 65, 67.

31. *EM*, p. 62.

32. *EM*, pp. 67–68.

33. *EM*, pp. 71, 72.

34. Osborne provides a fine brief discussion of Leroy-Beaulieu and kindred thinkers in his "Social Science at the Sciences Po: Training the Bureaucratic Elite in the Early Third Republic," *Historical Reflections* 8, 1 (Spring 1981), pp. 51–76.

35. *The Modern State in Relation to Society and the Individual* (London: S. Sonnenschein, 1891).

36. These included *De la Colonisation*, the *Traité de la Science des Finances*, the *Précis d'Economie Politique*, and a second edition of *L'Etat Moderne*. Aside from an added chapter in *De la Colonisation*, these books appeared without any significant additions. The 1893 editions of *Le Collectivisme* and the *Précis* were simply reprints.

37. Cauwès characterized the Established Liberals as the Anglo-French, doctrinaire, and orthodox school. Paul Cauwès, *Cours d'économie politique: professé à la Faculté de Droit de Paris; contenant avec l'exposé des principes l'analyse des questions économiques* (Paris: Larose et Forcel, 1893), vol. 1, pp. 28, 55.

38. Cauwès, *Cours*, vol. 1, pp. 21–26.

39. Cauwès, *Cours*, vol. 1, pp. 29–30.

40. Cauwès, *Cours*, vol. 1, p. 5.

41. Cauwès, *Cours*, vol. 1, p. 23.

42. Cauwès, *Cours*, vol. 1, pp. 27–28.

43. Cauwès, *Cours*, vol. 1, p. 8.

44. Cauwès, *Cours*, vol. 1, p. 9.

45. Cauwès, *Cours*, vol. 1, p. 10.

46. Cauwès, *Cours*, vol. 1, p. 10.

47. Cauwès, *Cours*, vol. 1, pp. 208–9; vol. 3, pp. 95–96.

48. Cauwès, *Cours*, vol. 1, pp. 1, 4.

49. Cauwès, *Cours*, vol. 3, p. 55.

50. Cauwès, *Cours*, vol. 3, pp. 87–88.

51. There is no question, Cauwès declared, that excessive hours compromise health, shorten life, and interfere with the family. *Cours*, vol. 3, p. 98). In the light of later developments it is significant that Cauwès did not propose a social-security insurance system. In his view obligatory social insurance would involve administrative and financial problems on such a

scale that the system might not work. Yet he was tentative rather than peremptory in his judgment since he recognized that a successful system might be developed. Moreover, in contrast to the bitter opposition of Leroy-Beaulieu and other Established Liberals, he accepted the principle of obligatory contributions, stating that government would not violate workers' freedom of decision if it required them to contribute to a pension system (vol. 3, pp. 515–17). Regarding workers, he argued that the threat of strikes inhibits employers from oppressing their employees and makes industry more peaceful and more just (vol. 3, pp. 129–31, 135–36). It seems odd that Cauwès would defend the right to form unions in 1893 when the law had already granted that right in 1884. Apparently he took the discussion of unions from his earlier treatises and did not thoroughly revise it.

52. Cauwès, *Cours*, vol. 3, pp. 98, 101, 110. In Cauwès's view the state was to ensure that a country become a "normal nation," one in which every feature of its national life would flourish. He took the concept of a "normal nation" from Friedrich List, his acknowledged master.

53. Cauwès, *Cours*, vol. 1, p. 187.

54. Cauwès, *Cours*, vol. 1, p. 186.

55. For example, Leroy-Beaulieu accepted the use of the term "capitalism," whose coinage he attributed to Marx. *Traité théorique et pratique d'économie politique* (Paris: Guillaumin, 1896), vol. 1, p. 268. Hereafter cited as *TEP*.

56. A major feature of this subtext is its fragmentary but revealing description of what we could call the "state of nature." A series of references enables us to reconstruct quite fully Leroy-Beaulieu's sense of the primitive past, and to see the degree to which his justification of the present rests upon quasi-historical assumptions that he surely shared with many of his contemporaries. The story is one of progress, the progress of production and freedom. Early human beings lived in a state of "primitive denudement," but humankind began its rise out of its aboriginal poverty because of the virtues of the few in early times who accumulated capital and made inventions.

57. *TEP*, vol. 1, p. iv. He wrote that studies by empirical economists had the greatest value because a researcher (*savant*) who is a "spectator" can attain greater impartiality than an experimenter can.

58. *TEP*, vol. 1, pp. 19, 128.

59. On economics as a science of observation, see *TEP*, vol. 1, pp. 5–6, 24, 57–61.

60. *TEP*, vol. 1, pp. 95–96.

61. *TEP*, vol. 1, p. 141. In *L'Etat Moderne* he mentioned a variety of such motives. Devotion to family, loyalty to country, and a desire for honors, luxurious tastes, and the ambition for power, he declared, account for some choices in the areas of production and consumption. Civilized human beings, he claimed, have more needs than barbarous ones because

the former aspire to higher and higher levels of existence. *EM*, pp. 35, 268–69; see also *TEP*, vol. 1, pp. 69–76.

62. *TEP*, vol. 1, pp. 39–40.

63. *TEP*, vol. 1, p. 36.

64. On the long-range realization in history of the law of specialization of functions, see *TEP*, vol. 2, p. 187; for a general statement of the idea, see vol. 2, p. 246; in relation to wages, vol. 2, p. 249. Leroy-Beaulieu's approach parallels that of Alfred Marshall, whose *Principles of Economics* had appeared in 1890 and whose *Elements of Economics of Industry* (1892) Leroy-Beaulieu cites in vol. 1, p. 138.

65. *TEP*, vol. 1, p. 25.

66. *TEP*, vol. 1, p. 20. Emphasis added.

67. *TEP*, vol. 1, p. 20.

68. *TEP*, vol. 2, pp. 744–65.

69. Leroy-Beaulieu defended piecework as being "more in conformity with justice" because it gives "to each according to his work." But he stated clearly that the work must be uniform and that employers must be absolutely fair in their compensation. Moreover, he did not stop with an appeal to managerial honesty; rather, because of the frequent changes in methods of production and the subsequent need to change the basis for assigning value to products, he recommended that piecework rates be determined by committees made up of workers as well as of managers. This was the only place in his work where he accepted limitations on the decision-making power of owners and entrepreneurs. *TEP*, vol. 2, pp. 223–27, 231–34.

70. *TEP*, vol. 2, p. 244.

71. *TEP*, vol. 2, p. 345.

72. *TEP*, vol. 2, p. 294.

73. *TEP*, vol. 2, p. 242.

74. To demonstrate that productivity was the fundamental factor he presented a statistical study of wages and production from a wide range of years, countries, and industries. See, for example, his discussion of day wages in agriculture from 1700 to 1882 (*TEP*, vol. 2, p. 305).

75. The first chapter in the section on distribution defended the right of people with inborn talents to reap rewards even though nature rather than their own efforts was responsible for their abilities. Later, the chapter justifying the charging of interest is a model of Leroy-Beaulieu's argumentation in favor of capitalist practices. Basically he claimed that there are no substitutes for competition, the free market, contract, profit, and interest since both nature and civilization demand these institutions. Capital is "indefinitely productive of utilities," he pointed out (*TEP*, vol. 2, p. 97; see also p. 87), and for that reason it is appropriate to charge interest for its use. Furthermore, interest has existed in all societies because no one will surrender so valuable and useful a thing as capital without the expectation

of remuneration. The ineffectiveness of centuries of religious and philosophical condemnations of interest testifies that this practice is rooted in the natural psychological constitution of human beings and is thus inevitable (p. 88). Finally, civilized societies need the institution of interest since it helps society achieve that most important of goals, progress (pp. 103, 106). The important point here is that for Leroy-Beaulieu there was no open question, nothing to be said on any other side of the question. The matter was closed, demonstrated once and for all by a reasoning based on undeniable principles about nature, human nature, and the value of ever-increasing production.

76. *TEP*, vol. 1, pp. 345.

77. *TEP*, vol. 1, p. 507. The four chapters, in the first volume, that discuss these conditions are particularly valuable as statements of his overall perspective.

78. *TEP*, vol. 1, pp. 508–9, 510.

79. On unfree labor in contrast with free labor, *TEP*, vol. 1, pp. 509ff., 526–28; on unions, vol. 2, pp. 465–75.

80. On the *livret* and other disabilities, *TEP*, vol. 1, p. 531; on profit sharing, see vol. 2, chap. 17, as well as the following chapter on cooperatives.

81. Leroy-Beaulieu wrote in April 1895, "La liberté ne va pas sans quelques inconvenients pour ceux qui ne savent pas s'en servir." "Les aperçus du delegué ouvrier français à la conférence de Berlin," *EF* 18 (26 April 1895), pp. 514–15.

82. This discussion occupies the first ten pages of the chapter on capital. Then in another thirteen pages midway in the chapter (vol. 1, pp. 205–18) he commented on such topics as Stanley Jevons's and Eugene Böhm-Bawerk's concept of time as an element in capital.

83. *Capital: A Critique of Political Economy*, vol. 1, pt. 8: "So-Called Primitive Accumulation."

84. *TEP*, vol. 1, p. 201; emphasis added.

85. See *TEP*, vol. 1, chap. 4: "Le capital—La nature et la genèse du capital," esp. pp. 198–200, in which Leroy-Beaulieu describes in a "thought experiment" how capital emerged from the initiative of enterprising individuals in primitive times.

86. Originated by Nassau Senior in the first half of the nineteenth century, this theory was adapted in France by such Established Liberals as Bastiat.

87. *TEP*, vol. 1, p. 220.

88. *TEP*, vol. 1, p. 275.

89. *TEP*, vol. 1, pp. 288–89.

90. *TEP*, vol. 1, p. 508.

91. *TEP*, vol. 1, pp. 533–34.

92. *TEP*, vol. 1, p. 538.

93. *TEP*, vol. 1, pp. 553–54.

94. *TEP*, vol. 1, p. 535.

95. *TEP*, vol. 1, pp. 589–90.

96. *TEP*, vol. 1, p. 510.

97. *TEP*, vol. 1, pp. 612–15.

98. *TEP*, vol. 1, p. 622.

99. Leroy-Beaulieu wrote: "that person who is so important, so diverse in situation and origins, so ordinarily confused with the capitalist but who is often distinct and who, in any case, is very different from the passive capitalist, that is to say the industrial entrepreneur." The eighteenth-century writer Cantillon preceded Say in pointing to the entrepreneur as a key figure in the economy, but his work remained unknown for a long time.

100. The central chapter on the entrepreneur is "La Mission de l'Entrepreneur" (*TEP*, vol. 1, pp. 292–315). Leroy-Beaulieu considered the theory of entrepreneurship developed by J.-B. Say and his successors to be one of the chief achievements of the French school of economic thought. Within the production side of economic life, the entrepreneur is the "centre nerveux qui lui donne la vie, la conscience, la direction. L'entrepreneur c'est le point capital, la force motrice de la structure sociale" (p. 294). The individual who organizes and directs production is the person "si important, si divers de situation et d'origine, que l'on confond ordinairement avec le capital, mais qui en est souvent distinct, qui en tout cas est très différent du capitaliste passif, à savoir l'entrepreneur d'industrie" (p. 303).

101. *TEP*, vol. 2, pp. 189–97.

102. Capital is "rebellious to all subjection," Leroy-Beaulieu wrote, meaning that savings and investment would decline unless the owners of funds knew that they could control the use of those funds. *TEP*, vol. 1, pp. 299–300.

103. *TEP*, vol. 1, p. 304.

104. *TEP*, vol. 1, p. 298.

105. *TEP*, vol. 1, pp. 508–10.

106. *TEP*, vol. 1, p. 507.

107. *TEP*, vol. 1, pp. 314, 508.

108. *TEP*, vol. 1, p. 644. The ideas I summarize in this paragraph come from pp. 639–45.

109. *TEP*, vol. 1, p. 639.

110. *TEP*, vol. 1, p. 645.

111. He elaborated, "Since no energetic human is deprived of hope under this system, and no man who has arrived at the highest rank is completely free from fear, it follows that human activity is raised to the highest possible point." *TEP*, vol. 1, pp. 640–41.

112. *TEP*, vol. 1, p. 647. Admitting that the operations of the market sometimes can cause inconveniences, Leroy-Beaulieu claimed that the

"intelligent initiative either of individuals or of associations can surmount them" (p. 674). This is one of the few places where Leroy-Beaulieu speaks positively of reliance on human judgment rather than on automatic economic mechanisms.

113. *TEP*, vol. 1, p. 667ff. He did approve the newly passed American laws that regulated railroad rates.

114. *TEP*, vol. 1, p. 674.

CHAPTER 8: THE LAST TWENTY YEARS

1. For example, he lectured several times on the problem of population in France. See the preface to *La question de la population en France* (Paris: Alcan, 1913).

2. On Russian bribery see Aumercier, p. 204, and Arthur Raffalovitch, *"L'abominable vénalité de la presse": d'après les documents des archives russes (1897–1917)* (Paris, 1931). Raffalovitch reprinted letters to his superiors in which he reported on his bribery of various periodicals (pp. 125–31), but he made it clear that he never had to offer money or excessive advertisements to Leroy-Beaulieu, who favored loans to Russia and did not demand money for acting on his convictions. As Aumercier points out, Leroy-Beaulieu did not depend upon the income from his journal. On his warnings to investors see the preface to *TSF*, 8th ed. (Paris: Alcan, 1912).

3. Despite his dissatisfaction with the regime and his electoral defeats, Leroy-Beaulieu's ideas found their way inside the halls of the legislature. For instance, in a 1903 debate pitting advocates of compulsory versus voluntary old-age insurance programs, a deputy named Arnal quoted extensively from Leroy-Beaulieu on the distinction between a moral duty and a legal right. "Legal requirements," he quoted Leroy-Beaulieu as saying, "can only apply to certain very precise and limited types of human actions, for otherwise the entire domain of spontaneity and liberty would disappear, to the enormous detriment of the moral worth of the individual as well as of the very progress of society as a whole." Henri Hatzfeld, *Du paupérisme à la sécurité sociale, 1850–1940: essai sur les origines de la sécurité sociale en France* (Paris: Colin, 1971), p. 73.

4. Leroy-Beaulieu served on their executive boards, though he was by no means the dominant figure. C. M. Andrews and A. S. Kanya-Forstner, "The French 'Colonial party': Its Composition, Aims, and Influence, 1885–1914," *Historical Journal* 14 (1971), pp. 102–3, and C. M. Andrews, "The French Colonialist Movement during the Third Republic: The Unofficial Mind of Imperialism," *Transactions of the Royal Historical Society*, 5th ser., 26 (1976), pp. 143–66.

5. Leroy-Beaulieu promoted organizations that campaigned for tax reductions and was president of the tenth convention of the Union de la

Propriété Batie, a national organization devoted to lobbying against government legislation that would require owners of buildings to improve the sanitary facilities and safety features of their property. His activity in these areas is described in "Toast de M. Paul Leroy-Beaulieu," *Congrès National de la Propriété Batie, Paris 5–8 mai 1913. Organisé par le Chambre Syndicale des Propriétés Immobilières de la Ville de Paris sous le patronage de Union de la Propriété Batie de France* (Orleans: Pigelet, 1913), pp. 544–48. I am grateful to Professor William B. Cohen of Indiana State University for calling my attention to this organization and to Leroy-Beaulieu's role in it.

6. "Depression ou progression: l'impôt sur les successions au Sénat," *EF* 26 (12 February 1898), p. 198; "Modérés et radicaux: les projets de bouleversement simultané des contributions directes," *EF* 26 (25 June 1898), pp. 873–75; *TSF* 8th ed., p. 605. See also "L'impôt global et personnel sur le revenu," brochure no. 47 of the Comité de Défense et de Progrès Social (Paris: 1904), p. 5.

7. In May 1890 Leroy-Beaulieu wrote: "A new sect of sophists has recently appeared which has contributed, notably in Austria, to the development of prejudices and unlimited aspirations among ordinary people (*la classe populaire*); it is the sect of antisemites. These fanatics, augmented sometimes by schemers, have portrayed . . . all industrial and commercial wealth as detestable, all work by directors and idea-men as parasitical. It is fortunate that the people of Paris have not let themselves be caught by the snares of this new school." "Les déchets de la production contemporaine: à propos de la manifestation ouvrier du ler mai," *EF* 18 (3 May 1890), p. 547.

8. Aumercier, p. 69 n. 1.

9. Leroy-Beaulieu was president of the Comité de Surveillance from 1891 to 1916. Aumercier, p. 19.

10. On the formation of the Ligue de la Patrie Française, of which Brunetière was a founding member, see *JDD*, 1 January 1899, p. 2; 7 January 1899, p. 2; "Appel à l'Union," 24 January 1899, p. 2; also 25 and 26 January, p. 2, for new adherents to this Appeal, which was a plea for moderation and acceptance of the decision, yet to be announced, by the Cour de Cassation.

11. Pierre was deputy from the Hérault from 1907 until 1914. "Leroy-Beaulieu, Pierre," *Dictionnaire des parlementaires français . . . de 1889 à 1940* (Paris: PUF, 1968), vol. 5, pp. 2255–56; Aumercier, p. 16.

12. Report of the meeting of the Société d'Economie Politique of 5 January 1912, *JDE*, vol. 270 (15 January 1912), p. 140.

13. Paul Leroy-Beaulieu to Ferdinand Brunétière, 21 March 1905; see also letter of 6 December 1903 and 13 March 1904. Fonds Brunétière, Bibliothèque Nationale, n.a.f. 25043.

14. The award was the Jean Reybaud prize, and the reporter for the committee was the noted philosopher Emile Boutroux. Leroy-Beaulieu

used the money to set up a prize for "the most effective propaganda work for reviving the birth rate in France." Stourm, "Notice," p. 180; Stourm, "PLB," p. 546.

15. In 1896, in a publication in English, Leroy-Beaulieu restated his humanitarian position: "I see no reason to regret having been one of the pioneers of the colonial movement in France. The member for Rochdale [i.e. Richard Cobden] ignored the tutorial mission of Europe, in the present epoch, in relation to most of the Asiatic nations, and to the scattered and uncivilized tribes of Africa. His conception of the relations between a great civilized nation and the primitive races unable to work the vast areas they occupy is far too narrow. For certain races, and within certain climes, civilization must be introduced from without; a benevolent and persevering guardianship is necessary to develop it amongst them. . . . Colonization must be rendered moral and not absolutely vetoed; it must be purged of barbarous incidents, so far as the nature of man will allow. It is lamentable to see the excesses of Pizarro and Cortez renewed in our own time; but it is a good thing to extend the civilization of Europe over the plains of Africa, and to turn to account the resources of a continent abandoned to sloth, massacre, and devastation. . . . We can only hope that an enlightened public opinion . . . will impose on all the founders of colonial empire more of moderation and good faith in the accomplishment of their mission." Paul Leroy-Beaulieu, "Richard Cobden: His Work and the Outcome of His Ideas," in Henry Dunckley et al., *Richard Cobden and the Jubilee of Free Trade* (London: Unwin, 1896), pp. 122–24.

16. "De la nécessité de l'annexion totale de la Tunisie," *EF* 9 (9 April 1881), p. 439.

17. "La politique africaine, les irrésolutions et le danger croissant," *EF* 9 (9 July 1881), p. 34.

18. "De la nécessité de l'annexion," p. 438. On the following page he quoted approvingly a cynical phrase of Bismarck: "Of all the beatitudes there is not one which has more truth on the earth than the beatitude to which M. de Bismarck alluded two years ago when he cried in the midst of the Reichstag: Beati possidentes!"

19. On the founding of the society see G. de Molinari, "Chronique économique," *JDE*, 4th ser., 18 (June 1882), p. 485. Molinari explained the purpose of the organization: "The extension of civilization has almost always been harmful to indigenous races. . . . Thus we can only applaud the efforts that are made to the end of making civilization more merciful to those races for which its domination is so hard."

20. "Le développement de la puissance coloniale de la France" (pt. 1), *EF* 8 (1 May 1880), p. 530.

21. *L'Algérie et la Tunisie*, 2nd ed. (Paris: Guillaumin, 1897), pp. xii, xiv (from the preface to the first edition).

22. *L'Algérie*, pp. vii, viii.

23. *DLC*, 4th ed. (Paris: Guillaumin, 1891), pp. 841–42.

24. *L'Algérie*, p. 295.

25. *DLC* (1882), pp. 312–13.

26. *Le Sahara, le Soudan et les chemins de fer transsahariens* (Paris: Guillaumin, 1904), pp. 16–17, 18.

27. *DLC* (1908), p. xii (preface to the 4th edition of 1891).

28. *DLC* (1908), p. ii.

29. Société d'Economie Politique, Réunion du 5 juin 1884, "Discussion: où la femme, au point de vue économique, est-elle mieux placée, au foyer de la famille ou dans l'atelier?" *JDE* 26 (1884), pp. 451–52.

30. "Discussion," pp. 446–50.

31. "Discussion," pp. 458, 459.

32. "Discussion," pp. 456.

33. "Discussion," pp. 452–54.

34. *Question de la population*, pp. 476ff. His general principle was that "Le privilège ne peut être exclu d'une société" (p. 455) and so he also called for reserving scholarships only for those who came from families with numerous children (p. 456); for specific tax breaks for philanthropic societies engaged in providing inexpensive housing solely for "normal families," i.e., those with three or more children (p. 457); plural votes for fathers of large families (p. 463); and an "inexorable" rule that public service jobs should only go to fathers of "normal families" (pp. 469–71).

35. *Question de la population*, p. 13.

36. "La question de la population en France" (pt. 1), *EF* 5 (7 April 1877), esp. p. 419; "Du mouvement de la population en France" (pts. 1 and 2), *EF* 8 (2 and 9 October 1880), pp. 405–7, 433–35; "The Influence of Civilization upon the Movement of Population," *Journal of the Royal Statistical Society* 54 (1891), pp. 372–84 (trans. from *L'Economiste Français*, 20 and 27 September 1890), esp. p. 377 on religion and other causes of population decline.

37. For the most complete of his many discussions of civilization, see *Question de la population*, pp. 184–85.

38. "La question de la population et la civilisation démocratique," *RDM* 143 (15 October 1897), pp. 872–73; see also "La question de la population en France" (pt. 2), *EF* 5 (14 April 1877), p. 451.

39. "La question de la population et la civilisation démocratique," p. 871.

40. "The Influence of Civilization," p. 382.

41. "La question de la population et la civilisation démocratique," p. 871.

42. See Karen M. Offen, "Depopulation, Nationalism, and Feminism in Fin-de-siècle France," *American Historical Review* 89 (June 1984), pp. 652–53.

43. "Du mouvement de la population en France" (pt. 2), pp. 434–35.

44. "La question de la population et la civilisation démocratique," p. 888.

45. E. Aubert, Paul Leroy-Beaulieu et al., "Hygiène sociale," *Séances et Travaux de l'Académie des Sciences Morales et Politiques* 178 (1912), p. 468.

46. *Question de la population*, pp. 270, 271, 273.

47. *Question de la population*, pp. 272–73.

48. *Question de la population*, pp. 328–29, 337, 439–42.

49. QO, p. 122.

50. Jacques Flach, professor of Comparative Legislation at the Collège de France, declared that the effort to "arrest the propagation of the species is a crime of *lèse* humanity as it is of *lèse patrie*." Paul Leroy-Beaulieu et al., "La question de la population en France," *Séances et Travaux de l'Académie des Sciences Morales et Politiques* 179 (1913), p. 464. Leroy-Beaulieu's readings from his chapters take up pages 381–445 of the volume; the discussion of his ideas, which took place on February 8, 15, 22, and March 1 and 8 and concluded with remarks by Leroy-Beaulieu, is recorded on pp. 445–501. The most purely Established Liberal voice was that of Eugène d'Eichtal (pp. 484–90), who denounced reliance of any kind on the state and who insisted, as Leroy-Beaulieu would have done forty years earlier, that population would grow if only the obstacles preventing industrialists from increasing production were removed. Among the barriers he mentioned were laws that restricted too narrowly the employment of children and women and the 1884 law that legalized unions and permitted them to exclude women from workplaces. Eichtal also warned against the proposed minimum wage for women who do work at home, because he said that law would make it too expensive to employ them. Alexandre Ribot, a former prime minister, spoke (in more general and less politically damaging terms) along the same lines, poking holes in all the proposals to use state powers for either repression or encouragement (pp. 456–63).

51. This translates as the Union of Fathers and Mothers Whose Sons Died for the Nation. Paul Leroy-Beaulieu to Henri Poincaré, 18 November 1916, Poincaré papers, Bibliothèque Nationale, n.a.f. 16006, f. 477. In this letter Leroy-Beaulieu, as president of the organization, asked Poincaré to participate in an observance held by the group.

52. Eichtal, "PLB," p. 7.

CHAPTER 9: LEROY-BEAULIEU IN THE HISTORY OF LIBERALISM

1. Stourm, "PLB," p. 533.

2. QO, p. 125.

3. The original reads: "souple, éveillée, où l'instruction, les connais-

sances scientifiques et les notions techniques se répandent, où des combinaisons nouvelles éclosent à chaque instant." *TEP*, vol. 2, p. 103.

4. *QO*, pp. 184, 186.

5. *TEP*, vol. 2, p. 105.

6. *TEP*, vol. 1, p. 479.

7. *TEP*, vol. 1, p. 478.

8. *AL*, pp. 60–61.

9. *EMO*, p. 70.

10. *QO*, pp. 75–78, 107–9.

11. *TEP*, vol. 1, p. 38. See also p. 81, where Leroy-Beaulieu sums up the truths taught by political economy.

12. For Leroy-Beaulieu's most extensive discussions of science and of natural laws, see the first four chapters of *TEP*, vol. 1, esp. pp. iv–v, 11–13, 18–20, 23. On p. 7 he praised the pioneers of economic science who "helped establish that the production and distribution of wealth are subject to natural laws and not the changeable fantasies of lawmakers."

13. The quotation from Montesquieu comes from *EMO*, p. 115. *Things* is a key word in the statement. For Leroy-Beaulieu, as for the philosophical materialists of his time, the physical world was made up of separate objects with well-defined boundaries and clearcut parts. Nature was a realm of individual phenomena, or independent, circumscribed objects and events, that were accessible to the eyes of observers.

14. For example, *TEP*, vol. 1, p. 65: "No one, among those who are sensible, impartial, and possessing some [intellectual] authority, denies in principle" the truth of the basic laws economists had identified for almost one hundred years.

15. On complications of reality, see *TEP*, vol. 1, pp. 25, 34, 36–37, 38, 90–91.

16. See *EM*, pp. 336–50, esp. pp. 340, 345–46; also *TEP*, vol. 2, pp. 354, 368, 486.

17. The comment on Comte is in "De l'oeuvre colonisatrice de la France et les écueils à éviter," *EF* 10 (25 November 1882), p. 671.

18. *JDD*, 2 September and 22 September 1871.

19. "De la représentation des intérêts industriels et commerciaux en France," *EF* 2 (7 November 1874), pp. 565–66.

20. *TEP*, vol. 1, pp. ii, vii.

21. Gaëtan Pirou, *Les doctrines économiques en France depuis 1870* (Paris: Colon, 1925), p. 115.

22. *TEP*, vol. 1, p. 142.

23. *TEP*, vol. 1, p. 19.

24. *TEP*, vol. 1, p. 56.

25. *TEP*, vol. 1, pp. 48, 54.

26. Paul Cauwès, as we have seen (Chapter 7 above), argued the

opposite: that selfish motivation becomes less prevalent as civilization develops.

27. *EM*, p. 208.

28. *EM*, p. 5. See also pp. 268–69; and *EP*, vol. 1, pp. 69–76.

29. *EM*, p. 35.

30. *TEP*, vol. 1, pp. 104, 108–9.

31. For a key example of this attitude, see the doctrine of competition in *TEP*, vol. 2, chap. 7.

32. On these thinkers (except Ward) see James T. Kloppenberg's magisterial *Uncertain Victory: Social Democracy and Progressivism in European and American Thought, 1870–1920* (Oxford: Oxford Univ. Press, 1986).

33. *EM*, pp. 249–50.

34. The comment on Jesus is in *TEP*, vol. 1, p. 105, and the quotation is from *DLC* (1874), p. 41. See also *TEP*, vol. 4, p. 284.

35. *TEP*, vol. 1, pp. 682–83.

36. *QO*, p. 88.

37. *EM*, p. 89.

38. *TEP*, vol. 1, p. 297.

39. *TEP*, vol. 1, p. 508.

40. *TEP*, vol. 1, p. 293ff. Yet, as was pointed out in an earlier chapter, when Leroy-Beaulieu engaged in a "thought experiment" and reconstructed the scene of the building of the first canoe, he did not picture a number of fisher folk talking the idea over and then cutting down a tree together and hollowing it out through joint effort.

41. *EM*, p. 315.

42. *QO*, p. 293.

43. *EM*, p. 50. See also *TEP*, vol. 1, pp. 638–45, 681–87.

44. This commitment was too strong for him ever to grasp the insight eloquently stated in our time by C. B. Macpherson that no one is fully responsible for his or her own self-development, that we all were able to train ourselves because others did their daily work and kept society going, often sacrificing their own self-development because of economic pressures. On this conception of human solidarity, see various works by C. B. Macpherson on democracy and Liberalism.

45. This is why the genetic method had an important place in nearly all of Leroy-Beaulieu's books. In *L'Etat Moderne* (p. 39) he stated outright that in order to know a phenomenon one must trace it back to its origins in the past.

46. His most extensive statement of this view appeared in *AL*, chap. 3.

47. One aspect of Leroy-Beaulieu's doctrine of historical forces was ambiguous if not contradictory: his view of the role of the mind in shaping events and developments. "Ideas give birth to facts," he wrote in *EMO*,

p. 16. This statement is in disaccord with his emphasis on instinct as the force of change in history.

48. See above, pp. 192–93.

49. *QO*, p. 288.

50. On the development of rights he wrote: "An exact analysis testifies that law creates no right; it recognizes a right, defines it, . . . sanctions it, . . . makes it precise. . . . At the outset one finds the act, the instinctive act, a whole repetition of more or less uniform acts, [which] . . . develop and become precise . . . because they conform to the necessities of human and social life. . . . Language, exchanges, rights are born spontaneously by the development of successive embryos. . . . If, to bring about the development of humanity, it was necessary to wait for the vacillating, uncertain, contradictory decisions of speculative reason (*la raison raisonnante*), humanity after many centuries would hardly have raised itself above an animal level" (*EM*, p. 109). See also pp. 45–46 on the origin of medieval commercial codes.

51. *EM*, p. 29.

52. *EM*, p. 89. See also his dramatic exclamation in *TEP*, vol. 2, pp. 393–94: "O that our country might no longer be a collection of scattered molecules that can not resist the slightest wind."

53. *TEP*, vol. 1, p. 505.

54. On the inadequacy of this label see chap. 1, note 9 above. I believe the term should be replaced by such labels as Reformist Liberalism and Welfare Liberalism.

55. *Le Collectivisme*, p. 409.

56. *TEP*, vol. 1, p. 184.

57. Guy Baret, *Le Figaro* (15 December 1982), p. 1.

58. Aumercier, in her multivolume dissertation on Leroy-Beaulieu, interprets him primarily as a shrewd observer of economic realities.

59. I am grateful to Professor David Gordon of the University of North Carolina at Charlotte for the comments and some of the wording I have used here.

Selected Bibliography

PRIMARY SOURCES

From the Archives Nationales

Batbie, Anselme. Dossier. AJ 16 947.

Chevalier, Auguste et Michel, correspondance addressée à. AB 19 3357.

Elections, Chambre des Deputés, 1881–1884, Hérault, arrondissement de Lodève. C 3507.

Leroy-Beaulieu, Paul. Dossier, "Candidates for the Chair of Political Economy, Collège de France." F 17 13556.

———. Dossier de presse, *L'Economiste Français*. F 18 343.

———. Dossier, Légion d'Honneur. LH 1610.

Régistre de la Faculté de Droit, 17 April and 29 April 1872. AJ 16 1791.

Simon, Jules. Papers. 87 AP 4; 87 AP 6; 87 AP 10.

Société des Caves et des Producteurs Réunis de Rocquefort. Dossier, 65 AQ R 429.

From the Bibliothèque Nationale

Brunétière papers, n.a.f. 25043.

Lacroix, Paul de. "Pierre-Paul Leroy-Beaulieu, membre de l'Institut," *Autographes du XIXe siècle*, vol. 9; n.a.f. 22862.

Leroy-Beaulieu, Pierre. "Aux électeurs des arrondissements de Lisieux et de Pont L'Evêque," Paris, 16 February 1852. LE 77.23 Fol.

Poincaré papers, n.a.f. 16006, f. 477.

From the Archives de l'Institut de France

Leroy-Beaulieu, Paul. Letter of candidature, 12 June 1878. Paul Leroy-Beaulieu dossier.

WORKS BY PAUL LEROY-BEAULIEU

Books (by date of publication)

De l'état moral et intellectuel des populations ouvrières et de son influence sur le taux des salaires. Paris: Guillaumin, 1868.

L'administration locale en France et en Angleterre. Paris: Guillaumin, 1872.

Guerres contemporaines, 1853–1866. Paris: Librairie Internationale, 1869.

Recherches historiques, statistiques et économiques sur les guerres contemporaines, 1853–1866. Paris: Librairie Internationale, 1869.

La question ouvrière au XIXe siècle. Paris: Charpentier, 1872.

Le travail des femmes au XIXe siècle. Paris: Guillaumin, 1873.

De la colonisation chez les peuples modernes. 1st ed. Paris: Guillaumin, 1874.

Traité de la science des finances, 2 vols. 1st ed. Paris: Guillaumin, 1877.

Essai sur la répartition des richesses et sur la tendance à une moindre inégalité des conditions. Paris: Guillaumin, 1881.

De la colonisation chez les peuples modernes. 2nd ed. Paris: Guillaumin, 1882.

Le collectivisme: examen critique du nouveau socialisme. 2nd ed. Paris: Guillaumin, 1885.

L'Etat moderne et ses fonctions. Paris: Guillaumin, 1889.

Un chapitre des moeurs electorales en France en 1889–1890. Paris: Guillaumin, Librairie Chaix, 1890.

Traité théorique et pratique d'économie politique, 4 vols. Paris: Guillaumin, 1896.

L'Algérie et la Tunisie. Paris: Guillaumin, 1897.

Le Sahara, le Soudan et les chemins de fer transsahariens. Paris: Guillaumin, 1904.

De la colonisation chez les peuples modernes, 2 vols. 6th ed. Paris: Alcan, 1908.

Traité de la science des finances, 2 vols. 8th ed. Paris: Alcan, 1912.

La question de la population en France. Paris: Alcan, 1913.

Major Articles

"Les ressources de la France et de la Prusse." *RDM,* 2nd per., 89 (1 September 1870), pp. 135–55.

"La province pendant la siège de Paris: II. Sa situation politique et sociale." *RDM,* 2nd per., 92 (15 March 1871), pp. 144–77.

"La réforme municipale en France: la Commune et le self government."
RDM, 2nd per., 93 (15 May 1871), pp. 248–79.
"Une enquête anglaise sur la condition des travailleurs." *RDM*, 2nd per.,
97 (1 December 1871), pp. 651–81.
"Les ouvrières de fabrique d'autrefois et d'aujourd'hui." *RDM*, 2nd per.,
97 (1 February 1872) pp. 630–57.
"The influence of civilization upon the movement of population." *Journal
of the Royal Statistical Society* 54 (1891), pp. 372–84 (translated from
L'Economiste Français, 20 and 27 September 1890).

Articles Relating to Imperialism

"La colonisation française et la colonisation anglaise." *EF* 2 (15 August
1874), pp. 181–83.
"La colonisation de l'Algérie" (pts. 1 and 2) *EF* 2 (22 and 29 August 1874),
pp. 212–14 and 245–47.
"L'Egypte et les intérêts français." *EF* 6 (9 February 1878), p. 163.
"La situation en Egypte et les intérêts français." *EF* 6 (28 September
1878), p. 385.
"De la colonisation et de l'exploitation du continent africain." *EF* 7 (1
February 1879), pp. 129–31.
"De la fondation d'une union douanière occidentale." *EF* 7 (11 October
1879), pp. 433–35.
"Les intérêts de la France et de l'Italie en Afrique." *EF* 8 (28 August 1880),
pp. 249–51.
"L'Algérie et la Tunisie: de la nécessité de protege efficacement les intérêts
françaises à Tunis." *EF* 9 (19 March 1881), pp. 345–47.
"De la nécessité de l'annexion totale de la Tunisie." *EF* 9 (9 April 1881),
pp. 437–39.
"La politique africaine, les irrésolutions et le danger croissant." *EF* 9 (9
July 1881), pp. 33–35.
"Le développement de la puissance coloniale de la France (pt. 1)" *EF* 8
(1 May 1880), pp. 529–31.
"La politique continentale et la politique coloniale." *EF* 9 (7 May 1881),
pp. 565–67.
"Les intérêts coloniaux et exterieurs de la France et la situation
gouvernementale." *EF* 11 (10 February 1883), p. 157.

OTHER SOURCES

Ageron, Charles-Robert. *France coloniale ou parti coloniale*. Paris: PUF, 1978.
Andrews, C. M. "The French Colonialist Movement during the Third
Republic: The Unofficial Mind of Imperialism." *Transactions of the
Royal Historical Society*, 5th ser., 26 (1976), pp. 143–66.

Andrews, C. M., and A. S. Kanya-Forstner. *The Climax of French Imperial Expansion, 1914–1924*. Stanford, Calif.: Stanford Univ. Press, 1981.
———. "The French 'Colonial party': Its Composition, Aims, and Influence, 1885–1914." *Historical Journal* 14 (1971), pp. 102–3.
Ashford, Douglas E. *The Emergence of the Welfare States*. Oxford: Basil Blackwell, 1986.
Aubert, E., Leroy-Beaulieu, Paul, et al., "Hygiène sociale." Discussion of infant mortality at the Académie des Sciences morales et politiques. *Séances et Travaux de l'Académie des Sciences Morales et Politiques* 178 (1912).
Aumercier, Giselle, "Paul Leroy-Beaulieu, observateur de la réalité économique et sociale française: L'Economiste français 1873–1892." Thèse, doctorat du troisième cycle, 4 vols. Paris, 1979.
Béchaux, A. *Les écoles économiques aux XXe siècle*, 2 vols. Paris: Rousseau, Guillaumin, 1902, 1907.
Bertocci, Philip. *Jules Simon: Republican Anticlericalism and Cultural Politics in France, 1848–1886*. Kansas City: Univ. of Missouri Press, 1978.
Blet, Henri. *Histoire de la colonisation française*, vol. 2: *Les étapes d'une renaissance coloniale, 1789–1870*. Paris: Arthaud, 1946.
Block, Maurice. "La crise économique." *RDM*, 3rd ser., 32 (15 March 1879), pp. 433–59.
Bodley, John Courtenay. *France*, 2 vols. London: MacMillian, 1898.
Bouchard, L. "Le budget de la République et les reformes financières." *RDM*, 2nd per., 94 (1 July 1871), pp. 71–99.
Bourcier de Carbon, Luc. *Histoire de la pensée et des doctrines économiques*, 3 vols. Paris: Montchrestien, 1971–1979.
Boutrouche, Robert R. "Quelques aperçus sur l'opinion anti-coloniale en France depuis le XVIIIe siècle." *Revue Africaine* 74 (1933), pp. 377–402.
Bouvier, Jean. "Aux origines de la Troisième République: les reflexes sociaux des milieux d'affaires." *Revue Historique* 210 (1953), pp. 271–301.
Brouilhet, Charles. *Le conflict des doctrines dans l'économie politique contemporaine*. Paris: Alcan, 1910.
Campbell, Stuart L. *The Second Empire Revisited: A Study in French Historiography*. New Brunswick: Rutgers, 1978.
Caro, Elme. "L'idée de la patrie: ses défaillances et son reveil." *RDM*, 2nd per., 91 (15 January 1871), pp. 243–62.
———. "La république et les républicains." *RDM*, 2nd per., 93 (1 June 1871), pp. 516–46.
Cauchy, E. "Rapport sur le concours relatif à l'administration locale en France et en Angleterre." *Séances et Travaux*, 5th ser., 23 (July–September 1870), pp. 73–156.
Cauwès, Paul. *Cours d'économie politique: professé à la Faculté de Droit de*

Paris; contenant avec l'exposé des principes l'analyse des questions économiques, 4 vols. Paris: Larose et Forcel, 1893.

————. *Précis d'un cours d'économie politique: professé à la Faculté de Droit de Paris; contenant avec l'exposé des principes l'analyse des questions économiques*, 2 vols. Paris: Larose et Forcel, 1879; 2nd ed. 1879–1880.

Christopher, John B. "The Dessication of the Bourgeois Spirit." In E. M. Earle, ed., *Modern France: Problems of the Third and Fourth Republics*. Princeton: Princeton Univ. Press, 1951.

Daniel, André. *L'année politique 1885*. Paris: Charpentier, 1886.

de Broglie, Gabriel. *Histoire politique de la "Revue des Deux Mondes" de 1829 à 1979*. Paris: Perrin, 1979.

————. *L'Orléanisme: La ressource libérale de la France*. Paris: Perrin, 1981.

de Mazade, Charles. "Chronique de la quinzaine" (regular column). *RDM*, 1 January 1870 to 15 October 1885.

Degoix, Paul (Ingénieur). "Les grèves et la question ouvrière." *JDE*, 4th ser., 3 (August 1878), pp. 177–87.

Deschamps, Hubert. *Méthodes et doctrines coloniales de la France*. Paris: Colin, 1953.

Desjobert, Amédée. *La question d'Alger: politique, colonisation, commerce*. Paris: Duffart, 1837.

Dictionnaire des parlementaires français . . . depuis ler mai 1789 . . . jusqu'en ler mai 1889. Paris: Bourloton, 1891.

Dictionnaire des parlementaires français . . . de 1889 à 1940. Paris: PUF, 1968.

Digeon, Claude. *La crise allemand de la pensée française (1870–1914)*. Paris: PUF, 1959.

Durckheim, Emile. *Le socialisme*. Paris: PUF, 1971.

Duval, Jules (d. 1870). "Les fonctions économiques de l'Etat." *JDE* 17 (March 1870), pp. 382–96.

Duverger, Maurice. *Sociologie de la politique*. Paris: PUF-Themis, 1973.

Eichtal, Eugène d'. "Les grèves des ouvrieres et les conseils d'arbitrage en Angleterre." *RDM*, 2nd per., 93 (June 1871), pp. 188–213.

————. "Paul Leroy-Beaulieu." *Revue des Sciences Politiques* 37 (January–June 1917), pp. 1–7.

Elwitt, Sanford. *The Making of the Third Republic*. Baton Rouge: Univ. of Louisiana Press, 1976.

Feilbogen, S. "L'évolution des idées économiques et sociales en France depuis 1870." *Revue d'Histoire des Doctrines Economiques et Sociales* 3 (1910), pp. 1–10, 347–72.

Flach, Jacques. "La vie et les oeuvres de M. Edouard Laboulaye." *Revue Politique et Littéraire (Revue Bleue)* 21 (17 May 1884), pp. 610–18.

Fontpertuis, Adalbert Frout de. "L'Afrique centrale: son exploration et sa colonisation." *JDE* 7 (October 1879), pp. 10–27.

————. Review of Paul Leroy-Beaulieu's *Répartition des Richesses*. *JDE*, 4th ser., 13 (March 1881), pp. 500–505.

Frankel, S. Herbert. *The concept of colonization.* Oxford: Clarendon, 1949.

Fustel de Coulanges, Numa. "La politique d'envahissement: Louvois et M. de Bismarck." *RDM*, 2nd per., 91 (1 January 1871), pp. 1–29.

Garnier, Joseph. "Chronique économique" (regular column). *JDE*, 1871–1880.

———. "Observations sur l'article précédent." *JDE* 17 (March 1870), pp. 396–98.

Gide, Charles, and Charles Rist. *A History of Economic Doctrines, from the Time of the Physiocrats to the Present Day*, trans. R. Richards and Ernest F. Row. 2nd English ed. New York: D.C. Heath, 1948.

Girard, Louis. *Les Libéraux français, 1814–1875.* Paris: Aubier, 1985.

Girardet, Raoul. *L'idée coloniale en France de 1871 à 1962.* Rev. ed. Paris: Livre de Poche, 1978.

Girvetz, Harry. *The Evolution of Liberalism.* Rev. ed. of *From Wealth to Welfare.* London: Collier-MacMillan, 1963.

Guillen, Pierre. *L'expansion (1881–1898).* Paris: Imprimerie Nationale, 1985.

Guiral, Pierre. *Prévost-Paradol, 1829–1870: pensée et action d'un libéral sous le Second Empire.* Paris: PUF, 1955.

Hanotaux, Gabriel. *Histoire de la France contemporaine*, 4 vols. Paris: Société d'édition contemporaine, 1903–1909.

Hatzfeld, Henri. *Du paupérisme à la sécurité sociale, 1850–1940: essai sur les origines de la sécurité sociale en France.* Paris: Colin, 1971.

Hendrick, Robert M. "Frédéric Bastiat, Forgotten Liberal: Spokesman for an Ideology in Crisis," Ph.D. diss., New York University, 1987.

Jardin, André. *Histoire du libéralisme politique: de la crise de l'absolutisme à la constitution de 1875.* Paris: Hachette, 1985.

Joughin, Jean. *The Commune in French Politics, 1871–1880, the History of the Amnesty of 1880*, 2 vols. Baltimore: Johns Hopkins, 1955.

Kloppenberg, James T. *Uncertain Victory: Social Democracy and Progressivism in European and American Thought, 1870–1920.* Oxford: Oxford Univ. Press, 1986.

Laveleye, Emile de. "L'exploration de l'Afrique Centrale et la conférence géographique de Bruxelles." *RDM* 20 (1 April 1877).

———. "Les tendances nouvelles de l'économie politique et du socialisme." *RDM*, 3rd ser., 45 (15 July 1875), pp. 445–68.

Léon, Pierre. "L'affermissement du phenomène d'industrialisation." In Ferdinand Braudel and E. Labrousse, eds., *Histoire économique et sociale de la France.* Paris: PUF, 1976. Book 3, vol. 2, pp. 475–618.

Leroy-Beaulieu, Paul, et al. "La question de la population en France." *Séances et Travaux de l'Académie des Sciences Morales et Politiques* 179 (1913), pp. 381–501.

Le Van Lemesle, Lucette. "La promotion de l'économie politique en France au XIXe siècle jusqu'à son introduction dans les Facultés." *Revue d'Histoire Moderne et Contemporaine* 17 (1980), pp. 270–92.

Levasseur, Emile. "Rapport sur le concours pour le Prix Léon Faucher." *Séances et Travaux de l'Académie des Sciences Morales et Politiques* 29 (May–June 1870), pp. 315–57.

———. "Rapport sur le concours pour le prix fondé par Mme. Léon Faucher (lu dans la séance du 19 mars 1870)." *Mémoires de l'Académie des Sciences Morales et Politiques de l'Institut de France* 13 (1872), pp. 471–510.

Logue, William. *From Philosophy to Sociology: The Evolution of French Liberalism, 1870–1914.* DeKalb: Northern Illinois Univ. Press, 1983.

Loubère, Leo A. *Radicalism in Mediterranean France: Its Rise and Decline, 1848–1914.* Albany: State Univ. of New York Press, 1974.

Lutfalla, Michel. "Aux origines du libéralisme économique en France, le *Journal des Economistes*: analyse du contenu de la première série, 1841–1853." *Revue d'Histoire Economique et Sociale* 50 (1972), pp. 494–517.

Masson, André. "L'opinion française et les problèmes coloniaux à la fin du Second Empire." *Revue Française d'Histoire d'Outre Mer* 49 (1962), pp. 366–435.

Mayeur, Jean-Marie. *Les débuts de la Troisième République, 1871–1898.* Paris: Seuil, 1973.

McDougal, Mary Lynn. "Working Class Women during the Industrial Revolution, 1780–1914." In Renate Bridenthal and Claudia Koonz, eds., *Becoming Visible: Women in European History.* Boston: Houghton Mifflen, 1977. Pp. 262–65.

Merivale, Herman. *Lectures on Colonies and Colonization.* 2nd ed. 1861; rpt. London: Oxford Univ. Press, 1928.

Michel, Henri. *L'idée de L'Etat.* 2nd. ed. Paris: Hachette, 1899.

Mill, John Stuart. *Principles of Political Economy*, 2 vols. London: J. W. Parker, 1848.

Mohrt, Michel. *Les intellectuels devant la défaite, 1870.* Paris: Correa, 1942.

Molinari, Guy de. "L'Année 1880." *JDE*, 4th ser., 13 (January 1881).

———. "Chronique économique." *JDE*, 4th ser., 16 (October 1881), pp. 324–25.

———. "Chronique économique." *JDE*, 4th ser., 18 (June 1882), p. 485.

Moon, Parker Thomas. *Imperialism and World Politics.* New York: Macmillan, 1939.

Morel, L.-A. *Clément-Joseph Garnier, 1813–1881: l'homme et l'oeuvre.* St. Germain-en-Laye: Penot, 1906.

Mullins, Willard. "On the Concept of Ideology in the Political Sciences." *American Political Science Review* 66 (1972).

Murphy, Agnes. *The Ideology of French Imperialism, 1871–1881.* Washington: Catholic Univ. of America Press, 1948.

Osborne, Thomas R. *A Grande Ecole for the Grands Corps: The Recruitment and Training of the French Administrative Elite in the Nineteenth Century*. New York and Boulder, Colo.: Social Science Monographs, 1983.

Palmade, Guy. "Le *Journal des Economistes* et la pensée libérale sous le Second Empire." *Bulletin de la Société d'Histoire Moderne* (May 1962), pp. 9–16.

Parieu, E. de. "Discours d'ouverture prononcée à la séance publique annuelle du samedi 28 décembre 1867." *Séances et Travaux*, 5th ser., 13 (January–April 1868), pp. 209–25.

Passy, Hippolyte. "Prix Bordin: rapport sur le concours." *Séances et Travaux*, 5th ser., 12 (July–September 1867), pp. 5–24.

Pirou, Gaëtan. *Les doctrines économiques en France depuis 1870*. Paris: Colin, 1925.

Power, Thomas Francis. *Jules Ferry and the Renaissance of French Imperialism*. New York: King's Crown Press, 1944.

Proust, Marcel. *A la recherche du temps perdu*. Paris: Gallimard, 1954. Vol. 2: *Le côté de Guermantes*.

Plessis, Alain. *The Rise and Fall of the Second Empire, 1852–1871*, trans. Jonathan Mandelbaum. Cambridge: Cambridge Univ. Press, 1985.

Raffalovitch, Arthur. *"L'abominable vénalité de la presse": d'après les documents des archives russes (1897–1917)*. Paris, 1931.

Renouvin, Pierre. *La politique extérieure de la IIIe République de 1871 à 1904*. Paris: Centre de Documentation Universitaire, 1948.

Reybaud, Louis. "Rapport sur le concours ouvert dans la Section de Morale relativement à l'instruction et au salaire des femmes dans les travaux d'industrie." *Séances et Travaux de l'Académie des Sciences Morales et Politiques* 24 (October–December 1870), pp. 169–92.

Roberts, Stephen H. *History of French Colonial Policy (1870–1925)*, 2 vols. London: P. S. King, 1929.

Rudelle, Odille. *La république absolue, 1870–1889*. Paris: Publ. de la Sorbonne, 1982.

Say, Jean-Baptiste. *Cours complet d'économie politique*. 2 vols. 2nd ed. Paris: Guillaumin, 1840.

———. *Traité d'économie politique*. 6th ed. Paris: Gallimard, 1841.

Schéfer, Christian. *La France moderne et le problème coloniale*. Paris: Alcan, 1907.

———. *L'Algérie et l'évolution de la colonisation française: la politique coloniale de la Monarchie de Juillet*. Paris: Champion, 1928.

Schelle, G. "L'oeuvre de Paul Leroy-Beaulieu." *JDE*, 6th ser., 54 (April–June 1917), pp. 20–36.

Schlesinger, Arthur, Jr. "Is Liberalism Dead?" *New York Times Magazine*, 30 March 1980, pp. 42–43ff.

Schnerb, Robert. "La politique fiscale de Thiers: I. Un demi-siècle de luttes autour de l'impôt." *Revue Historique* 201 (1949), pp. 186–212.

Scott, John R. *Republican Ideas and the Liberal Tradition, 1870–1914.* New York: Columbia Univ. Press, 1951.

Seeley, John R. *The Expansion of England.* Boston: Roberts, 1883.

Seliger, Martin. *Ideology and Politics.* London: Allen & Unwin, 1976.

Smith, Adam. *The Wealth of Nations,* ed. Edwin Cannon. New York: Modern Library, 1937.

Smith, Michael Stephen. *Tariff Reform in France, 1860–1900.* Ithaca, N.Y.: Cornell Univ. Press, 1980.

Société d'Economie Politique. "Discussion: Les causes de la crise actuelle." Meeting of 5 December 1877, *JDE,* 3d ser., 48 (December 1877), pp. 446–56.

Société d'Economie Politique. "Discussion: Où la femme, au point de vue économique, est-elle mieux placée, au foyer de la famille ou dans l'atelier?" Meeting of 5 June 1884, *JDE* 26 (1884), pp. 445–59.

Soltau, Roger. *French Political Thought in the Nineteenth Century.* New Haven, Conn.: Yale Univ. Press, 1931.

Stourm, René. "Notice historique sur la vie et les travaux de M. Anatole Leroy-Beaulieu." *Séances et Travaux de l'Académie des Sciences Morales et Politiques* 83 (January–June, 1915), pp. 169–91.

———. "Notice historique sur la vie et les travaux de M. Paul Leroy-Beaulieu." *Séances et Travaux de l'Académie des Sciences Morales et Politiques* 89 (9 December 1918), pp. 151–84.

———. "Paul Leroy-Beaulieu." *RDM* 38 (1 April 1917), pp. 532–53.

Teste, Louis. *Les monarchistes sous la Troisième République.* Paris: Rousseau, 1891.

Thornton, Archibald. *The Imperial Idea and Its Enemies: A Study in British Power.* London: Macmillan, 1959.

Thuillier, Guy. *L'ENA avant L'ENA.* Paris: PUF, 1983.

Vacherot, Etienne. "Les nouveaux Jacobins." *RDM,* 3rd ser., 40 (1 July 1880), pp. 40–74.

Vallette, Jacques. "Note sur l'idée coloniale vers 1871." *Revue d'Histoire Moderne et Contemporaine* 14 (1967), pp. 158–72.

Vapereau, G., ed. *Dictionnaire universel des contemporains.* 6th ed. Paris: Hachette, 1893.

Ventre-Denis, Madeleine. "Sciences sociales et Université au XIXe siècle." *Revue Historique,* no. 520 (October–December 1976), pp. 321–42.

Vidal, Roger. *Batbie: homme politique, économiste, juriste.* Paris: Pichon, Durand-Auzias, 1950.

Vesin. "La colonisation d'Algérie (suite et fin)." *JDE* 6 (June 1879), pp. 406–39.

Walch, Jean. *Michel Chevalier, économiste saint-simonien, 1806–1879*. Paris: Vrin, 1975.

Weill, George. *Histoire du parti républicain en France, 1814–1870*. Paris: Slatkine Reprints, 1980.

Index

À la Recherche du Temps Perdu
(Proust), 3
Académie des Sciences Morales et
Politiques, 3–5, 10, 18, 22–25,
27–29, 37–39, 48, 53, 62,
83–84, 107, 134–35, 142, 147,
150–51, 175
Africa, French colonization in,
79–83, 85, 87, 89–101, 133,
136–38, 159
Ageron, Charles, 81, 87
Algeria, 79–80, 82–83, 85–87,
89–91, 94, 97, 99, 101, 136–37,
159
Alsace, 42, 82, 86, 102–3
Annam, 96
Anti-Semitism, 133
Arrazat, Eugène, 73–74
Asia, French colonization in,
79–82, 84, 86, 92–94, 96,
99–100, 133, 137
Association pour la Défense de la
Liberté Commerciale, 62
August Decrees, 177
Augustine, 161

Aumercier, Giselle, 133
Austria-Hungary, 98, 136

Baret, Guy, 174–75
Bastiat, Frédéric, 20–21, 33–34, 118
Bastille, fall of, 152
Batbie, Anselme, 20, 48
Belgium, 101, 145
Bertillon, Jacques, 144
Bey of Tunis, 94, 136
Bismarck, Otto von, 44, 115
Blanc, Louis, 21
Block, Maurice, 5
Bluntschli, Johann, 118
Bodley, E. C., 108
Bonaparte, Louis-Napoléon. *See*
Napoléon III
Bonaparte, Napoléon. *See* Napo-
léon I
Bonapartists, 16, 22, 41, 46–47,
51, 74
Bourbons, 75
Bourcier de Carbon, Luc, 174
Boutmy, Émile, 48
Bouvier, Jean, 46

Brentano, Lujo, 66
Britain, 66, 115, 120, 145, 154,
    160; colonial policy, 79, 81–83,
    91–92, 94, 98, 135, 138; income
    tax in, 48, 72; local government
    in, 16, 28, 31–32, 38; social re-
    forms, 173–74; trade treaty with
    France, 17; work week in, 140
Broglie, Victor de, 15–16, 67
Brunétière, Ferdinand, 133–34
Budget, national, 50–51, 55
Buffon, Georges-Louis Leclerc de,
    120
Buloz, François, 15–16, 25, 47, 51
Bureaucracy, role of, 32, 34, 36,
    68, 114–15, 166

Callac, Junilla de, 12–13
Canada, 79
Capitalism, 6, 14, 29, 38, 58, 70,
    110, 178; abstinence theory, 127;
    and colonies, 88–89, 97; effec-
    tiveness of, 126–27, 129; and
    entrepreneurs, 17, 21, 39, 100,
    117, 127, 129; free labor,
    124–25; large-scale enterprises,
    5–6, 17, 44, 52; natural laws,
    19–20, 122, 126; production,
    109, 126, 128
Caro, Elme, 43, 45
Cassagnac, Paul de, 74
Catholic Church, 68, 70, 74–75, 134
Cauchy, E., 37–38
Cauwès, Paul, 66–67, 116–18,
    120, 173–74
Caves du Rocquefort, 62
Centre Droite, 46–47, 75–76
Centre Gauche, 46–47, 51–53, 64,
    67–68, 73–74, 76, 151
Chamberlain, Joseph, 164
Chamber of Deputies, 51, 53,
    63–64, 71–72, 74, 76–77, 82,
    133–34, 174–75
Chambers of Commerce, 156

Chevalier, Michel, 4, 17, 20–21,
    24–26, 53, 62, 118, 167
Cheysson, Émile, 139–41
China, 84, 98
Classical Liberalism, xiii, xvi, 18,
    158–59, 173, 176
Cochin China, 80
Collège de France, 4, 18–19, 22,
    62, 64, 106, 132, 134, 142
Colonialism, 3, 5–6, 28, 30,
    78–105, 135–38; administration,
    84; and capitalism, 88–89, 97;
    colony, defined, 78, 81, 99;
    continental policy, 86–87,
    94–95, 104; and emigration, 86,
    88; expansion, 87, 90–91,
    93–96, 101–4, 133; exploitation
    of colonies, 98; and nationalism,
    79, 86, 91, 98, 102–3, 136–37;
    reconciled with Liberalism,
    78–79, 99, 165; reform of, 85;
    self-government, 88, 136; trade,
    80–81, 83, 85, 87–88, 97; and
    war, 84–85, 137–38
Comité de l'Afrique Française,
    133
Comité de l'Asie Française, 133
Comité de Défense et de Progrès
    Social, 177
Comité de Surveillance, 133
Communards, 40, 42–47, 50, 56,
    58–60, 65, 73
Commune. See Paris Commune
Communitarians, 5
Comte, Auguste, 31, 156
Comte de Chambord (Henri
    Dieudonné d'Artois), 75, 173
Comte de Paris (Louis-Philippe-
    Albert), 75
Condorcet, marquis de (Marie-Jean
    de Caritat), 23
Congo, 101
Conseils Généraux, 31–32, 38, 53,
    63, 151

Conservatism, 8, 46, 75, 114, 152, 169, 173
Conservative Republic, 41–60, 69, 76
Conservatoire des Arts et Métiers, 22
Constant, Benjamin, 19, 31
Constitutionnels, 46–47, 72, 151
Continental expansion policy, 86–87, 94–95, 104
Correspondant, Le, 83
Coulanges, Fustel de, 45
Cours d'Économie Politique (Cauwès), 116
Cousin, Victor, 18
Credit, regulation of, 20–21
Crimean War, 19

Darwin, Charles, 120, 165
Debt, national, 52
Decentralization, government, 17, 38, 43, 50, 55
Declaration of the Rights of Man and Citizen, 177
Delpon de Vissec, Charles, 74
Democracy, 31, 71–72, 115, 118
Depressions, economic, 69–70, 89, 92, 100
Desjobert, Amédée, 82, 88
Dewey, John, 160
Distribution; of income and wealth, 20, 52, 109, 117, 124; of political power, 72
Doctrinaire Liberalism, 173
Dreyfus, Alfred, 133–35
Dunoyer, Charles, 20–21
Dupont-White, Charles, 65
Duran, Carolus, 63
Duval, Jules, 82–83, 99

Écho de Lodève, 72, 74
École des Ponts et Chaussées, 22
École Libre des Sciences Politiques, 4, 48, 51, 106, 150

École Polytechnique, 21
Economic laws, 121–22
Economic Man, 113, 116, 120, 124, 131, 158
Economics, study of, 22–23, 62, 116, 119–22
Economiste Français, 4, 49–51, 53, 57, 62, 66, 91, 94, 132, 134, 142, 148
Education, 18, 49–50, 65–66; consideration of opposing sides of issues, 151; government role in, 21, 27, 35; and peace, 31; and productivity, 21; provided by private sector, 20, 33; to transform working class, 36
Egypt, 92
Éléments d'Économie Politique (Laveleye), 122
Emigration, 86, 88
England. *See* Britain
Enlightenment, xiii
Entrepreneurs, 17, 21, 39, 100, 117, 127, 129
Established Liberalism, xiii–xvi, 4–5, 9, 30, 32, 35, 38, 40, 45, 48, 50, 53, 61, 68, 70, 110, 119, 134, 150–52, 156, 157, 160, 161, 166; academic monopoly, loss of, 66–67; on colonialism, 82, 104; comprehensiveness of, 23, 138, 176; in contemporary France, 174; defense of existing social order, 37, 59, 65; economic and political heritage of, 21–22; on economics as science, 119–120, 158; effect of civil strife (1870–71) on, 27, 42, 59; on form of government, 47; on free labor, 124; on free trade, 28; hostility toward authoritarian regimes, 31; on individualism, 31, 117, 122, 135; on interest rates and profits, 109; and

intervention by the state, 39, 45, 55, 167–68, 170–71; on liberty, 25; limitations of, 176; on nationalism, 41–42, 146–47; nonpolitical remedies for social problems, 57; origin of, 173; on peace, 64; on productivity, 36, 135, 159; rival doctrines, 67, 116–17; on women, 141

Expansion, colonial/continental, 87, 90–91, 93–96, 101–4, 133

Exploitation colonies, 97–98

Fashoda incident, 135, 137–38

Ferry, Jules, 46, 94, 102–3

Figaro, Le, 174–75

First International, 45, 65

Forcade, 15–16

Foreign policy, 24, 28, 31, 53–54, 64, 69, 94–95, 99, 103. *See also* Colonialism

Fournier de Flaix, E., 139–41, 145

France Nouvelle, La (Prévost-Paradol), 16

Franco-Prussian War, 27, 29, 40–47, 50, 54, 56, 58–59, 84–86, 101

Free labor, 124–26, 141

French Revolution, xiii, 3–4, 8, 11, 17–19, 37, 46, 71, 79, 114, 142, 151–52, 177

French School of Economics, 107, 120–21

Freycinet Plan, 75

Frout de Fontpertuis, Adalbert, 49

Galtier, Auguste, 73–74

Gambetta, Léon, 46, 68–69, 74, 102–3

Garnier, Joseph, 19, 24, 47–48, 64, 71

George, Henry, 110, 157

Germany, 13, 24, 55, 65–66; control of Alsace-Lorraine, 82, 102–3; Franco-Prussian War, 27, 29, 40–47, 50, 54, 56, 58–59, 84–86, 101; power of, 83, 85, 91, 98–99; prospects of war with, 104, 135, 142, 147; World War I, 148

Gide, Charles, 66, 107, 116

Girardet, Raoul, 78

Gold standard, 20–21, 50

Government; decentralization of, 17, 38, 43, 50; local, 16, 28, 31–32, 37–38; role of, 16, 20–21, 27, 33–36, 55–56, 111–15, 166–69; self-, 30, 32, 59, 88, 136, 166

Government of National Defense, 42

Grande Bourgeoisie, 3–4, 6, 8, 10–11, 26, 37, 46, 48, 58–59, 61–62, 69–72, 104–5, 108, 134, 150–51, 171–72, 177–78

Grande Encyclopédie, 107

Green, T. H., 160

Grévy, Jules, 67

Guesde, Jules, 65

Guilds, medieval, 125

Guillaumin publishing firm, 19, 22, 50

Guizot, François, 11–12, 16–18, 33, 39, 89, 115, 165, 173

Guyot, Yves, 158, 167–68

Historical processes versus natural processes, 164–65

Historical School of Economics, 65–66

Hobhouse, J. L., 160

Identity cards (*livrets*), abolition of, 125

Ideology, defined, 7–8

Imperialism. *See* Colonialism

Income taxes, 45, 52, 58, 72, 109, 132–33

Indépendant de Lodève, 72–73
India, 79, 81, 83
Individualism, xiv–xvi, 30, 35–36,
   39, 67, 117, 154, 163–64, 169,
   176
Indochina, 80–81, 84, 92, 94, 96, 99
Industrial Revolution, 8
Industrialization, 17, 31, 44, 69–70,
   167
Inheritance taxes, 128
Institut de France, 4, 18, 22–23,
   38, 62
International Association of Work-
   ing Men, 59–60
International League for Peace,
   24–25, 31
Italy, 136

"Jacobins," 59
James, William, 157
Janet, Paul, 48
Jews, 133, 137
Journal des Débats, 4, 22–23, 48,
   53, 62, 91, 150
Journal des Économistes, 5, 19, 47,
   59, 64–65, 67, 71
July Monarchy, 5, 11, 18, 37, 48,
   59, 82, 151

Keynes, John Maynard, 4

Labor unions. *See* Unions
Laboulaye, Édouard, 24
Laissez-faire, xiii–xvi, 19, 21, 27,
   30, 35, 37, 39, 55–56, 108, 113,
   131, 167–71
Lamarck, Jean-Baptiste de, 165
Land ownership, 128–29
Large-scale enterprises, 5–6, 17,
   44, 52
La Salle, Robert Cavelier de, 97
Lassalle, Ferdinand, 5, 110, 119,
   126, 170
Laveleye, Émile de, 66, 110, 122

Le Chapelier, Isaac, 17
Left Republicans, 67–68
Legislative Assembly, 12, 16
Leopold II, 101
Le Play, Frédéric, 107
Leroy-Beaulieu, Anatole (brother),
   12–14, 70, 133–34, 148, 177
Leroy-Beaulieu, Cordelia (wife),
   25–26, 62–63, 73, 148
Leroy-Beaulieu, Marguerite
   (mother), 12
Leroy-Beaulieu, Paul, 3–5, 10–14,
   25–26, 63, 107–8, 148
—general: on civilization, 152,
   154, 171; class base of his ideology, 39, 153–154, 171–72; conception of ideal society, 36–37,
   153; confidence in capitalism, 6,
   38, 58, 70, 110, 178; on family
   issues, 29, 36, 55, 142–45, 146,
   161, 164; history seen as progress, 33, 153, 165; hostile conception of the state, 33–34; as
   ideologist, 4–9, 151–52, 165–66;
   and Liberal tradition, xiii–xvi,
   3–5, 9, 149–50, 173–75; as
   member of Grande Bourgeoisie,
   3–4, 6, 8, 10, 26, 48, 58–59,
   62, 72, 108, 150; on modern society, 30, 59–60; moralistic
   views of, 58, 160; pace of reform 33–34; in Proust's *À la
   Recherche*, 3–4, 63; on radicalism, 71; reconciliation of Liberalism and imperialism, 78–79,
   86–88, 96–99; religious views
   of, 51, 70, 73, 161–62; as representative figure, 149–50, 175;
   rigid honesty of, 133; on superficiality of the French, 45–46,
   56; thought processes of, 57; on
   truth, 155, 157–58; unity and
   continuity of his views, 149–51
—career: as capitalist landowner,

62; during Conservative Republic, 41, 44–60; decline in authority, 134; elected to Académie, 62; elected to Institut and Collège de France, 62; during Franco-Prussian War, 41–44; as journalist, 49–50, 62, 132; last twenty years, 132–48; as member of Conseils Généraux, 53, 63, 151; prizes awarded by the Académie, 10, 24–25, 37–38, 53, 135; as publicist, 14–15, 18, 24–25, 27–40; during Republic of the Republicans, 61–76; seeks election to Chamber of Deputies, 51–53, 63–64, 72–74, 77, 133, 151; as teacher at Collège de France, 62, 64; as teacher at École Libre des Sciences Politiques, 48–49

—writings, 10, 24–25, 38–39, 106–7, 115, 132, 157; *L'Administration Locale*, 28, 31, 35, 50; *L'Algérie et la Tunisie*, 136; *Le Collectivisme*, 106, 110–11, 114, 119, 125, 129, 131; *De la Colonisation*, 28, 50, 62, 77, 84–87, 89–92, 95–99, 106, 132–33, 135, 137–38; *L'État Moderne*, 106, 111–15, 119, 131, 159–60, 162, 168–69; *L'État Moral*, 27, 29, 35–37, 39, 56, 108, 153; *Guerres Contemporaines*, 24, 28, 31, 84; *"La Question Ouvrière"* (articles), 25, 29–30, 40, 147, 171; *La Question Ouvrière* (book), 50, 56, 58–59, 66, 108–11, 129, 132, 134–35; *La Question de la Population*, 142–47, 152; *Réparition des Richesses*, 72, 106, 108–10, 131; *Traité d'Économie Politique*, 106–7, 115, 118–21, 131–32, 134, 154, 156, 162, 172; *Traité des Finances*, 50–53,

55, 57, 72, 115; *Le Travail des Femmes*, 29, 35, 50, 139, 164
Leroy-Beaulieu, Pierre (father), 11–13
Leroy-Beaulieu, Pierre (son), 134, 148
Levasseur, Émile, 48, 83–84, 134
Liberalism: Catholic, 134; Classical, xiii, xvi, 18, 158–59, 173, 176; "cosmopolitan," 25; Doctrinaire, 173; emergence of critiques of, 61, 65–67, 116; New, 171; Orleanist, 15–16, 18, 51, 59; range of opinion, 20–22, 173–74, 177; Reformist, xiii–xvi, 5, 159, 173–74; tradition of, xiii–xvi, 3–5, 7–9, 18, 115, 172–75; welfare, xiii–xv, 4, 173–74. *See also* Established Liberalism
Liberal Regime, 151, 154, 157, 165
Liberty, 15–16, 25, 29, 32, 35, 71, 129, 131, 168, 177
Limited-liability companies, 17
Livingstone, David, 101
Local government, 28, 31–32, 37–38
Lorraine, 42, 82, 86, 102–3
Louis-Philippe. *See* July Monarchy
Lycée Bonaparte, 13

MacMahon, Patrice, 53, 67, 74
Malthus, Thomas R., 20, 37, 88, 120, 142
Manchester School, 115, 120
Markets, 130–31, 174
Marshall, Alfred, 121
Marx, Karl, 3, 5, 66, 110, 119, 126, 157, 170
Marxism, 65, 79
Materialism, 156
Mazade, Charles de, 16, 42, 45, 47, 51, 68–69, 71
Metternich, Klemens von, 115

Michelet, Jules, 139
Middle classes, position of, 33, 39
Mill, John Stuart, 83, 88, 124
Molinari, Guy de, 71, 158, 167–68
Monarchism, 46–47, 64, 74–76
Montesquieu, baron de (Charles-Louis de Secondat), 23, 32, 155
Montplaisir, 62–63, 107, 161
Morocco, 138, 142
Moslems, 136
Mun, Henri de, 173
Murphy, Agnes, 86, 96

Napoléon I (Napoléon Bonaparte), 79
Napoléon III (Louis-Napoléon Bonaparte), 12, 15–19, 24–25, 42–43, 46, 80
Napoleonic Wars, 79
National Assembly, 42–45, 48, 53, 59
Nationalism, 28, 41–43, 45, 54–55, 79, 82, 85–86, 89, 91, 98, 102–4, 135–37, 141–42, 149, 166, 169
Natural laws, 19–20, 23, 32, 34, 65, 120–22, 124, 126, 154–55
Natural processes versus historical processes, 164–65
New Liberalism, 171
Newton, Isaac, 23
Nouveau Journal, 64
Nouvelle France (Prévost-Paradol), 82–83
Nouvelles couches sociales, 68, 70

Old Regime, 8, 18–19, 80–81, 115, 118, 152, 173
Ollivier, Émile, 15, 42
Opportunists, 67–68, 75
Orleanists, 12, 15–16, 18, 21–24, 47, 51, 59, 69, 72, 75, 151
Osborne, Thomas R., 115
Ouvrière (Simon), 138

Paine, Thomas, 112
Palmade, Guy, 23
Panama Canal, 133
Paper currency, 20–21
Paris Commune, 27, 40–47, 50, 56, 58–60, 65, 74, 104
Party of Order, 12
Passy, Frédéric, 5, 25, 104, 138–41, 144
Passy, Hippolyte, 23, 27, 34, 37, 82
Patriotism. See Nationalism
Peace, 19, 24–25, 28, 31, 43, 45, 54, 64, 137
Phylloxera, economic problems caused by, 44
Physiocrats, 19, 119
Pirou, Gaëtan, 158
Population growth, 50, 69; and birth rate, 55, 142–47; and colonialism, 86, 88–89, 91, 102; and infant mortality, 144–45; promoted by state, 55, 113; and wages, 20; and women, 138, 145
Positivism, 156, 158
Précis d'Économie Politique (Cauwès), 66, 116
Prévost-Paradol, Lucien, 16–17, 22, 31, 47, 82, 85, 91, 99
Production, and capital, 126, 128
Productivism, economic, 100
Productivity, 21, 36, 39, 109
Progress, history as, 33, 153, 165
Property, private, 127–29
Proudhon, Pierre-Joseph, 66
Profits, 109, 111, 130
Profit sharing, 29, 126
Proust, Marcel, 3–4, 63
Prussia. See Germany
Puritanism, 14

Radical Party, 73–75
Radical Republicans, 43, 68, 71, 73, 103, 132
Raffalovitch, Arthur, 132

Railroads, 20–21, 50, 52, 56, 69, 94, 138
Reformist Liberalism, xiii–xvi, 5, 159, 173–74
Refoulement, 80
Renan, Ernest, 46
Renouvier, Charles, 65
Republic of the Republicans, 61, 64, 69, 79, 166
Restoration, 18
Revolution. *See* French Revolution
Revolution of 1830, 18
Revolution of 1848, 12, 21
Revue Contemporaine, 24
Revue des Deux Mondes, 4, 15–16, 23, 25, 29, 36, 40, 42–43, 47–48, 51, 59, 67–68, 71, 106, 133–34, 142–45, 150
Revue Nationale, 24
Ricardo, David, 20, 66, 120
Robespierre, Maximilien, 11
Rossi, Pellegrino, 4
Royer-Collard, Pierre-Paul, 173
Russia, 14, 53, 61, 64, 82–83, 91–93, 98, 100–101, 132–33, 142
Russo-Turkish War, 92, 100–101

Saint-Simon, Henri de, 5, 19, 31, 82, 101
Savoie, 82
Say, Jean-Baptiste, 4, 19, 21, 39, 66, 81, 118, 129
Say, Léon, 5
Schäffle, Albert, 110, 157
Second Empire, 6, 12, 14–19, 27, 29, 32, 41, 59, 71–72, 78, 80, 84, 150–51, 167
Sedan, battle of, 43, 84
Self-government, 30, 32, 59, 88, 136, 166
Self-interest, as motivating force, 159–60
Seliger, Martin, 8
Senate, 46–47, 67, 75–76, 133

Senegal, 80, 89–90, 94
Senior, Nassau, 111
Simon, Jules, 5, 35, 53, 74, 138–41
Sismondi, Sismonde de, 19
Slavery, 79–80
Smith, Adam, 3, 21, 52, 81, 88. 119–20
Social contract theory, 112
Social Darwinism, 136
Socialism, 29, 65–66, 69, 157, 169–70; appeal for workers, 56, 71; on labor, 123; rise of, 5, 14; strikes inspired by, 30, 65; as threat, 111, 135; Utopian, 19
Socialist Party, 174
Socialists of the Chair, 65–66
Social Question, 17–18, 22, 27, 29, 41, 49–51, 56–57, 65, 67, 69, 71, 104, 107, 109–10, 118, 139, 171
Société d'Économie Politique, 19–20, 22–24, 62, 65, 134, 138, 150, 175
Société d'Economie Sociale, 107, 156
Society for the Protection of the Natives in the Colonies, 136
Solidarist movement, 144
Sorel, Albert, 48
Spencer, Herbert, 115, 160
Statistique Humaine de la France (Bertillon), 144
Stourm, René, 25–26, 63, 72, 108, 149
Strikes, 18, 27, 29–30, 50, 65, 109
Sudan, 91, 93–95, 98–99, 138
Suez Canal, 83, 93, 97
Suez Canal Company, 62
Suffrage. *See* Universal suffrage
Sugar, prosperity from, 79–80
Sumner, William Graham, 160

Taine, Hippolyte, 46, 48
Tariffs, 17, 21, 52, 58, 67

Taxation, 21, 50–52, 55, 69; income taxes, 45, 52, 58, 72, 109, 132–33; inheritance taxes, 128; to redistribute income, 109; of wealthy, 58
Taylor, Frederick, 108
Temps, Le, 24
Thiers, Adolphe, 17, 44, 48, 52, 68, 70, 72, 87
Third Republic, 5, 11, 44–48, 53, 61, 68–70, 74, 133, 166–67. *See also* Conservative Republic; Republic of the Republicans
Tocqueville, Alexis de, 16–17, 24, 33
Tonkin, 94, 96
Trade; with colonies, 80–81, 83, 85, 87–88, 97; foreign, 52, 58; free, 5–6, 17, 19, 21, 30, 39, 67, 81, 83, 87–88
Trade unions. *See* Unions
Transportation, 21, 44; railroads, 20–21, 50, 52, 56, 69, 94, 138; steamships, 44
Trilling, Lionel, 7
Tunisia, 62, 94, 136
Turkey, 53, 61, 64, 92, 100–101

Union Libérale, 76
Union des Pères et Mères dont les Fils Sont Morts pour la Patrie, 148
Unions, 5, 17, 27, 29–30, 65–66, 117–18, 123, 125
United States, 50, 154–55, 160; economic depression in, 53; politics in, 51; power of, 82, 91; reforms in, 173–174; working conditions for women, 29
Universal suffrage, 6, 15–17,

31–32, 46–47, 70–71, 76–77, 133, 166–67
Utopian Socialism, 19

Verne, Henri, 83, 85, 91, 99
Vocational education, 21
Vue sur le Gouvernement de la France (Broglie), 15

Wages, 20–21, 24, 27, 32–33, 36, 67, 109, 118, 123–26
Walras, Léon, 65
War, 19, 24–25, 28, 31, 45, 54, 69, 84–85, 138
Ward, Lester Frank, 160
Wealth of Nations (Smith), 81
Welfare Liberalism, xiii–xv, 4, 173–74
Women, 138; and birth control, 146–47; and birth rate, 142–45; clerical jobs for, 144; as free economic agents, 141; as homemakers and mothers, 139–40; legal protection for, 45, 139; working conditions for, 29, 38, 139–41
Work, 27, 33, 36, 39, 139–40, 161
Workday, 118, 140, 156
Working class, 38–39, 58–59; discontent of, 5–6, 17, 29, 109, 171–72; education of, 33, 36–37; free labor, 124–26, 141; improvidence of, 110; moral level of, 27, 37; movements, 45; quiescence of, 44, 50; security for, 57, 118; and Socialism, 14, 56, 65–66; strikes, 18, 27, 109; unions, 17, 27, 117, 123; wages, 33, 36, 67, 109, 118, 123; working conditions, 21, 33, 68, 118
World War I, 148